TALKING AND LISTENING
A guide to the helping interview

TALKING
AND LISTENING

A guide to the helping interview

Laura Epstein

Professor, School of Social Service Administration,
The University of Chicago,
Chicago, Illinois

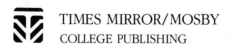
TIMES MIRROR/MOSBY
COLLEGE PUBLISHING

ST. LOUIS • TORONTO • SANTA CLARA   1985

Editor: Diane L. Bowen
Editorial Assistant: Jane E. Kozuszek
Project Editor: Karen Edwards
Manuscript Editor: Kathy C. Hickman
Designer: Nancy Steinmeyer
Production: Margaret B. Bridenbaugh

Library of Congress Cataloging in Publication Data

Epstein, Laura.
  Talking and listening.

  Includes index.
   1.   Interviewing—Handbooks, manuals, etc.
2.   Social case work—Handbooks, manuals, etc.
I.   Title.
HV43.E68   1985   361.3'22   84-19058
ISBN 0-8016-1547-X

A/VH/VH   9   8   7   6   5   4   3   2   1   02/B/256

PREFACE

This book provides a framework for interviewing in the helping professions. It is a guide for starting an interview and continuing it along lines that are helpful and productive for the person being interviewed, who is a client or applicant for service.

Experience strongly suggests that some issues are fundamental to interviewing practice. Students are learning to interview in the fields of mental health, physical health, and child welfare and are dealing with differences among people caused by social class, age, sex, and special needs associated with cultural and ethnic backgrounds. They are trying to help clients who may be involuntary, unwilling, or hostile. Many colleagues have spoken to me about the need for a textbook that would discuss fundamentals — basic knowledge that comes before advanced technique. Such knowledge is needed not only by undergraduate students, but also by beginning graduate students and newly hired practitioners who staff the large public organizations that dispense human services.

Human services today need staff members who have an organized repertoire of skills. The staff members need a firm understanding of services that they will dispense and for which their employing organizations will be held accountable. Human services have become a vast enterprise; effective services are expected by the public in return for the large amounts of money expended. Young practitioners are aware of these expectations and desire to be productive, competent, and helpful. To help young practitioners, educators attempt to organize knowledge efficiently, develop new knowledge to replace the obsolete, and take advantage of discoveries from their own experience and from research.

Within the social science disciplines that form the basis of human services practice, there are substantial differences of opinion about what knowledge is fundamental and how it can best be taught. Although these differences cannot be definitely settled, progress can be made by taking a fresh look at new interpretations. It is the intention of this book to present an approach to interviewing that addresses the fundamentals. Interviewing is seen as part of the problem-solving process involving social interaction, various types of human encounters and communication processes, and basic helping processes. Within this broad framework specific guidelines are presented that attempt to pinpoint what has to be heard, said, and done to alleviate a particular problem. To describe those guidelines concisely an interviewing model has been constructed. The main components, that is, the ones without which the interview will falter, are identified. Interested students and practitioners will take the initiative to go beyond the fundamentals and will grow from their own experience and the study of advanced techniques in other works.

I have tried to be straightforward in presenting the material, using some but not too much professional jargon. Numerous interview transcriptions are given for illustration and analysis and to stimulate discussion. All the vignettes except one are taken directly from recordings of real interviews with the participants' permission, although they have been disguised. Since the illustrations are real, they accurately represent the kinds of things that happen in the world of interviewing and have the interest, ambiguity, and complexity of actual events.

The transcribed interviews touch on content that often comes up in classes and seminars in today's practice world. Particular attention is paid to how to get started, how to confront the strangers we need to interview, how to reach for an understanding of many different types of people, how to handle our own feelings of apprehension, and what the encounter is all about. Features having to do with beginning the interview, developing the middle, and arranging for an orderly ending are considered in detail. Because practice always takes place in a specialized setting, there is coverage of the unique aspects of interview settings and how they influence and affect the interview. Special attention is given to interviewing children, old people, and people of minority status, as well as other special groups.

Practice and practice theory are subject to many fast-paced changes that are often difficult to understand. I have tried to present the most current information, indicating that which adds to or supplants tradition. To help keep readers up-to-date I have referred to available research on interviewing, which includes current knowledge about working relationships, advice giving, dealing with violence, and the influence of treatment models.

In keeping with present ideas about the importance of systematic practice I have tried to outline the material in a logical fashion. Starting with the recognition of the strong impact that interviewing has on the learner, the text proceeds to a view of the surrounding context of interviews. Organizational settings, values, intentions, and helping theories are reviewed. A model of interviewing and its details is given, followed by the application of the model to specialized settings and populations. The text concludes with a survey of what happens after the interview, that is, planning and recording.

The text provides aids to teaching and learning in the form of delineated sections, cross-referencing to related information, summaries, and charts to visualize various processes. Each chapter provides selected bibliographies that are immediately relevant to the content of that chapter.

Normally students have limited time for extensive extra reading, whether they are attending a class, practicum, or in-service workshop. In this book I have tried to limit bibliographies to work that is immediately related to the material in the text. I would like to call attention to two works that provide superior additional material and extensive bibliographies. I have relied on these two works to supplement this text in my own teaching:

> Kadushin, Alfred. *The Social Work Interview*. 2nd ed. New York: Columbia University Press, 1983. Contains a comprehensive bibliography. Accompanied by an instructor's manual offering 132 pages of teaching resources.

> Marshall, Eldon K.; Kurtz, P. David; and Associates. *Interpersonal Helping Skills*. San Francisco: Jossey-Bass Publishers, 1982. Notable for succinct summaries by numerous well-known developers of different models of conceptualizing helping skills, including interviewing, and extensive lists of teaching materials and audiotapes. Gives addresses at which materials can be obtained. Also contains a comprehensive multidisciplinary bibliography.

There are inherent difficulties in texts dealing with the subject of interviewing. Diverse terminologies exist within disciplines and across disciplines. Also, despite considerable consensus, authorities dispute the correct or most appropriate way to conceive of and implement interviewing. These difficulties are not avoidable. Rapid development and pervasive differences of opinion represent the state of the art.

I considered appending glossaries, charts, and other devices for comparing terminologies from different sources and also for devising a means to show development from fundamental to advanced skills. However, I gave up this attempt as being impractical. This text attempts to deal with divergence by striving for the difficult, if not impossible, middle-of-the-road position, emphasizing problem-solving intentions and the logic of chronology in the interviewing process. The phases of beginning, middle, and end are used as benchmarks for organizing the material.

PLAN OF THIS BOOK

Because this book intends to teach the conventions of interviewing, it starts with an introduction to concepts in Chapter 1. In Chapter 2 it proceeds to investigate and discuss four common practice problems in getting started in interviews. Chapter 3 returns to matters of a general type, that is, the various contexts of interviews.

Chapter 4 depicts the interviewing model, which is described, explained, and illustrated in more detail in Chapter 5. Chapter 6 develops adaptations of the general interviewing model to groups and family interviewing.

The balance of the book, Chapters 7 through 11, discusses a number of special interviewing conditions. Chapter 7 explores the effect on the interview of the organization under whose auspices it takes place. Chapter 8 explains how interviews vary depending on the age, sex, and social class of the client. Chapter 9 discusses available information about adjustments needed in interviews with people whose cultural and ethnic background are different from dominant groups. Chapter 10 grapples with the problem of dealing with people who are being interviewed but do not want to be involved, at least not in the way the agency and practitioner prefer. In Chapter 11 interviewing's relationship with planning, organizing, and reporting will be reviewed.

To summarize, this book offers a general model for interviewing and a set of specific guidelines for following the model and adapting it to a variety of commonly encountered conditions. It provides a source for studying the fundamental attributes and skills of the interviewing process. Underlying theory and research, when available, are related to the guidelines. The purpose of this book is not to analyze the many theoretical, research, communication, and linguistic issues that are connected to the subject of interviewing, but to concentrate on presenting fundamental practices that form the basis of an interviewing style. The contents conform to a common learning pattern that allows students to move from general to specific ideas in a nonlinear manner. However, depending on individual styles of both instructors and students, the order can be rearranged because each chapter emphasizes a coherent set of ideas.

ACKNOWLEDGMENTS

I would like to express appreciation to colleagues at the School of Social Service Administration, University of Chicago. Special appreciation goes to Gwendolyn Graham and Edwina Simmons for their expert manuscript preparation, to Eileen Libby for superb help in identifying specialized literature for me in the library, and to my colleagues, especially Jon Conte and Lynn Vogel, who generously shared information. For their enlightening comments on the manuscript of this book while it was in preparation, I would like to thank the publisher's reviewers:

Horace O. Black, Golden West College
Melvin B. Drucker, Georgia State University
Dorothea Leonard, Miami-Dade Community College, South

L. Dennis Madrid, University of Southern Colorado
Winston Miller, University of Missouri in St. Louis
Florence L. Phillips, Texas Tech University
Carol Pribula, De Paul University
Richard L. Swaine, Southern Illinois University in Edwardsville

I am grateful to my students who suffered with an early version of this book and helped me make revisions.

Laura Epstein

CONTENTS

CHAPTER 1

Understanding interviewing

Beginnings and endings
Taking turns
Signals
Interruptions
Adjacency pairs
Topic changes
Body motion: in general
Body movement and gestures
Facial expressions and visual interaction
Eye contact
Paralanguage
Spatial behavior
Multichannel communication
Composition of an interview

Interviewing is directed conversation. Information is given and received. The interviewer and the person or persons being interviewed affect one another through their social interactions. Usually, the interviewer intends to create some change in the client's knowledge and understanding, in his* relationship with important other persons or in his environment. The interviewer also needs to carry out objectives of a school, hospital, clinic, welfare agency, or other human service organization. Communication and linguistics theories suggest that interviewing processes may be composed of interplays among human speech mechanisms and many social and cultural elements.

Basic definition and description of interviewing
SHORT DEFINITION

An interview is an event composed of a sequence of physical and mental experiences that occur when and where a helping professional practitioner and a client talk to one another. The interviewing event may occur once or repeatedly, over long or short periods of time. The interview is a product of what is said, or the content of the interview, and how it is said, or the process. In real life, content and process are always combined. They will be separated only for the purposes of analysis and study.

---

*Male and female pronouns are used randomly throughout the text, for both client and practitioner.

EXPLANATION OF THE DEFINITION

The interview is a directed conversation. It is an oral exchange of sentiments, objectives, opinions, information, and ideas. The interview reveals values, norms, hopes and expectations, and personal feelings and attitudes. It is intended to obtain and give information, and to influence, persuade, and enable an interviewee to solve a social problem at some level. The interview is expected to carry out one or more objectives of the service organization, which might be a school, hospital or clinic, welfare agency, or employment service.

An interview is a conversation that organizes thoughts that lead to some consequence, such as getting resources to a person or changing a person's mind. Knowledge may be added and rearranged. Attitudes, beliefs, feelings, ways of thinking may be altered and expanded. In this way, the interview is a means of intervention. It is one of the ways in which an intervention is accomplished.

Interviewing by itself is not an intervention. Action taken by a practitioner to introduce information, to interrupt some event or train of events, to interfere with some actions going on, to mediate some conflict, to intercede on behalf of the client — these are interventions. Interviews are instruments that make the occurrence of an intervention possible. In addition to interviewing, resources and strategies for change are instruments for intervention.

A good interview follows a logical course and is sensitive to what a client says, does, and means. There is a consensus in the helping professions that a bad interview is one that fails to make sense, that moves aimlessly, that does not explore the client's experiences and needs, that is too much focused on the practitioner, and that ignores the rules and expectations of the agency. Keeping track of the logic of content and being aware of the process will help to make the interview sensible and sensitive.

SIX MYTHS

Here are some flat assertions about interviewing ideas that are false. The sources of these myths are difficult to trace, but the myths are prevalent.

Myth 1. Getting the right information from the client will unlock mysteries. This is *false.* There is no right or wrong information: there is just information, some more instructive, some less. There are no mysteries, but there are practical limits on what can be learned and known about a client at a certain time under given conditions.

Myth 2. The interviewer's private personality is the most important part of the interview work. False. Wisdom, courtesy, decency, and kindness are great attributes that serve one well in the human services. Stupidity, rudeness, insensitivity, and brutality are unacceptable in this work. After considering these extremes, there is room for a wide variety of different personalities.

Myth 3. Interviewing and counseling are always one and the same thing. False, although they overlap. If interviewing and counseling are thought of as being the same thing, we have severely complicated the nature, boundaries, and substance of our subject. We have made it difficult to identify and study interviewing processes that are essentially skills. We have advanced beyond the process of interviewing into the realm of counseling with its many and varied theories, models, purposes and values. In order to analyze our subject, it is advisable to separate interviewing skills from counseling, to break out a sector that is encompassable. However, interviewing is never without content. Counseling theories, models, and objectives influence the interviewing situation.

Myth 4. An interview concerns only the two or several people who are physically present. False. Interviews are always public, to some degree, and are reported to other people in other places. The happenings of an interview always have a social context and influence a social situation or condition.

Myth 5. Without interpersonal rapport, the interview will fail. False. Rapport helps, but it is not everything. Sometimes it cannot even be achieved.

Myth 6. The nonverbal exchanges in an interview escape consciousness to a large extent. False. We can become highly aware of nonverbal exchanges, in which a great deal of information is contained.

The interview event

Interviewing is one of the basic means for providing human services. The other basic means are allocating and providing resources and designing and implementing strategies for changing persons, their environment, or both.

WHO INTERVIEWS AND WHO IS INTERVIEWED

In the United States the organization of work has changed significantly since the 1940's. In 1940, half the work force was engaged in production. By 1980, the estimate is that nearly three-quarters of the workers in America were service providers (Gartner 1976, p. 18). Millions of workers are in occupations that serve people, providing them with necessities or benefits that increase the quality of life. In the private sector, interviews to provide services often have a selling ingredient that may involve blatant manipulation. In the public sector, interviewing involves persuasion, that ought not to be full of tricks or use insidious means, but that should be straightforward and in the client's interests. There are profound dilemmas about the propriety, morality, and ethics of guiding, advising, and exploring the thoughts and lives of other persons. Interviewing sometimes raises difficult questions of social and moral theory that go beyond technique and are the subject of concern, uncertainty, and debate.

Because of the prominence of service activities in keeping the social system afloat, our society has become saturated with multitudes of talking encounters, or interviews. The dominant participants in people-serving interviews are the clients and the human service professionals. Clients may be inquirers, that is, people wanting information. They may be applicants or supplicants. They may demand services to which they are, or are not, entitled. Clients may be voluntary, that is, they may come for the service by choice. Or they may be involuntary, meaning they are required to participate. They may be under a degree of coercion, having been ordered to use a service by a court or other authoritative agency of the state. It may have been put to them in a strong way that they should use the service, even though the clients themselves have reservations.

Human services professionals may be in private practice, in which case their clients are nearly always voluntary. Mostly, however, human services professionals are employed by public agencies in fields organized by the health, education, and welfare branches of the social system. Human services professionals are established within a large number of professions, the most prominent being medicine, nursing, physical and occupational therapy, teaching, social work, law, and vocational guidance.

The socioeconomic status of clients affects the interviewers. People whose incomes are low are overrepresented among clients. Frequent clients also include those discirminated against because of age, race, gender, religion, or nationality.

WHERE INTERVIEWS TAKE PLACE

Interviews occur either on the premises of the agency or practitioner providing the service or in the home of the client. It is not uncommon, however, for interviews to occur on the street of the neighborhood where the client lives, in a coffee shop, or on a bus.

Interviews that take place in a natural setting have the merit of providing a practitioner with a great deal of information about the all-important context in which the client lives. Interviews that take place on an agency's premises are more economical and can be better controlled. In some instances the only place to have access to a client is on agency premises as in instances where the client is hospitalized, is in school, or is placed in an institution.

WHY INTERVIEW?

Regardless of the branch of human services, interviewing is the means by which it is decided if applicants are eligible to receive services, if they should be referred elsewhere, and what kind of services should be suggested and provided. The interview is the means by which the decision to intervene is negotiated with the client, and in which the interventions are installed. The interview is the means for monitoring if the service is being used appropriately by the client and if the service is effective for the client. If the service includes counseling, the interview is the means by which clients are taught, guided, enabled, or persuaded to change in behavior, thinking, attitudes, feelings, and perceptions of themselves and their world.

Some services do not require interviews unless problems arise. These are services to which citizens are entitled by rights established in legislation that are distributed by specific rules. Basic social security payments, for example, are obtained by making a telephone call, filling out a form, and mailing it. Most service delivery, however, is mediated by a social interaction between a practitioner and a client because there is a discretionary process used to allocate services. The practitioner and client must weigh the rules of eligibility, the choices among services, and the risks and benefits to all concerned—client, practitioner, agency, public. Wherever there is discretion to be exercised and there are options to be chosen, there must be an interview in order to obtain information, explain the conditions, understand the implications, and decide.

An applicant is nearly always an unknown quantity to the practitioner, who must become minimally acquainted with some of a client's characteristics in order to decide on acceptance. The practitioner will possess knowledge of the rules and procedures for justifying service delivery. It is characteristic in the human services for the rules governing eligibility and the choice of services to contain large amounts of uncertainty, creating ambiguity that requires complex judgments. The knowledge base that supports human services is a developing entity with many gaps, requiring judgments on the part of the practitioner. Generally, practitioners acting for their employing organizations have a large amount of discretion because they are allocating scarce resources for which there is high demand.

Counseling services must be provided through interviews that convey personal communications between client and practitioner. Counseling services, provided alone or in combination with concrete resources, involve changing people and rearranging their environments, both difficult things to accomplish. Interviews are the only means by which private problems can be explored and assessed, and by which the client or important people in the environment can be persuaded and encouraged to think differently, feel differently, and behave differently. There are many models of counseling, but they all depend on communication and hence, on interviewing.

WHAT DOES THE INTERVIEW CONSIST OF?

An interview contains social interactions, or interpersonal occurrences; communication processes, or a series of linguistic actions leading toward a result that is cognitive, affective, and behavioral; and interventions of a problem-solving nature. Language patterns, or linguistics, along with social interactions, influence people to modify their attitudes and actions. When an interview is over, two or more persons will have interacted. They will have conversed together in the form of a discussion. The practitioner will have attempted to make an alteration in the circumstances of a client's problem to reduce that problem. The client will have responded positively, negatively, or in a mixed manner.

It is the custom to think of interviewing as a blend of interaction, conversation, and intervention. The effective and appropriate blend is thought to evolve through learning and practice, over a good deal of time. The blend is the product of a practitioner's thoughtfulness and accumulating knowledge. Sensitivity and skill in social interactions, or interpersonal competence, is thought to result from normative psychological processes and the kind and quality of the personality of the practitioner (Briar 1979, p. 181).

In the past it was considered mechanical, hence undesirable, to construct and put into effect strict rules for interacting with clients. It was feared that machinelike actions would be cold, uncaring, and inauthentic, defeating the qualities of client-worker relationship. Today, as intervention processes have become more methodical, it is regarded as probably mistaken to think that systematic description and learning of techniques will necessarily cause social interventions to be mechanical, automatic, detached, and dehumanized. Great painters, musicians, and poets are master technicians as well as artists. There is no question that interviewing is an exceedingly complex phenomenon. Without verified competency standards, it has been, and continues to be, necessary to rely on a variable composite of knowledge and intuition in order to study the subject. Newer trends in human service knowledge, however, are developing many ideas to demystify the subject (Dong Yul Lee 1975; Ivey 1974; Marshall, Charping, and Bell 1979; Matarazzo and Wiens 1972; Matarazzo 1978; Schinke et al. 1978; Zastrow and Navarre 1979).

Social interaction in interviews

Interviewing is a set of social interactions or interpersonal occurrences carried out and carried forward by communication. Linguistic actions are initiated and carried out in order to positively influence the client and effect some type of problem solving. The communication process consists of words, phrases, and sentences exchanged in order to influence the outcome of the communication. Communication is the medium by which interventions in the thoughts, behaviors, and life-styles of clients are expected to take place.

Interactions in interviews are often distressing. George Konrad reflects on his reactions to client-worker social interactions thus:

> *Who am I, I sometimes ask myself, that I should question them so, that they should tell me their threadbare histories? Who do they take me for that they should bring me things to repair that would have made even the Galilean craftsman raise his arms to high heaven? Where did this drab serial of misfortune begin? With the statistical accidents of their cellular systems? With the mistaken ideas that were drummed into them? At what remote phase of their past? And when I say that something is bad, compared to what is it bad? (Konrad 1974, p. 90).*

The social interactions in interviews can be understood in terms of several overlapping areas. There are encounters in which the participants meet. There is a professional posture that establishes particular ways for a practitioner to behave in the meeting. There are general processes that occur and reveal what is happening in the encounter. And there are lines of action, including skills, which form the basic processes.

ENCOUNTERS

Social interaction between an interviewer and an interviewee begins with some kind of encounter. They meet, collide, embrace, or do battle. They share the interviewing activity. The two encounter one another in a situation that is potentially meaningful for one or the other, or both. The situation differs for each of the participants. One typical example of differing perceptions between interviewer and interviewee is incongruity of purpose. The interviewer may come to the encounter with a belief about what the client is, needs, and should do; but the client comes with a different view.

Interviewer and client can be expected to have an impact on each other. Each can be expected to try to change the other's perception of the situation, so as to elicit the desired response from the other. This process may or may not be conscious and deliberate. It could be manipulation, although it need not be. The client has an authentic perception of herself and her life situation and her needs. The practitioner's perception of a line of action depends on professional style and beliefs, and on the instructions of the agency.

In the interview client and practitioner work out a definition of the situation. They collaborate in a mediating process that bridges the distance between them. They reach a tacit agreement, one that is only implicit at first. They attempt to discover the identity of the other person in the interviewing situation.

DEFINING THE SITUATION

The practitioner and the client act on one another. Each attempts to influence the other's definition of the situation. Effective interpersonal skill is judged by whether one can successfully affect the way the other person defines the situation. The practitioner uses words, phrases, and sentences that will hopefully create a pattern of meanings leading to a desired response in the client. The classic puzzle for interviewers is how to get a client to tell certain things, listen to other things, change his mind partly or in whole, and come to some position that is believed by the practitioner to be appropriate. What the practitioner says does not necessarily create the effects hoped for. Ordinarily the most agreeable of clients is not compliant and reveals an independence, stubbornness, or resistance that sets up a dissonance or perhaps a conflict with the practitioner.

MEDIATING PROCESS

The ambiguity and uncertainty existing between the mind sets of the practitioner and the client are due to "mediating processes" (Weinstein, 1969). This means that stored memories of past experience plus the vividness of current impressions combine, and may result in competing, conflicting, and supporting meanings. Since both parties are responding to the mediating process, the practitioner must take her own response into account as well as the client's meaning. The assumption is that if we know what makes the other person tick, we can select lines of action that lead to the desired goal and reach it. Unfortunately, it is often impossible to guarantee successful prediction of what someone else is going to think, feel, or do. The practitioner can make an educated guess, however. Good fortune, talent, and experience facilitate the prediction of human behavior.

TACIT AGREEMENT

In the interview, practitioner and client strive to come to a tacit agreement regarding issues that will be temporarily recognized as important. They agree for the time being about what reality will be and what definition of the situation they jointly subscribe to, always retaining reservations. As the participants converse, each line of the conversation somewhat modifies the meaning of the situation. This modification of meaning as the conversation proceeds may change the definitions held by the participants. However, the tacit agreement provides boundaries from moment to moment. It provides limits to the conversational activities thought to be reasonable at the moment. The tacit agreement is the working consensus, necessary for the maintenance of interaction. Without a working consensus the interview will break down (Weinstein 1969).

The participants in the social interaction of an interview should reach a common notion, part of the working consensus, about what they want to accomplish together. What the participants talk about is normally called *focus,* and what they decide to accomplish is normally termed a *goal.* Only when interviewing has progressed enough to achieve a reasonable exploration can we formalize a contract to guide the whole work. In the beginning, the tacit agreement is flexible, fleeting, and changeable, becoming firmer as the participants gain confidence.

SITUATIONAL IDENTITIES

In an interaction each person has an identity that is relatively specific to the situation. There are basically four situational identities in every dyadic interview. There is the practitioner's perception of who she is; there is the client's perception of who the practitioner is; there is the practitioner's perception of who the client is; and there is the client's perception of who he is. Both client and practitioner usually emphasize selected aspects of themselves. These establish the particular identity that they want to possess and display in the interview.

The practitioner may assign an identity to the client. A practitioner may perceive the client as undeserving, manipulative, defensive, or cooperative. Conversely, the client may perceive the practitioner as all-knowing, benign, or aversive. The parties come to an interview with ready-made definitions of each other, referred to as *stereotyping.*

PROFESSIONAL POSTURE

The practitioner's skill in establishing and maintaining a desired identity is a crucial element in competent behavior in interviews. Practitioners often refer to this skill as "behaving professionally." A key feature of the practitioner's situational identity is professional posture.

According to Weinstein (1969), skill in establishing and maintaining the professional posture depends on three variables. First, the practitioner should be able, at least in part, to take the role of the client fairly accurately. The practitioner judges the impact that his behavior and conversation will have on the client. This is one of the features of empathy. Second, the practitioner should possess a substantial repertoire of possible lines of action that can be brought into play and tested out for utility, or discarded, or rearranged and tried again. This repertoire can be developed through training and experience. Third, the practitioner must possess "intrapersonal resources." That is, she must have enough courage, common sense, and personal security to take some risks, to compromise, or to alter tactics. Techniques for developing lines of action and for adapting one's personal resources to interview situations will be discussed in detail in Chapters 4 and 5 of this book.

The general process: what goes on in an interview?

There are at least two people, and frequently more, in the interviewing event. We will discuss the client's side of the interaction later on in this book, particularly in Chapters 8 through 10. At this point, we concentrate on the practitioner in order to study interviewing as it is perceived by her.

Practitioners normally have an image of the kind of response or set of responses that they are attempting to elicit from the client. The desired response might be a pleasant reception from the client, or having the client contain anger, or a change in the client's mind. There are many other sorts of hoped-for reactions.

The ability to accomplish the interviewing purpose is a function of the interviewer's skills at evaluating, monitoring, pursuading, influencing, and enabling the client in a constructive manner without coercion. It can be argued that any kind of influencing of clients is wrong or unethical in some way, that it attacks clients' rights to self-determination or otherwise invades a client's privacy. Nevertheless, in order to extend help and get a job done, we must influence clients. In modern practice, it is understood that persuasion is part of helping and healing (Frank, 1974). Whether the process of persuasion is coercive or not depends on whether we manipulate someone for our own ends, or whether we have openly and thoroughly created a climate in which the other person's perceptions and interests are legitimate and in which intentions and objectives are clear.

While interviewing the practitioner conducts an internal conversation to answer the question: *What's going on here?* The way the interviewer answers the question — in other words, the way the interviewer defines the situation — creates a judgment which suggests the lines of action to pursue.

> We are interviewing Mr. and Mrs. L.* She is 40 years old, is skinny, wears high heels, and has frizzled hair. Her clothes are expensive but gaudy. Her face is taut. Mr. L. is also 40 years old. His natty clothes are old, comfortable, and expensive. He has a round face and neat beard. He is affable. Mrs. L. leads the way into the office, looking around, picking her way. Mr. L. ambles in. The counselor is restrained, her demeanor relaxed, watching. They sit at a table.

What is going on here? (Or, what social interactions are taking place?) The first five minutes are important. A high proportion of clinicians make up their minds about the client within the first ten minutes. After that, they are filling in their information and testing out the appropriateness of the first impressions (Kendall 1975, pp. 56-57).

> To start with, there are conventional greetings. ("Hello. Take off your coats and put them there. Have a seat.") There is tension, caused by uncertainty, worried expectations, and attentive watching of one another. Situational identities are being established. Mrs. L. is presenting herself as chic and capable. Mr. L. is presenting himself as the casual professional. The counselor is comfortable and controlled.
>
> After they all sit down, the counselor starts the conversation by stating her understanding of what the couple have come for.

Typescript	*Diagram of practitioner inputs*
P: (a)† I gathered from Mrs. L.'s phone call that you are having problems about Mr. L.'s not getting a job. (Both nod and say "yeah, yeah." They stop. Neither says anything more. Both look expectantly at P.)	(a) P starts by stating her perception of the reason for their visit, which is based on the initial phone conversation with Mrs. L.
Mrs. L: (breaks the silence) It has ups and downs. Never seems to go smoothly. John looked like he was going to get this full-	

*All client-identifying information in this book has been disguised completely and occasionally fictionalized to prevent recognition.
†Small letters refer to points in the right-hand column.

Typescript	*Diagram of practitioner inputs*

time job and then he didn't get it and I felt very disappointed about it. (voice breaking) Clara — my boss — she knew John and she suggested we see you.

P: (b) This was all recently.

Mrs. L: Yes, recently.

P: (b) When exactly?

Mrs. L: A month and a half ago, before Easter.

(b) She asks a question that tries to establish when the problem arose.

P: (c) So you sort of trace the crisis from the issue that arose about this full-time job.

Mr. and Mrs. L: (in unison) No!

Mrs. L: It was never a full-time job.

Mr. L: It was in order to fill up this gap in the use of my time.

(c) She makes a statement to focus attention more specifically on when the problem arose.

(Silence)

Mr. L: Can I give you a more overall picture?

P: (d) Please. Go ahead.

Mr. L: I think that we've had issues which have dogged us from the very beginning of our marriage that have come up in different ways. I think they have really been the same issue all along. She thinks I should not be active in affairs like the Kiwanis Club, Independent Voters Club, and things like that. I should be home with my wife. Then that I should not be out overnight. I had a job where I had to travel. Then there was a hot issue maybe three or four years ago of how much Chris should criticize me. I thought she shouldn't criticize me at all. I wanted to be accepted the way I was (large sigh).

(d) She gives a prod or push to show that she wants the couple to say more about what the problem is.

P: (e) Was it the other way around also? About how much you criticize her?

Mrs. L: No. It's not that he's never criticized me (laughs sarcastically). He's too critical of my criticism.

Mr. L: I'll criticize her in reaction to something, but I tend — I probably accept all kind of rot that I shouldn't accept. I don't enjoy being critical, and I don't think it does any good. My job stability . . . I guess

(e) She asks questions that try to pin down further when the problem arose and what the problem is about.

Continued.

Typescript	*Diagram of practitioner inputs*

my capacity to hold a job has been an issue.

Mrs. L: (grimly) He's never really picked
when he leaves.

The practitioner's input is organized by the intention to explore the problem and to begin to acquire an assessment. Given that intention, the words, phrases, and sentences of the practitioner are geared (1) toward encouragement of the clients to talk about the area to which their attention is directed; and (2) toward influencing them to organize their information as directed. What the problem is and how long it has existed are topics the practitioner wants to talk about first.

But what is going on here between the practitioner and the couple? The three participants quickly defined a situation in which the interviewer is reaching for an understanding of what the problem is and how long it has existed. Mr. and Mrs. L. are describing how the problem is occurring at present, with occasional references to its being of long duration. The interviewer is behaving in a neutral but interested way. The clients appear to accept her role and quickly reveal troublesome conditions. The practitioner is attempting to alleviate the tension of unfamiliarity (mediating), and is attempting to grasp a sense of what the clients are talking about. A tacit agreement quickly develops that the issues of concern relate to the couple's marital relationship.

INTERVIEWING SKILLS

Interviewing skills are a developed aptitude for using spoken language in the performance of a helping job. It is impossible to divorce the language from its social and psychological contexts.

Interviewing style is an attribute of individual interviewers or of a group of similar interviewers. Style is the way that skill is displayed. Style develops as an interviewer's habits and manners are shaped by training and experience, and by the conditions in the places where he has worked. The client, patient, or pupil who is the object of the interview is a formidable shaper of the speech of the interviewer. There are styles for interviewing children that sound different from the language styles used with adults. There are language styles for sick people, for applicants, for husbands, for wives, and for the mentally defective. Style accounts for the coolness of a psychiatrist in a clinic and for the friendliness of a volunteer paying a call in a nursing home.

Interviewers are engaged in verbal behavior. Their skills are performed through words, phrases, and sentences, that is, through language. Spoken language varies a little or a great deal from place to place, from time to time, from person to person, and from culture to culture. There are almost no words, phrases, or sentences that are always right or always wrong. There are forms of expression that are better or worse than others in specific instances.

The two basic categories of verbal behavior in interviewing are talking and hearing. Practitioners talk, hear themselves, and hear others. Clients talk, hear themselves, and hear the practitioner. The words, phrases, and sentences people say must be arranged in a competent fashion. What is said has meaning. There are consequences to speech that have practical results. It is not advisable to approach this subject as if it were a matter of memorizing particular words, phrases, and sentences in order to unlock secrets, change someone's mind, clear up confusion, or eliminate conflict of interest. It is advisable to think in terms of conveying meaning, which is transmitted by various words and behavior.

Lines of action in interviews

The interviewer tries to construct lines of action (see box below) that will clarify or modify the client's understanding. The client may be attempting the same thing toward the practitioner. How is this done?

AGREEMENT ON FOCUS

Client and practitioner achieve a tacit agreement about what issues will be focused upon. That consensus stabilizes the flow characteristic of every interview. The tacit agreement provides temporary boundaries to the moment-to-moment changes in definitions of the situation. Agreement on focus gives boundaries to all the activities. Although boundaries should be flexible, they must exist if an interview is to avoid excess anxiety and

---

LINES OF ACTION
1. Agreement on focus
2. Getting an idea of the other person
3. Being empathic
4. Tactics
   a. Norms
   b. Clear speech
   c. Listening
   d. Flexibility

floundering. A clumsy focus on which there is basic disagreement creates an impasse to the discussion and is confusing and bewildering to both client and practitioner.

GETTING AN IDEA OF THE OTHER PERSON

People in an interview need to get an idea about each other's role, and social and personal attributes. What we expect from another person comes from notions we have about normative behavior. Therefore, we classify the other person, which leads to the development of expectations and the formulation of approaches that might be appealing.

BEING EMPATHIC

It is believed that empathy is one of the important conditions for managing the social interactions of an interview. Empathy is difficult to define and describe. Experts vary in their discussions. There is, however, a good deal of theory on the subject (Fischer 1978; Truax and Mitchell 1971; Weinstein 1969).

Empathy is considered to be the accurate assessment of another person's definition of a situation, while conveying that understanding in a genuine manner, with personal warmth. Empathy seems to depend on the correctness of the practitioner's grasp of what the client feels and means. To grasp and map meanings, the practitioner must keep several possible perspectives in mind at the same time, juggling them to achieve harmony between what the client means and what the practitioner understands. The practitioner attempts to answer the question: *Which among several possibilities best depicts to me what the other person is going through?*

Another characteristic of empathy is *cue sensitivity*. This means extracting, from a number of immediate cues, the reality of a situation as the client sees it. This ability has to be learned, mostly from experience, but also through laboratory drills. To start with, we take as background what we know about people from our personal lives, our education, and our previous employment. Our past collection of experiences will have taught us to define the meaning of many gestures, facial expressions, common voice inflections, and feeling states.

Empathy is a heightened cue sensitivity that helps us to recognize and discriminate subtle differences in what is going on between people in various situations. We learn this heightened sensitivity from repeated exposure to circumstances. We judge how right and how wrong we are, store up a repertoire of discriminations, and draw on them for understanding.

It is possible to overgeneralize what we perceive if we exclude relevant cues because they are discrepant. We can err by focusing only on a narrow section of what the other person is saying, or if we ignore non-verbal signals and contradictions in what the individual is saying. Words are easily falsified, accidentally or deliberately, so they must always be understood in their context. An interviewing attitude of cautious defensiveness and closed-mindedness inhibits cue sensitivity, leading to stereotypical perceptions. An open-minded and moderately self-confident attitude is best.

Empathy is not an interviewing technique. It is part of the context of interviewing. It is an integral part of every interview situation. Empathy is generally recognized as part of the relationship between practitioner and client. It comes into being in the social interactions during interviewing. There are differences of opinion among psychotherapy researchers about the content of the empathic relationship and about its specific effect on the outcomes of psychotherapy (Matarazzo 1978). Although the research and theory development about empathy has been conducted on "client-centered psychotherapy," the ideas have been adopted, to a greater or lesser extent, throughout many of the human services. Empathy theory has delineated the special value and necessity of forming a helpful relationship with clients.

Despite a good deal of uncertainty among research findings, there is virtual agreement that the following qualities of practitioner posture toward clients are desirable and probably necessary (Truax and Mitchell 1971):

1. Behaving in a nonphony, nondefensive, and authentic or genuine manner.
2. Providing a nonthreatening, safe, secure atmosphere by accepting the client, regarding her positively, and being warm and nonpossessive.
3. Having a high degree of accurate empathic understanding of the client on a moment-to-moment basis.

A REPERTOIRE OF TACTICS FOR SOCIAL INTERACTION

The interviewer needs a repertoire of tactics that can be called into play selectively to construct individual actions. This book will provide the fundamentals of such a repertoire.

The basic repertoire for interviewing consists of the following parts.

NORMS OF INTERVIEWING

Interviewing norms are the rules of the game. They provide a general idea of the parameters of reasonable and effective interviewing practice. Norms alone are not sufficient to carry one through an interview. While having the normative structures in mind, the interviewer must exercise thought, raise questions (either verbally or silently), consider several possible explanations and lines of action, and flexibly adjust to the persons being interviewed. There is variation among experts on how to state and describe interviewing norms.

CLEAR SPEECH

The interviewer's choice of words and phrases should be straightforward English, without jargon. Clear speech comes from logical thinking, possession of facts, and understanding reputable theory. Professional speech is a dialect used by members of a professional subculture as a shorthand way of communicating with one another. Jargon is a way to attract attention and display elitism. Professionals have a hard enough time understanding one another without inflicting their confusion on clients. All jargon used in human service work in interviews can be translated into plain English, and should be. The only exception is jargon that has entered into common usage, such as "freudian slips."

One does not need to be a skilled logician to communicate logically. We do, however, need to approximate a condition where what we say is demonstrably connected to what has previously been said and to ordinary speech norms and conventions. Our speech should be relatively complete so that the client can know what we are talking about.

Clear speech also results from having some basic facts straight so as to minimize vagueness and error. A firm grasp of an acceptable and generally understandable theory of human behavior and of professional practice aids clear speech. It will provide an elemental order that will enable the interpretation of interview events.

LISTENING BEHAVIORS

Listening is the vehicle by which most information is acquired from clients. No listening — no interview. Listening requires thinking while paying attention to the client. We want to collect information and think about what it means. Listening is the process by which facts are obtained so that clear speech may result.

Rules for good listening have been stated ably by Kadushin (1972, pp. 187-200). Slightly modified, these rules are:

1. Be attentive to general themes rather than details.
2. Be guided in listening by the purpose of the interview in order to screen out irrelevancies.
3. Be alert in order to catch what is said.
4. Normally, don't interrupt, except to change the subject intentional-

ly, to stop excessive repetition, or to stop clients from causing themselves undue distress.

5. Let the silences be, and listen to them. The client may be finished, or thinking, or waiting for the practitioner, or feeling resentful. Resume talking when you have made a judgment about what the silence means, or ask the client if you do not understand.

FLEXIBILITY

It is wise to go into an interview with a preferred plan plus one or two backup plans. It is never possible to predict exactly what will happen. It is best to be prepared to change in the course of interviewing. Flexibility takes practice. Departing from plans should not be a whim but, since plans are variable, they should not be adhered to when they seem to be failing. Lack of flexibility can result in undesired consequences, such as angering a client who perceives rigidity as an improper attempt to control, or failing to follow the client's thoughts and feelings, resulting in lack of communication from the client.

Communication processes in interviewing

Communication in interviewing is the transmission of messages regarding the reasons for the meetings between client and practitioner. This communication normally takes place through verbal language, facial expressions, body movements, and statements made about the situation and the encounter's aims and purposes.

COMMUNICATION AS THE CORE OF THE INTERVIEWING PROCESS

What goes on in communication is fairly straightforward. The communicator is getting across her message. The thought is put into language constructed according to the conventions of speech and the norms of social interactions. Speech conventions are the rules and agreements among speakers that identify common usage, so that one speaker understands another. A norm is similar in definition; it is a rule or principle. The practitioner should try to develop the ability to use language that the client will understand. However, the client's ability to understand the message being sent by the practitioner is not only a result of the practitioner's skill but is also the result of the client's characteristics, abilities, mind-set, and familiarity with speech conventions and norms of social interaction.

When we interview or are interviewed, we are communicating something to somebody. The modern science of communications is technical and complex, dealing with millions of words spoken by all kinds of people under a multitude of conditions. An enormous amount of research and conceptual and theory building work are needed to bring all the information under observation, sort it, and try to understand it.

Transferring and receiving information, such as facts, thoughts, attitudes, and emotions, is the business of communication. Spoken and written words and body motions, such as gestures, transmit content. The listener hears the interview content and mentally processes it. Signals of communication, such as words and motions, are transmitted and received. Thus is communication effected, with details such as sound, phrasing, turn taking, pausing, interrupting, nodding, and squirming. Communications research and theory building studies describe a range of factors such as social groups, social relations, personal attitudes, feelings, expectations, hopes, and traits. Interviewing can be thought of as a special form of communication with its own constraints and characteristics, created by the circumstances of a particular interview and the traits and conditions of the persons participating (Cross 1974; Hudson 1980).

SPEECH COMMUNICATION

The fundamentals of interviewing are talk; extralinguistic sounds such as tones of voice, sighs, and hesitations; and body movements and gestures. The modern systematic study of human speech behavior is of recent origin, dating from the 1940s, although early studies date back to the turn of the century. This field of research is in the process of identifying basic concepts and theory and developing satisfactory methodology.

Speech, or verbal communication, deals with individual speakers in interaction with listeners. The physical equipment that an individual uses to communicate consists of speech organs, hearing organs, arms and hands for gesturing, facial features, the nervous system, and the brain. Memory, which involves the psycho-physiological process of information storage and retrieval, is another part of communication. The way these components are constructed and the way in which they function greatly determine communication. The uses to which these components are put in social interaction result in the talking and listening roles and power positions that affect discourse.

Situational properties that surround communicators include environmental objects, other people, culture, attitudes, and history (Yngve 1975). Acts of communication include hundreds of thousands of sounds, arranged in a multiplicity of patterns, over time. The sheer amount of data staggers the mind and overwhelms theory builders and research methodologists. In addition to the physical properties and characteristics of speech, researchers study such phenomena as pauses, silences, hesitations, incoherences, grumblings, and filler sounds such as "ah" and "eh."

Interruptions have been studied to learn about their frequency, conditions, differences among individuals, and effects on interview productivity (Duncan and Fiske 1977; Goss 1973; Matarazzo and Wiens 1972; Pope 1979).

WORDS AND LANGUAGE

Language is a systematic means of communication, evolving over long periods of time. It is believed to have a biogenetic foundation (Smith and Wilson, 1979). It is a social phenomenon that varies among individuals and cultures. Language changes continually. Only literary language is smooth and logical. A standard literary form is usually developed from a local prestigious dialect. Grammarians, linguists, authors, and journalists establish the norms and conventions of an official dialect. Using standard English (or French, or any other language) is considered a mark of good breeding. Spoken language that appears substandard, which contains "bad grammar," is often considered a badge of ignorance and low status (Cherry 1966).

Spoken language is normally full of breaks, sighs, mumbles, grumbles, hesitations, and repetitions, and is replete with layers of meaning. Interviews show all the characteristics of spoken language, full of fractured sentences, tonal variations, and a certain lack of logic.

Typical examples of expected fractured speech are "Ah — ah — gulp — what — where — ah — when did it happen?" and "Depressed? Well — see — you know — ah depression sometimes is a — ah — ah — bad case of the blues."

The words used in interviewing are not necessarily exact. Some words tend to acquire magical properties and conjure up feelings of fear, wonder, and awe. Some words are taboo and have substitutes that hide or confuse meaning. Other words are "trendy" and are used for display purposes, to be in style, and often to pretend to be sophisticated.

An example is the word "sick." We say, "She is very sick." We might mean she has encephalitis. We might mean she acts weirdly, or carries out violent acts for which there is no obvious reason, endangering other people. Or we might mean she flunks all the easy courses but gets an "A" in mathematics. Or that she always seems to fall in with the wrong sort of men. Or that she has been diagnosed as psychotic. We might mean that we are compassionate about her undesirable social behavior and we want her to be helped and understood, not punished and judged. Or we might be unnerved because she is 13 years old and pregnant, so we say she is "P.G." — conveying her condition without specifying it. Or we might say she is "sick" because that word signifies that we have credentialed language, associating us with a profession. In some circumstances, such as a supervisory conference, calling her "sick" would generally convey some information. But if the hearers are not acquainted with our secret language or "lingo," they might not have any idea what we were talking about.

The simplest word signs denote unique, specific referents: names and social security numbers refer to people, license numbers refer to cars. The most common nouns, such as "man," "woman," "house," and "child," are somewhat vague but are reasonably definite for most purposes of description.

But then we get to another class of words that are open to an infinite variety of interpretations. The word "good" is an example. When we say somebody has a "good" relationship with his child, what exactly does that mean? We say someone is "troubled." Does that mean he just shot the president, stole a coat from a department store, or hit his wife?

Neither written nor spoken language is precise. We develop our own styles of language use, some more artistic than others. We all acquire some kind of language style that is composed of our choice of vocabulary and the demeanor we adopt in our delivery. Someone may use a lot of slang and still come across as a schoolteacher or a martinet. Someone else may use a high-toned collection of professional jargon and come across as chic, trendy, and important. Or both people may sound foolish.

Some exquisitely detailed studies of word usage have suggested that:

> the multitudinous conversations which are going on in this country at this moment, all the chatter and gossip, are largely independent individual events; yet as a whole they have a conformity which statistical analysis would reveal, corresponding to current topics and interests, conventional greetings, cliches, and platitudes. But each person is only as 'free to speak his mind' as his language allows. He may depart more and more from the statistics, from the rules, and his originality increases. So far but no farther; for if he departs too far, he fails to communicate (Cherry 1966, p. 107).

PATTERNS OF DISCOURSE

The flow of discourse in speech and in interviews reveals many patterns (Figure 1). The most common and the simplest patterns have received a good deal of research attention (Hudson 1980). Beyond those, however, complications arise. Every interviewer knows how complicated interview discourse can get, and communications researchers and experts find these matters just as complicated. We are a long way from discovering the kinds of speech regularities that might lead to exact rules. We are

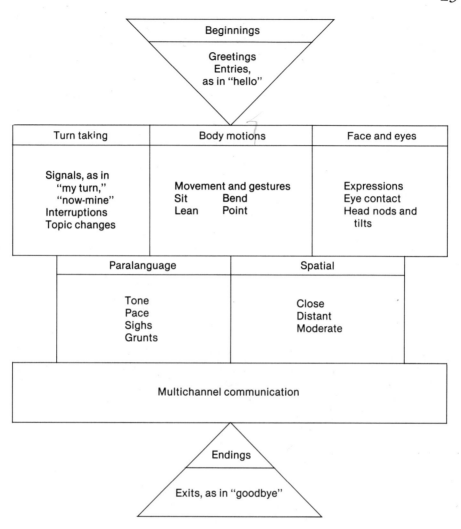

FIGURE 1   Patterns of discourse.

governed in our techniques by general and incomplete understanding of the state of the art of discourse.

BEGINNINGS AND ENDINGS

Greetings and farewells are the beginnings and endings of speech sections and are called *entries* and *exits,* respectively. In between is the *business.* Exits and entries indicate the tone of the participants' relationship. The greeting communicates that the other person is wanted, expected, and welcome, or unwanted, unexpected, and unwelcome, or that the reception is mixed. The greeting is an important piece of information for the client, who is usually unsure of the reception. The farewell communicates a reassurance that the relationship is unchanged or, if it has changed, how it has changed. All this is in the interest of minimizing misunderstanding and creating a healthy climate for the business at hand.

Entries and exits in a professional interview tend to be neutral. Interviewers' behaviors tend to be a compromise between what they really feel and what is expected of them in their occupational role, or their situational identity. There are many examples of wording for entries and exits, all of them good. What matters is that the greeting acknowledge that a new encounter has begun. The length of the greeting is generally proportional to the length of time since the last meeting. A short absence calls for a short greeting, and a long absence for a longer greeting. Important people tend to get a longer greeting than unimportant people. A client is likely to negatively perceive a practitioner as curt or abrupt if the greeting and the exit are short and cool.

TAKING TURNS

In conversation, turn taking is a central feature. In an interview involving two persons, it is assumed that each will take a turn to speak and each will take a turn to listen. Meanwhile, both can be expected to accompany their turn, either speaking or listening, with a variety of body motions, gestures, and facial expressions. The speaker will probably hesitate, repeat, be incomplete in expressions, and fill in with a variety of sounds, such as "ah." The listener will also usually make sounds.

SIGNALS

Direct statements may convey signals. Usually, conventional cues indicate that the speaker is about to yield or that the listener wishes to speak. Sensitive responses to these cues make for smooth transitions from speaker to speaker. Rules of etiquette recognize the value of cues. But because of pressures felt by either participant, cues for a change of turns may not be recognized or may be ignored. Then interruptions or simultaneous talk occur.

INTERRUPTIONS

Normally interruptions are frowned on in polite discourse, but they may result in informative and meaningful discussion, conveying large amounts of quality information. Interruptions may be power plays and may tell a good deal about the motives and misperceptions of the participants. It has been suggested in the research literature that when two people converse, they tend to obey conventions about identifying and responding to a fairly regularized system of turn taking. This procedure is advantageous because it coordinates the action. However, instead of smooth, coordinated turn taking, an interaction strategy can be followed that serves the purposes of competition, deceit, or ingratiation (Duncan and Fiske 1977).

A smooth, coordinated discourse is desired for most business interviews. Coordination depends a good deal on the quality and recognition of signals in the turn-taking system. Occasionally the signal is verbal: "I want to talk!" or "My turn." It may be nonverbal but vocal, such as throat clearing. Often the signal is a hand gesture; it is advisable for interviewers to watch for such gestures in order to pick up the cue. We should try not to confuse a signal with a movement taken simply to reduce an arm cramp or relieve pressure from clothing. Shy, withdrawn, or cautious participants may signal a desire for a turn by the quality of their gaze or the look in their eye. Signals indicating willingness to yield tend to be voice changes but could also be gestures.

If the interaction is to be smooth, signals should generally be permissive, not coercive. Nevertheless, attempts to coerce participation do occur. They do not normally lead to coordination, having a tendency to produce conflict. Conflict may occasionally be wanted in an interview, but normally it is not. It may occur, nevertheless, even if unwanted (Duncan and Fiske 1977).

Because discourse contains numerous layers of intent and meaning, turn taking is not simply a matter of mechanical changing of speaker and listener roles in some kind of orderly manner. In professional discourse there is often uncertainty about who should speak, or whether a turn should be given up by the practitioner. For example, if a client signals to break in on the practitioner's speech, should the practitioner say, "Let me finish"? Who should do most of the talking is another common question in interviewing. When should an interviewer interrupt and change the content? Turn-taking decisions are made with split-second timing and produce definite reactions in the other person.

ADJACENCY PAIRS

Adjacency pairs is a term for a type of turn taking consisting of statements that require a particular response. For instance, a question is normally followed by an answer. In interviews pairing is different from that in an oral test or in a classroom. Answers given in an interview may be statements of fact. They may also take the form of another question, a gesture such as a yes-or-no nod, a large body movement (standing up, clenching and shaking a fist, slumping into a chair), looking away or looking down, or a deceitful statement, to name only the most obvious.

A greeting normally is responded to with a greeting. If not, a whole world of negative meaning may be inferred. A complaint is normally followed by an apology, but it may be followed by a denial, an explanation, or an invitation to explore the subject. A summons is normally expected to receive a conventional answer; but it may receive a rejection, or a surprised or upset response. An invitation is normally supposed to receive an acceptance, but it may also receive a suspicious response.

TOPIC CHANGES

Another attribute of turn-taking activities in interviews is topic changing. It often seems that speakers never finish a subject, fail to explore the topic with logic and thoroughness, or fail to proceed from the general to the specific. Speech is frequently inconclusive, or firm decisions get made without the "i's" dotted and the "t's" crossed. It has been suggested that part of the looseness of discourse and frequency of topic change result from the large quantity of information possessed by the persons involved, and also from making assumptions about what others are saying or meaning without pursuing the details (Hudson 1980).

BODY MOTION: IN GENERAL

The way we stand, sit, bend, posture, and move may reveal what we are thinking. There are five ways in which we use our bodies to communicate. First, we use our faces to express messages, especially through gazing or glancing at others. Second, we use paralanguage, which consists of voice tones, pitch, inflection, and miscellaneous sounds that we make. Third, we use gestures. Fourth, we arrange our bodies within the space we have (proxemics). Fifth, by complex combinations of nonverbal behavior, we "leak" information that we do not speak (Weitz 1974).

Within cultures, and to some extent across cultures, there appear to be basic facial expressions that communicate messages about what we feel, and to some extent, about what we think. It is believed that these expressions are inborn, at least to some degree. It is relatively certain that we learn to "talk" with our faces through socialization experiences, and we learn to "read" faces through experience. By the time we are old enough to become interviewers we possess a basic supply of such signs.

Most interviewers and many clients depend on stereotyped facial expressions and gestures. It is comforting to depend on them to smooth the way through communication interactions with people we barely know or, perhaps, distrust. Interviewers tend to maintain a neutral, impartial, relaxed, pleasant, relatively immobile expression. This expression is considered to be best when interacting with a client, who is present for a service, not for social interaction for its own sake.

Still, interviewers are interested in reading the faces of clients to discover more about their thoughts and reactions. Clients are interested in reading an interviewer's face to find out how they are doing. Reading faces may be one of the crucial skills involved in the production of empathy.

BODY MOVEMENT AND GESTURES

It has been estimated that the human face can produce over 20,000 different facial expressions. Ray L. Birdwhistell (1974), one of the most prominent researchers studying movement, asserts that the following types of body movements have been isolated in studies of Americans:

1. Head nods: one nod, two nods, three nods
2. Head sweeps: one sweep and two sweeps
3. Head cock
4. Head tilt
5. Head raise and hold
6. Head position hold
7. Eyebrow lifts: lifted brow, lowered brow, knit brow, single brow movement
8. Lid closure: over-open, slit, closed, squeezed
9. Laugh lines
10. Nose movements: wrinkle-nose, compressed nostrils, bilateral nostril flare, uninostril flare or closure
11. Mouth: compressed lips, protruded lips, retracted lips, withdrawn lips, snarl, lax open mouth
12. Chin: chin thrust, lateral chin thrust, puffed cheeks, sucked-in cheeks

Depending in part on their cultural background, speakers often use characteristic body, hand, and face movements to mark out the arrangement in their speech, almost as if the movement were an integral part of the talk and its meaning. For example, the lifted shoulders and spread-out arms of Pierre Trudeau convey a nonverbal communication that says: "Isn't that so?" "Right?" "How else could it be!" Ronald Reagan's famous lateral head sweeps convey open and honest certitude. Alexander Haig's jutting chin says, "I am determined" and "It is so." Humphrey Bogart, the master of the lifted eyebrow, conveys paragraphs questioning your naivete and deceit. It has been theorized that these movements, and others, may in fact represent organized language that is not yet deciphered!

Listeners' movements affect the speaker. An interviewer can be thrown off balance by a client who drums her fingers, looks around, or nods in an unusual way. Such listener movements may give us an impression that we have not "gotten through" or communicated, or we just might not know what effect we had. A client can convey enough meaning through movements to cause an interviewer to change course. A listener's movements are feedback to the interviewer, affecting how the speaker proceeds. A listener, whether interviewer or client, tends to anticipate or make a prediction about what the speaker will say, at least over the short term, and starts to prepare a response ahead of time (Kendon 1974).

FACIAL EXPRESSIONS AND VISUAL INTERACTION

As interviewers, we need to pay attention to eyebrow flashing (or winking) and eyebrow lifting, both our own and the client's. There is a wide assortment of winks, blinks, and furrows. There are interesting studies that have analyzed the eyebrow lift as communicating surprise, as an accompaniment to asking a question, as expressing curiosity, and also as expressing indignation, arrogance, disapproval, or negation. A flashing eyebrow or winking eye is thought to express something positive such as approval, greeting, flirting, seeking confirmation, thanking, or emphasizing (Eibl-Eibes 1974). Consideration of the many possible signals that can be expressed by eyebrow movements alone shows us that we have to be conscious of our facial movements. The approved neutrality of expression that is the general rule for interviews is one of the ways we attempt to control facial expressions so that we minimize sending messages that are inappropriate.

Clients also guard their facial expressions, making it difficult for us to read them. To the extent, however, that clients are unguarded, we can pick up clues to their thoughts and feelings by observing their eyebrow movements. Because of the wide array of possible meanings, however, we ought not to jump to conclusions about what clients' faces are telling. We should obtain evidence from verbal statements to confirm or reject a hypothesis regarding their nonverbal communication.

There is some credible evidence that women are more effective than men at sending and receiving information via facial expressions. Related research indicates that persons who themselves have relatively inexpressive faces nevertheless are capable of effectively sensing other people's affect. It seems probable that such people have learned to inhibit affect but remain sensitive. They can feel "inside" what another person is communicating with his expressions (Buck et al. 1974). It would appear to be a reasonably safe hypothesis that even though interviewers inhibit their own facial expressions they do not lose touch with their perceptions of clients.

EYE CONTACT

Eye contact is one of the most complex facial expressions used in interactive power plays and also in sensing preferences and attractions (Exline 1974). It seems quite certain that people resent being stared at. The good manners taught to us in childhood are supported by research, leading to one interviewing rule that probably has no exceptions: *don't stare.* Being stared at is usually reacted to as a threat. It has been found that people seem most comfortable with moderate eye contact, and least comfortable with the extremes of either never being looked at or being stared at.

Assuming that the interviewer will make moderate eye contact, what might we assume if the client stares or persistently looks away? Research studies on reactions to these two types of eye contact suggest that the nonlooking listener is perceived as disinterested or rejecting, and the silent starer is perceived as deviant. It is not known for certain if these perceptions are correct, but it is common knowledge that interviewers find nonspeakers who stare or look away ("avoid eye contact") to be troublesome clients.

The research reported on eye contact behaviors of persons suggests that eye contact behavior is among the most difficult to decipher. This difficulty has been recognized in our general appraisal of interaction by such expressions as "the eyes are the window of the soul." We sometimes think that if we could read the other person's gaze, we would know all we need. From an empirical standpoint, we do not know enough about the forms and meanings of eye contact to offer a dictionary of meanings.

PARALANGUAGE

Paralanguage deals with tone of voice, pacing of speech, sighs, grunts, and similar nonverbal accompaniments to words. Tone of voice and manner of vocal delivery convey immense amounts of information. In fact tone, under many circumstances, tells more than the words themselves. It seems reasonable to suggest that a good tone, together with relevant words, enhance interview communication. It is likely that subtle but real messages are sent by interviewers through paralanguage. These messages affect interaction with clients and elicit or restrain client feelings of trust, expectation, and attraction (Weitz 1974). Tone is a vehicle through which empathy is conveyed.

SPATIAL BEHAVIOR

Proxemics refers to the study of patterns of interpersonal distance in face-to-face encounters (Erickson 1975). How the client spontaneously positions himself in an interviewing space is a source of interest for the interviewer. But very little is known about spacing the body in interviews beyond the level of interviewing folklore. A few bits of insight can be gleaned from research in this field. Hall (1974) refers to three categories of space in face-to-face interactions: fixed, semifixed, and dynamic. Walls and other territorial boundaries are fixed features, such as the office of the interviewer, the place occupied by his desk, the home of the client, and the schoolroom of the teacher.

The space between persons is usually a fluid or dynamic feature of the interview. Anxiety can be generated by sitting or standing too close or far apart for the norms and preferences of others. It is not all right for an interviewer to move too close to, breathe on, or touch most clients. As with facial expressions, it is advisable to be moderate until experience with a client develops signals that tell how close or how distant is enough. Clients, of course, might move in or move away from an interviewer, creating a need for the interviewer to take some protective measures.

Furnishings of a room may be considered semifixed when they are easily movable. A good example of a semifixed informal interviewing arrangement is when people sit around a coffee table, walk around, and move chairs. A fixed furniture arrangement is one where the space is organized to demonstrate the superiority or power of the interviewer. The standard procedure of putting the client at the other end of the desk is the typical arrangement to protect the interviewer's authority and induce a feeling of submission in the client.

Cultural background appears to play a large part in how people place themselves with others. Most North Americans stay outside the olfactory space of the other person, but some cultures have a preference for being able to sense smells. People vary a good deal with respect to their tolerance for noise and stimulating sights. They will position themselves to achieve comfort at whatever level is right for them. It is believed that there is no known universal distance-setting mechanism.

MULTICHANNEL COMMUNICATION

Some communication uses a variety of verbal and nonverbal channels simultaneously. Confronted with a live interviewee, we rarely if ever consider channels of communication separately. What we have is a combined phenomenon, a person using all or most verbal and nonverbal channels of interpersonal communication. What we hope is that with luck and skill we may decode what is going on with all the channels operating. The various communication channels "leak" into one another. Several channels may support one another affirmatively or contradict one another. The words

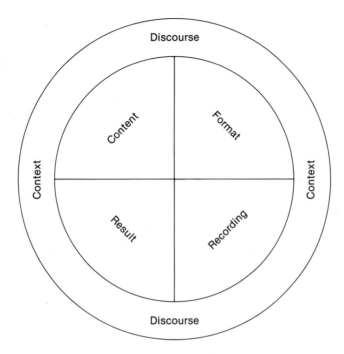

FIGURE 2   Composition of an interview.

say one thing and the eyes another. The pleasant friendly demeanor may belie the clenched fists and the head movements. It is because of the multichannel signaling phenomenon that interviewers need to be alert observers and have a good mixing mechanism — that is, listening.

COMPOSITION OF AN INTERVIEW (Figure 2)

An interview is made up of patterns of discourse, which are speech and body motions. Discourse takes place within the context of surrounding environment, has content, and has a format, or arrangement. The format consists of a particular interview mode, its planned or accidental sequence, and its organization, all designed to deliver a service or to influence and change a client. The process ends with a recording for administrative purposes. The balance of this book deals with identifying the various parts that make up the interview.

Summary: understanding interviewing

Every interviewer perceives that there are a multitude of happenings in the encounter with a client. Before looking into details about how to interview, it is advisable to observe, identify, and understand the arena in which interviewing takes place. Such understanding provides a map for interviewing details.

Interviewing is a fundamental occurrence for provision of human services of all kinds. Yet the scientific study of interviewing has only recently begun. Although some research and theory has been developed, the scholarly study of interviewing is in its infancy.

Interviewing is a primary activity for understanding people and their problems; it is a conversation between a professional practitioner and people who wish to receive help of a problem-solving type. Interviewing organizes thoughts in order to improve a problem situation and is an essential part of the problem-solving process. During the interview the allocation and provision of resources can be organized, and the implementing of strategies for changing people and their environment can be initiated.

An interview consists of social interactions and communications processes. Interviewers and interviewees encounter one another in places and under conditions where one is expected to provide help and the other to obtain help. In the process of this interaction, each one attempts to define the situation, to size up and understand the other. They arrive at a preliminary, tacit agreement about their purposes and their situational identities. The interviewer adopts a professional posture that includes responsibility for analyzing what seems to be going on, as well as responsibility for establishing and guiding the helping process constructively.

Certain lines of action normally organize the interview. An agreement on the focus should occur, as should a perception about what kind of person the client is. Following interviewing norms, the practitioner should project an empathic spirit during the interview, speak clearly in order to be understood, listen attentively, and adopt an attitude of flexibility.

Communication is the core of the interviewing process. It consists of transferring and receiving information such as facts, thoughts, attitudes, and emotions. Verbal communication is the medium for interviewing. Language — words, phrases, and sentences — is the means for conveying information. Verbal language is augmented by body motions, gesture, voice tones and timbre, and by spatial arrangements of people. Speech customs, personal styles, and cultural characteristics give particular form to an individual's speech. The language used by an interviewer is his personal language, formed by upbringing, education, and experience. Personal language is augmented and changed by knowledge about interviewing norms.

Verbal discourse tends to follow patterns. Greetings and farewells usually begin and end the discourse, carried out with ordinary social conventions. The face communicates nonverbal messages through facial expressions, eye contact, nods, and head tilts. Although we depend on the face for communication, it sometimes gives uncertain and ambiguous messages.

Discourse depends on customary turn-taking behaviors, which create order as interviewer and interviewee talk about various topics. Meanwhile body motions add content to messages. Tones of voice and nonverbal sounds add meaning to verbal messages. The physical positions taken by people in an interview may contain messages that enhance or disguise what is being said.

Most verbal interchange simultaneously involves many types of communication instruments. Information received forms a pattern in which all elements are in flux. This complex of many communication elements, called multichannel communications, makes understanding complex. Experiencing the whole pattern will enhance our ability to grasp its meaning.

REFERENCES

Birdwhistell, Ray L. "Toward Analyzing American Movement." In *Nonverbal Communication,* edited by Shirley Weitz. New York: Oxford University Press, 1974.

Briar, Katherine H. "Interviewing: A Scientific, Artistic, or Mechanistic Process." In *The Pursuit of Competence in Social Work,* edited by Frank W. Clark, Morton L. Arkava, et al., 179-192. San Francisco: Jossey-Bass Publishers, 1979.

Buck, Ross W., et al. "Communication of Affect Through Facial Expressions in Humans." In *Nonverbal Communication,* edited by Shirley Weitz. New York: Oxford University Press, 1974.

Cherry, Colin. *On Human Communication.* Cambridge: The M.I.T. Press, 1966.

Cross, Crispin P. *Interviewing and Communication in Social Work.* London: Routledge & Kegan Paul, 1974.

Dong Yul, Lee, et al. "Development and Validation of a Microcounseling Skill Discrimination Scale." *Journal of Counseling Psychology,* no. 22 (May 1975): 468-472.

Duncan, Starkey, Jr., and Fiske, Donald W. *Face-to-Face Interaction: Research, Methods, and Theory.* Hillsdale, N.J.: Lawrence Erlbaum Associates, Publishers, 1977.

Eibl-Eibes, Feldt. "Similarities and Differences Between Cultures in Expressive Movements." In *Nonverbal Communication,* edited by Shirley Weitz, 20-33. New York: Oxford University Press, 1974.

Erickson, Frederick. "One Function of Proxemic Shifts in Face-to-Face Interaction." In *Organization of Behavior in Face-to-Face Interaction,* edited by Adam Kendon, Richard M. Harris, and Mary Ritchie Key. The Hague: Mouton Publishers, 1975.

Exline, Ralph V. "Visual Interaction: Glances of Power and Preference." In *Nonverbal Communication,* edited by Shirley Weitz. New York: Oxford University Press, 1974.

Fischer, Joel. *Effective Casework Practice: An Ecletic Approach.* New York: McGraw-Hill Book Company, 1978.

Frank, Jerome. *Persuasion and Healing.* New York: Schocken Books, 1974.

Gartner, Alan. *The Preparation of Human Service Professionals.* New York: Human Sciences Press, 1976.

Goss, Albert E. "Speech and Language." In *Handbook of General Psychology,* edited by Benjamin B. Wolman, 568-629. Englewood Cliffs, N.J.: Prentice-Hall Inc., 1973.

Hall, Edward T. "Proxemics." In *Nonverbal Communication,* edited by Shirley Weitz, 203-229. New York: Oxford University Press, 1974.

Hudson, R.A. *Sociolinguistics.* Cambridge: Cambridge University Press, 1980.

Ivey, Allen E. "Microcounseling and Media Therapy: State of the Art." *Counselor Education and Supervision,* no. 13 (March 1974):172-183.

Kadushin, Alfred. *The Social Work Interview.* New York: Columbia University Press, 1972.

Kendall, R.E. *The Role of Diagnosis in Psychiatry.* Oxford: Blackwell Scientific Publications, 1975.

Kendon, Adam. "Movement Coordination in Social Interaction." In *Nonverbal Communication,* edited by Shirley Weitz, 150-168. New York: Oxford University Press, 1974.

Konrad, George. *The Caseworker.* New York: Harcourt Brace Jovanovich, 1974 (paperback edition).

Marshall, Eldonk; Charping, John W.; and Bell, William J. "Interpersonal Skills Training: A Review of Research." *Social Work Research and Abstracts,* no. 15 (Spring 1979):10-16.

Matarazzo, Joseh D., and Wiens, Arthur N. *The Interview: Research on Its Anatomy and Structure.* Chicago: Aldine-Atherton, 1972.

Matarazzo, Ruth G. "Research on the Teaching and Learning of Psychotherapeutic Skills." In *Handbook of Psychotherapy and Behavior Change,* edited by S.C. Garfield and A.E. Bergin, 836-875. New York: John Wiley and Sons, 1978.

Pope, Benjamin. *The Mental Health Interview: Research and Application.* New York: Pergamon Press, 1979.

Schinke, S.P., et al. "Interview Skills Training: An Empirical Evaluation." *Journal of Social Service Research* 1 (1978):391-401.

Smith, Neil, and Wilson, Deidre. *Modern Linguistics.* New York: Penguin Books, 1979.

Truax, Charles B., and Mitchell, Kevin M. "Research on Certain Therapist Interpersonal Skills in Relation to Process and Outcome." In *Handbook of Psychotherapy and Behavior Change,* edited by Allen E. Bergin and Sol L. Garfield, 299-344. New York: John Wiley and Sons, 1971.

Weinstein, Eugene A. "The Development of Interpersonal Competence." In *Handbook of Socialization Theory and Research,* edited by David A. Goslin. Chicago: Rand McNally College Publishing Co., 1969.

Weitz, Shirley, ed. *Nonverbal Communication.* New York: Oxford University Press, 1974.

Yngve, Victor H. "Human Linquistics and Face-to-Face Interaction." In *Organization of Behavior in Face-to-Face Interaction,* edited by Adam Kendon, Richard M. Harris, and Mary Ritchie Key. The Hague: Mouton Publishers, 1975.

Zastrow, Charles, and Navarre, Ralph. "Using Videotape Role Playing to Assess and Develop Competence." In *The Pursuit of Competence in Social Work,* edited by E.W. Clark and M.L. Arkava, 193-204. San Francisco: Jossey-Bass, 1979.

CHAPTER 2

Four common problems and their solutions

Interviewing goes beyond intellectual understanding of concepts to the immediate impact of a personal encounter. The mediating processes referred to in Chapter 1 come into play at once. To overcome the tension aroused when two or more strangers start to interact, we call upon our backgrounds, or our "stored memories." The interviewer possesses a bank of interactional resources to draw from. The interviewer can depend on learning already acquired from past experience.

Other sources of strength for the interviewer are the quality of concern for the client's welfare, the existence of a basic or broad fund of specialized knowledge, and the sharpness of thought that comes from professional interest in the client's type of problem.

Some of the potential pitfalls of getting started will be described in this chapter, along with ideas about avoiding problems. Activities to ease the process of getting started will be suggested.

Preparation

It is advisable to spend 5 to 15 minutes preparing. That means remembering where the last interview ended, on what note it ended, and what the main substance of the interview was.

Every practitioner should have a notebook. In some agencies the practitioner makes brief notations on a log or chart (see Chapter 11). The practitioner remembers by looking over notes and trying to re-picture the interview's emotional climate. The practitioner then mentally notes and probably jots down on paper what is expected to be the key point or points of the upcoming interview. The key points are derived from a combination of (1) an understanding with the client on the next topic, as decided or tacitly indicated in the last interview; (2) the practitioner's reflections about information or direction needed; (3) the present position of the work in light of the agreed-upon or necessary goals; and (4) suggestions about the upcoming order of business from administrative, supervisory, or consultant discussions.

If this is to be a first interview, the interviewer will review any salient documents or verbal reports. If there are no documents or verbal reports — for example, in the case of a "walk-in" — the practitioner relies on past experience with walk-ins or on a fund of past experience with unexpected encounters. Several alternative scenarios should be prepared in skeleton form, to be thought about as the interview progresses.

Common problems and their solutions

Four common problems may occur when starting an interview: (1) "freezing," (2) talking too much, (3) not noticing, and (4) imagining things. There can be various explanations for these problems, but the author's explanations and recommendations will be provided here.

FREEZING

Freezing is a response often felt by inexperienced interviewers at the start of an interview. It may even continue into the body of the interview. What happens is that the interviewer senses being overwhelmed and inadequate, gets a "dry mouth" and butterflies in the stomach, does not know what to do with hands or feet, and forgets things. Freezing is stage fright. It afflicts most new workers and some experienced people. In his autobiography Laurence Olivier, an experienced actor, tells how he developed stage fright after many years of being on the stage. The affliction left him eventually, although he never knew why he got it or why it left.

The way this problem appears in interviews is that the interviewer feels stopped from speaking. He is inhibited and may be so tense that he cannot hear the client. There are numerous types of explanations for anxiety. A modest amount of this feeling when facing a new endeavor is normal and of short duration. Most adults who have coped with the multitude of fear-producing stimuli that accompany going to a university, taking examinations, meeting new people, and applying for jobs already possess a set of habits that come to the rescue when a new fear-inducing experience is at hand. Most beginning interviewers know their own system for quickly pulling themselves together and proceeding. But if the system fails, it is advisable to take stock.

The most appropriate explanation for freezing in an interview is that we think of ourselves as lacking in power to produce the desired effect. Expectations of personal efficacy determine whether coping behavior will be initiated, how much effort will be expended, and how long it will be sustained in the face of obstacles and aversive experiences. Just before freezing up, the interviewer will have confronted himself with the thought: *I can't do it. I will make a fool of myself.*

To deal with such a reaction a number of things can be done:

1. *Remember* that nearly every interviewer has felt this way and has overcome the feeling.
2. *Review other frightening experiences you have encountered,* starting with the most recent ones and going backward. Review the outcomes of anxiety attacks you remember. You will realize that you not only lived through them but that you also coped. Tease out what you did to help you get over the attack, and be prepared to repeat those activities. *Appraise your performance accomplishments.*

3. *Review any recent interviews you have observed being done by others.* Review as quickly as you can but do not rush. These could be interviews that you sat in on for training, interviews you have seen on training tapes or films, interviews you read in texts, or interviews you may have seen on educational television. Avoid using interviews filmed for commercial entertainment, such as those in movies and soap operas, where the interviewers are actors performing from a script. These provide unreal, false, and unreliable models. Particularly attend to memories of how the recalled interviews got started and how long silences were resolved. Take any ideas from these memories that spontaneously appeal to you.

   The aim is not to copy a model but to use the memory as encouragement, as you might depend on a friend to give you a little push to get you started on a ski run or get you off a diving board. *Get a grasp of your situation by reviewing vicarious experiences.* If this does not work, go back and arrange to sit in on or observe some interviews in progress, or look at some tapes, or read a text, or do whatever appeals to you as most comfortable. Avoid introspection of the type that assumes that your inhibition is due to underlying personality problems you may or may not have.

4. *Allow yourself to be persuaded that you will perform well.* Take comfort from friendly colleagues who reassure you. Stay away from unfriendly colleagues who might be gratified by your discomfiture. Accept reassurance from a friendly supervisor. Permit yourself to be dependent; the condition is only temporary.

5. *Get your body into a comfortable state.* Do some relaxation exercises, empty your mind, meditate before going into the interview. Open the window in the interviewing room (if you can find one that opens) to let in fresh air. Breathe deeply and evenly when you start to feel the freeze tighten you up. Wear comfortable clothes that you can ignore. Even if you are on a diet, eat something before the interview. Bring coffee into the room for yourself and your client.

6. *Above all: concentrate on your clients.* Listen acutely to what they are saying. Watch them to observe their appearances and actions. Make an effort to sense what they are thinking and feeling. Forget yourself.

TALKING TOO MUCH

How much talk is too much? The general answer is this: say everything you need to, no matter how much or how little, to put the client at ease, to present yourself, to ask the required questions, and to make the necessary comments.

On the other hand, be frugal and economical in the quantity of words and the amount of time used for practitioner talk. Excessive talking is a matter of style and anxiety. Select the essential questions and comments and leave out the rest. If you leave out something important that causes the client to misunderstand, you can fill it in later. Selecting what is most important comes from deciding on goals and a strategy for achieving them.

Some people are just more talkative than others. If the interviewer makes sense, clients are not put off by excess talk. They may become bored, but they will pay attention to sensible content. However, under anxiety conditions such as being an inexperienced beginner in interviewing, low-frequency talkers may freeze. High-frequency talkers may explode with verbiage. Some may do a little of both (see example at the end of this chapter). The central factor to keep in mind is that the client must be afforded the maximum opportunity to talk.

Clients vary in talkativeness just as practitioners do. There are laconic and restrained clients whose verbal productivity is naturally low. One way for a fearful client to preserve a feeling of safety is to say little.

Practitioner overtalking because of interview anxiety is an anxiety-reducing effort. Overtalking is controllable but it has to be recognized. If the client is overwhelmed he may look sleepy or bored and become silent. This may be a sign that the interviewer is talking too much (see example at the end of this chapter). Or the client may start up a process of interrupting without waiting for natural turn taking to occur. The best way to check for overtalking is to tape an interview and monitor the frequency of practitioner talk and the length of time used, and compare those findings to the importance of the subject. It is often possible to discover overtalking by self-observation. Often after a bout of too much talk a practitioner will feel embarrassed. That may be a signal that controls are in order.

To reduce overtalking it is necessary for the practitioner to give up, as much as possible, the illusion that clients can be controlled by words. The next thing is to exercise self-control. Make a check on quantity of practitioner talk. This should be followed by self-observation. By paying attention to and respecting their own feelings, practitioners can learn to anticipate what it feels like when they start talking too much. Having identified the signal of talking too much, they need to be willing to obey a self-imposed command to stop, for example, to finish a sentence and stop even if a thought is left in mid-air. Rarely will the client notice. If the practitioner has stopped too short, the client will give a communication signal, asking or showing that she wants the practitioner to go on.

NOT NOTICING

Noticing is used here to mean something more subtle than observation, although that is not meant to imply that observation is an easy or simple thing to do. It is probably artificial to make distinctions between these two words, but the intention is to note something special that can occur if a practitioner is overly anxious.

By observation we mean paying close attention, watching, and perceiving for a formal or official purpose. In an interview we can observe how a client looks, what his demeanor is, and what the dominant affect is as shown in facial expressions and obvious body motions. We can observe social interactions or individual behaviors. We can watch how a marital couple, parent and child, brother and sister, student and teacher, or family group interact if the participants are with us in the interview setting. We can watch how they quarrel, who starts, who maintains the quarrel, and what they seem to be quarreling about. We can watch how they support one another or frustrate one another. We can perceive sometimes who is misunderstanding whom and about what. We can observe the coming and passing of moods in an individual person. We can observe how a person reacts to the practitioner's role, questions, and comments.

We can observe indirectly by setting up a plan for the client or clients to make written records, or logs, of what is done at stated periods of the day, or in particular places such as work or home. Information can be obtained about problem or coping behaviors, their type and quality, and their frequency, antecedents, and consequences. From such records we can obtain observations that we ourselves do not make directly. We may get useful ideas from actual occurrences for understanding a problem or thinking about solutions. We can ourselves log client behaviors that we see, such as behaviors at playtime or eating time in a day care center or residential children's home. We can engage the cooperation of parents or staff in observing and logging behavior. These are the kinds of observations that we accumulate in the interests of assessment and in order to monitor possible effects of intervention. We can check if there are changes in behavior occurring possibly because of intervention.

Noticing, as used in this book, refers to discerning things that are not overtly obvious. It especially means recognition of some attitude, reaction, sentiment, or sensation that does not surface clearly, and that may be a product of the client's interaction with the practitioner or a response to something vague in the interview setting. Noticing or not noticing is another part of the mediating process that goes on between interacting persons.

Not noticing can happen to practitioners who are anxious because of being in a new and unfamiliar situation or because of great pressure and time shortage. Practitioners who do not have their anxiety under control may be preoccupied. The result is to miss important client-related information. Such practitioners are so occupied paying attention to their own thoughts and sensations that they cannot push attention outward to the client; they are self-absorbed instead of client-absorbed.

Under such conditions it is advisable to slow down, keep cool, and take time out. The practitioner can temporarily leave the interview to pull herself together, or she can make the effort to withdraw into herself for a moment to relax and redirect her attention outward.

We cannot, of course, notice everything even under the best of conditions. Under some conditions our anxiety and inattentiveness will be natural and unavoidable. The idea is to minimize inattention.

IMAGINING THINGS

Imagination is a great attribute. It is the ability to form a mental image of something we cannot actually see or directly perceive. Certain imaginations, however, can defeat an interview. The practitioner may infer that a client has certain characteristics or problems because the practitioner is committed to a persuasive but unhelpful ideology. The practitioner may imagine the client to have attributes of a certain kind because the practitioner wants him to. Both these examples of using imagination are natural and understandable. Everyone comes to an interview with a preordained body of information, impressions, and bits and pieces of disconnected knowledge, all of which compose an ideology. Clients, however, rarely fit the stereotype that results from prepackaged expectations and beliefs. Open-mindedness is called for.

If we imagine that the client is suffering from something hidden and disguised, we may not notice a need for practical services that are available and would reduce the problem.

Some people are afflicted by deep-seated problems of long duration that influence numerous facets of their lives. Usually, however, people are concerned with current and relatively obvious problems. Giving our imaginations excessive free rein to make premature judgments can deter us from concentrating our interview on what concerns the client.

An example

The following interview illustrates all four of the difficulties just discussed. Suggestions are given for better ways to have handled the interview. They are not necessarily the only good suggestions, but they are an improvement over what was actually done. Readers can study these interview interchanges and come to their own conclusions about what might have been said differently.

> Charles is a 13-year-old boy. He was referred to a school counselor because of low grades in English and science. The teachers assessed the youngster as intelligent but performing considerably below capacity. They are competent to make this assessment because of their knowledge of educational processes and experience with children.
>
> In the classroom and in his personal interactions with both the science and literature teachers, Charles is provocative and inattentive. His work is sloppy and inaccurate. Both teachers agree upon the hypothesis that Charles has an "authority problem." They conjecture that the problem is due to conduct problems originating in his relations with his parents. This is the conventional wisdom, they believe.

The excerpts below are from the second interview. (The statements are numbered for reference.) The transcript shows what was actually said, followed by comments and suggestions for better words, phrases, and sentences. The "Discussion of the Interview" will describe which of the four problems of getting started are present.

P is a school counselor whose work is to assess and intervene in a problem of poor academic achievement. At the time of the second interview she has seen the child in one other interview 3 weeks ago and has run into him casually once on the street. Today the child has been taken out of the classroom to work on his school problems with the counselor.

The interview is reproduced in phases. First a portion of the entire interchange is given to get the sense and flow without interruption. Each phase is followed by comments dealing with the four problems and suggestions for better statements. This format shows the discourse patterns as the topics flow.

*First phase**

1. **P:** Now we can just talk about what's been going on in the last couple of weeks, since I haven't seen you in 3 weeks, I almost think it has been.
2. **C:** I saw you when you were walking on the street.
3. **P:** Right. When you were on your way to go ball playing. That was pretty funny that we met there. I was ready to go home, and there you were. There was a woman with you. Was she a teacher from the school?

*P is the practitioner; C is the client.

4. **C:** That was Mrs. Bridges, Dave's mother.

5. **P:** Oh, I see, Was he there too? I didn't recognize him. Were they all kids from your class? Were they kids from the neighborhood?

6. **C:** Some of them were kids from my class. But not the big girl. She goes to a different school. She's at . . .

7. **P:** *(Interrupting)* That was awfully nice for your teacher to take everybody. Is that the first time you've been ball playing this year? Oh—you told me about one other time. I guess it was your second time.

8. **C:** Yeah. I lost my ball.

9. **P:** *(Quickly and upbeat)* Yougonnabuyanotherone??

10. *(Several interchanges about buying balls follow.)*

11. **P:** that sounds like fun. *(silence)* Do kids bring balls to school to play with during recess period?

12. **C:** Sam brought one to school.

13. **P:** Did he play?

14. **C:** Yeah.

15. **P:** That must have been fun.

16. *(Long silence)*

17. **P:** *(Upbeat)* So? What else have you been doing? Done any basketball lately?

18. **C:** Little bit.

19. **P:** After school or during recess time? After school?

20. *(More ball playing talk)*

21. **P:** You been keeping pretty busy, eh?

22. **C:** Yeah.

In this section, all four start-up problems are illustrated. The practitioner has stage fright and is frozen. She does not speak about Charles's academic problems and his undesirable behavior toward teachers. The practitioner has skipped conventional greetings, causing awkwardness in getting into the interview. She is talking too much to try to cover up her anxiety. The subject of the talk is baseball, which has nothing to do with the purpose of the interview. She imagines that the child has an underlying personality disturbance causing his poor performance, but she is not directing the conversation to find out what it is. She also imagines that Charles does not want to reveal himself to her, but she has not noticed that the child is polite and sensitive to her. Charles is playing along until something gets said about his problem. He is scrupulously following the linquistic rule of adjacency pairs by answering the practitioner's questions.

Charles might wonder if there is a secret purpose behind this survey of ball playing. He knows that he is present because of his poor grades. However, the practitioner is so attentive to her own anxiety that she is wasting time and possibly making Charles unnecessarily anxious.

The practitioner should have taken 5 or 10 minutes before the interview to review and relax a bit. She could have jotted down a few notes to bring into the room and glance at. The notes might have read:

Greeting
Apologize for 3-week delay
How is client?
Review purpose
Open up topic of goals
Other

Second phase

23. **P:** So tell me how schoolwork is going.
24. **C:** All right.
25. **P:** I think when we talked last there was mention of your getting into a tutoring situation. I think the slowness of getting things moving is a problem. I don't know about you, but many people get anxious or angry at delays. Possibly you feel that way. I should explain about my delay in getting back to you. I had to go to a meeting in another city to learn more about the psychology of children with academic achievement problems. You know you are hardly alone in that regard. There are many possible explanations. The school might be at fault and the child also. You really have to look at each situation individually. I am really sorry I did not get back to you to tell you I would be away. Perhaps I was thoughtless, but I was feeling rushed. Since we had just gotten acquainted and our relationship was so new, I thought perhaps you would overlook my not saying anything to you about going away.
26. **C:** Uh huh.
27. **P:** I'd like to run this by you and see what you think.
28. **C:** *(Pushy, quick)* Uh huh. All right. Go ahead!
29. **P:** We said something about a tutor. A tutor. That's what you feel. And I would agree. Yeah. You're going to need some tutoring to get you out. I think you could possibly benefit from working together with me just to devise ways of handling . . .
30. **C:** *(Interrupting)* Uh huh.
31. **P:** . . . using your tutoring to your best advantage, and

using some assistance figuring out exactly how you are
going to go about tackling your problems with English.

32. **C:** Mm-mm. That's no problem.

33. **P:** Hm? Could you give me an idea what you mean, that's
no problem?

The long speech (Interchange 25) is mostly unnecessary and is an example of talking too much. If the practitioner did rush off and the child had been expecting to see her, the child is owed an apology and a brief explanation, such as:

> *I was rude to rush off without letting you know. I am sorry. I had to go to a professional meeting. Did it put you out?*

Instead of Interchanges 27 through 31, a review summary could be substituted, for example:

> *Let me say what I think we discussed last time: that you are behind in English and science and that you thought the solution was to get a science tutor. I thought you also needed help in English.*

Third phase

34. **C:** *(Loud)* If I don't pass the class, it's no big thing. All I
have to do is just go. I just want a tutor to help me with
science.

35. **P:** So it's just a question of going to English.

36. **C:** Mm.

37. **P:** Do you feel like there's anything . . . *(long silence)* OK,
there's another thing I have to clarify, go back to that
. . . umm . . . that is . . . *(silence)* . . . my role as a counselor. What you've expected it to be, what you've been
led to believe it's going to be. As far as your personal
affairs are concerned, I don't care about those. Those
are only if you want to bring those up. And even then I
don't know if we are going to deal with those. The
important thing is that you get some quick input into
dealing with science and English.

38. **C:** Uh huh.

39. **P:** And I think together we can get some quick input. You
may get some quick input on your own, but . . . *(long
silence)*

40. **C:** Uh huh???

41. **P:** I guess — that's kinda it. *(silence)* I'd kinda like to get an
idea of what you're going to do.

42. **C:** I'm just going to do my work! *(irritated)* I'm going to classes now. I just really need tutoring in science.
43. **P:** Well, that's good.
44. **C:** I just need tutoring.
45. **P:** Have you seen anybody about getting a tutor?

Interchange 37 is a long, muddled speech. The subject is the practitioner's role. The statement in the middle ("I don't care about your personal affairs") is probably a way of telling the child, "I would like to work with you on matters of highest concern to you, such as your schoolwork." The practitioner is afraid that Charles will regard her as intrusive, so she asserts lack of interest in his affairs. This is an example of talking too much to disguise freezing, and also imagining a reaction of the child for which there is no evidence.

Fourth phase

46. **C:** No, not yet. My father's supposed to call up the office about it. My folks said I don't need a counselor. Just a tutor. *(starting to sound depressed)*
47. *(Very long silence)*
48. **P:** *(Voice getting very low pitched)* So your father's going to handle getting you a tutor.
49. **C:** *(Very sad, with a catch in his throat)* Probably I'll have to handle that myself. I'll just have to find a tutor. Hm, hm.
50. **P:** What I would like to do . . . *(silence)* I guess you need to know that if there's a service that I can perform for you . . . My basic service that I would offer is to help you organize getting your tutor and getting your work for English. That's the big thing.
51. **C:** *(Strong-voiced and reassuring)* YEAH.
52. **P:** Now, if you feel like having any assistance in just getting organized, *(using a pompous voice tone)* that's fine. That's the full extent of what I would do.
53. **C:** Listen, I need to get off this business of needing somebody to coach me to do my work. Now I need a tutor to get me up to par in science so I can go ahead on my own. I understand that what's wrong is that I haven't been doing my work. Which is ridiculous. I got a mental block or something. The science is hard to understand. And my teacher doesn't do good explanations. It's alright about the things we do in class. I understand that. But when it comes to reading this book *(points to textbook),* the words they use here just trip me up, I swear.

In Interchanges 46 through 53 the nature of the practitioner's anxiety becomes clearer. There are clues to what is causing communication problems.

The practitioner is talking about her role in the abstract. This was done previously in Interchange 37 and now is done in Interchanges 50 and 52.

The client is bored. With Interchange 51 Charles responds strongly ("YEAH") to what he sees as a solution—a tutor. After the vague speech of the practitioner (Interchange 52), the client starts on his own initiative to specify his problem. So there are two parallel scripts (from Interchange 46 through 53) being carried out without good communication. The client starts to depict the problem. The practitioner continues to discuss her role abstractly.

The situation would have been improved by such questions and comments from the practitioner as:

"What exactly is the trouble in your English (or science) class?"

"How do you feel about your teacher?"

"When do you do your homework?"

"Where do you do your homework?"

"What interferes with homework?"

"What makes your homework go well?"

"What are your ideas about things that could be done to raise your grades?"

"Do you know how to get a tutor? They are very hard to get, and someone has to pay. Do you know who would pay for your tutor?"

"What do you think you need in addition to a tutor?"

This phase suggests that the practitioner is worried about being rejected by the client. This conclusion is suggested by Interchanges 49 through 52. If the practitioner is absorbed in worrying about being accepted, she will not be able to attend to and notice the client's information.

Fifth phase

54. **P:** Um hum.

55. **C:** All these big words and the science terms, you know.

56. **P:** Well, I think what I'm basically driving at—time keeps running—well, I think perhaps—well, why don't I just say, what you should do is get it started right away.

57. **C:** That's what I will do. That's what I will do.

58. **P:** And the English thing? You said something about a mental block that you might have.

59. **C:** *(Giggling)*

60. **P:** Do you have some kind of a thing that's keeping . . .?

61. **C:** *(Strongly)* NO! When the teacher starts giving up on

the students because they aren't doing well, starts kinda giving up on the class, you know, makes it sort of like punishing, you know, then you have to work harder to win her confidence back. When the teacher starts helping me but she won't talk to me about what I'm doing. If I don't understand then I have to just rack my brains by myself. So then I start not going, and she gets mean . . .

62. **P:** *(Interrupting)* Do you think that's kinda what's going on, I mean?

63. **C:** No, not in English. My English teacher, he's just kinda stubborn, you know. I ask him a question and he just doesn't answer. Just looks at me like I am crazy. I just had to learn how to deal with him. If he asks me something and I don't know, I have to just stay with it and say to him *(loud)* "What's this word!" I just keep looking right at him and asking again. So finally he's started loosening up and telling me something.

64. **P:** Well, I can see how a tutor might help with that.

65. **C:** *(Loud)* Right!

66. **P:** The English thing . . . well, that's . . . well, the English thing . . . I think . . . well . . . that's the most logical thing where you and I could work. If . . . it's only a question of doing the work . . . then . . . there's something that's slowing you down. You haven't done the work. You're very capable. I know. We all know that. The thing is, is there a particular kind of organizational plan which you've got for doing your English?

67. **C:** Well, I do it right after school after the other kids come home. But the reason I didn't understand it was because it was Shakespeare. It uses all those funny words that I don't understand. I kept telling him so he let us read it in class. So now I understand it and it's not a problem. We discussed it in class and all the points got out. Then, I can ask the questions. But if I don't even understand what it says, I can't even ask a question. I had to rack my brain so hard. After, I just say "Oh — forget it." That's no good. That's just a bad habit I have.

In Interchanges 54 to 67, Charles uses his own initiative to clearly identify and specify his learning problems as he sees them. His description is clear and credible. He displays the way he carefuly studies and evaluates his teachers, himself, and his relations with teachers regarding his problems with schoolwork. There may be more to it than Charles expresses, but we do not know.

We also do not know exactly why Charles has started this detailed problem definition. He threw in the expression "mental block." The practitioner paid high attention to that phrase. The term "mental block" has no technical or scientific meaning. It is a colloquial expression that might be a code for or clue to an underlying complex problem.

The practitioner, despite her disavowals earlier of intrusiveness into Charles's privacy, has perhaps been wanting some indication of psychological subtlety to emerge. Maybe it has! There are several possible reasons for the client's words. Charles seems to be an expert reader of teachers' minds; he may be explaining his problem so carefully to educate the practitioner. On the other hand he may be trying to head her away from exploring a subtle psychological problem. He may also be making a pitch for some adult help in getting a tutor. "Mental block" could be a throwaway remark because of its common usage. Charles may just be trying to call the practitioner's attention to himself and away from the practitioner's abstractions. If that was Charles's intention, he succeeded. In Interchanges 55-68, the practitioner is more responsive.

Although the practitioner is showing less of the four problems, she could have improved the dialogue with the following statements substituted for what was actually said:

64. Tutors are scarce, and somebody has to pay them, unless we are lucky and locate a good volunteer. If you want, I can talk to the office and see who's available and how much it costs.

66. While we are waiting to get a tutor, you and I could schedule your homework time to get the assignments covered. I can help you with your English, but I'll have to see the science assignments to find out if I know enough to help you with those. How would you feel about my helping you with your homework? What would you think about my asking your parents to help you with homework?

Sixth phase

68. **P:** OK. What I do is treatment for a problem that the person has.

69. **C:** Mm.

70. **P:** It doesn't take much time. Like one session a week. And maybe we could do this until the end of the marking period. The next marking period. Whenever.

71. **C:** Mm.

72. **P:** Ah . . . What we try to do in a case like this . . . Let's say English. A person has a problem with English, or alge-

bra, whatever. They're having difficulty doing the homework . . . *(talking slowly, dragging it out)* . . . getting it in, they don't understand the work. What we can do is we can break that problem up into little bitty bits, attack it in small little pieces.

73. **C:** Mm.

74. **P:** Very easy to do. Attack it in small little pieces that are fairly easy to do. Get you somewhere. And there is very little exploration into your problems at home, only if we find a connection.

75. **C:** *(Coldly)* Yes, I understand.

76. **P:** So what I'm offering to you is not an hour of head shrinking.

77. **C:** Yes, yes, I understand. But what I was saying was right now I'm trying to concentrate on my schoolwork. And what I really need is a tutor. I don't need a counselor. My friend Bob has been going to a counselor for 3 years.

78. **P:** It sounds like you think your problem can best be handled by a tutor.

79. **C:** Right. *(placating)* I'm going to get this through. Do what I have to do.

80. **P:** How would you feel about coming down here one period a week . . . discussing how you're doing . . . with your tutor and with your English . . . and perhaps if you're having difficulty getting organized or getting the work in . . . talking about little ways that perhaps . . .

81. *(Very long silence)*

In Interchanges 68 through 80, the practitioner has not noticed that Charles wants politely either to rid himself of the practitioner or acquire some confidence that she can actually do something for him. The practitioner remains fixed on getting the youngster to commit himself to regular sessions.

Seventh phase

82. **P:** Well, I can't see that you have anything to lose. *(edge in her voice)* But that's up to you.

83. **C:** Well, you see, I don't know, like. I get out the sixth period.

84. **P:** Hm hm.

85. **C:** Then—I'll have to find time to see my tutor. And that's why I don't know about seeing you, whether I'll have the time. Maybe I'll have to go to the doctor sometime.

Maybe I'll have to take care of the little kids. Besides *(bringing in the big guns),* my mother doesn't want me to. I'll have to ask her. I'll have to ask her when I would have time to come.

86. **P:** *(Very loud)* HANG LOOSE. HANG LOOSE as far as time goes. I can be very loose. Like if you could only see me sixth period on Wednesday, or sixth period on Friday, or vice versa.

87. **C:** Mm.

88. **P:** It would be one—one period a week.

89. **C:** Mm . . .

90. *(Very long silence)*

91. **P:** Well, the service is an organizational thing.

92. **C:** *(Very coy)* Oo . . oo . . oh . . oh . . eee . . . . Awright?

93. **P:** *(Breaks up laughing)* Say yes or no. You make me feel like I am twisting your arm.

94. **C:** I hate to let people down. If I say yes but I don't come, then I let you down and make you feel bad. Then I'll feel funny, you know. Then I don't really know how my schedule is going to work out.

95. **P:** OK. I can understand that. The thing of letting you down or letting me down, there's a lot of different feelings going on in there. Yeah. You won't be letting me down. Let it go at that. You won't be letting me down. I'm not going to be here next week.

96. **C:** Going on vacation?

97. **P:** Yeah.

98. **C:** Where you going?

99. **P:** Los Angeles.

100. **C:** Oh! I'd love to go to Los Angeles. I've never been anywhere. Sometimes I think I'll join the Navy to travel all over.

101. **P:** Well, I'll be back the week after next. OK! OK! *(Very slowly and pedantically)* WATCH! WATCH how you're doing, particularly in English because that is where you have to make up work. If you find that you're not getting your work made up, then you should do some serious thought about seeing me and we'll see about getting you organized. That's the whole thing . . .

102. **C:** *(Interrupts)* Right!

103. **P:** That's what I'm here for, if you want it, if you need me.

104. **C:** All right.

105. **P:** OK.

106. **C:** All right. *Whew!*

107. **P:** Bye.
108. **C:** Bye.
109. **P:** Have a good weekend.

• • •

This illustration shows what may happen if all the four problems of getting started are present: freezing, talking too much, imagining things, and not noticing.

These problems are only partly a matter of specific words, phrases, and sentences. Suggestions have been given for better statements in the discussions of each phase.

Summary

The well-intentioned practitioner in the illustration wanted to be helpful. She seemed overly worried about the client's seeming disinterest in establishing a regular plan of meetings together. She may herself have had a reluctance to set up regular meetings, not having a clear idea about what they would be for. The freezing (anxiety) reflects her tension brought about by uncertainty about purpose and appropriate interventions. She talked too much to disguise her uncertainty. She made assumptions (imaginations) that lacked evidence. And she sometimes did not notice the client's reactions because she was too much absorbed in herself.

The interviewing problems depicted in the illustration can occur especially in starting up. The problems can be controlled by increasing one's self-confidence, attending carefully to the client, and restraining a tendency to make too many inferences.

CHAPTER 3

Helping processes and their relationship to interviewing

In every interview the social interactions are affected by factors in addition to the participants' verbal discourse. Certain features of the helping processes greatly influence client-practitioner communication. These features are organizational environment, practice theories and guidelines, and client and practitioner characteristics and qualities.

Organizational environment of interviewing

Interviews are conducted in an organization such as a welfare agency or other agency, clinic, hospital, school, housing authority, employment and training facility, or correctional facility. The organization influences the way in which the interview is conducted (see Chapter 7). For instance, the organization emphasizes work in a particular service domain. It sets limits on privacy. It affects the substance of the communication between client and practitioner. The organization establishes the terms and conditions for the availability of resources needed in the helping process.

SERVICE DOMAINS

The domains of the helping professions are divided according to broadly defined, sometimes overlapping, problem clusters: ill health, education problems, poverty, marital conflict, parent-child conflict, loneliness, existential confusions, unemployment, old age, single parenthood, problems of the handicapped, mental illness, and incorrigibility, to name the most prominent.

Organizations need to provide for those of its problem population who are in need, meet eligibility requirements, and are good candidates for staff services. The establishment of a domain consensus for each organization, its departments, or its other organizational entities serves the purpose of dividing up available resources in the local human services system.

Agencies adopt positions that tend to favor some practices over others because of their history, the quality of their relationships with other service organizations, and the strong influence exercised by leading officials who often build up reputations in some specialty. An organization's preferences are revealed in training materials and requirements for the focus and scope of assessment and intervention practices.

Organizations not only have theoretical preferences but also specialize in defined problem areas. Although quality varies a good deal and viewpoints change, there are relatively well-defined bodies of knowledge in particular problem areas. This knowledge will guide organizations in giving priority to areas of assessment and intervention in specific domains.

PRIVACY OF INTERVIEWS

An interview is both a public and private event. When client and practitioner participate in an interview, they bring to it ideas, beliefs, and wishes, and they have been influenced by other people such as colleagues, teachers, authorities, and friends. In this sense, the individuals in an interview are not there alone. Furthermore, the interview events are nearly always reported to others in official reports and in conversations with supervisors, consultants, and colleagues.

What is told to others about an interview is always selected information. Our minds automatically combine and reduce events to explain them and make them comprehensible. Selection is normal. It may also be deliberate, if we judge it inadvisable to reveal some things. Unless there is a videotaped record, some things will be left out and other things added. However, even a videotape is not a true recording. People being taped are influenced in their behavior and conversation by the presence of the technical crew and equipment.

Because an interview can never be reported with absolute accuracy, it is in some respects an intensely private transaction. The privacy component of an interview gives the interviewer the power to exercise judgment with a great deal of independence from supervision, scrutiny, and control. An interviewer has private control over what he says, how it is said, what he thinks, and what he decides. How much power will be exercised is an important decision. Nearly always the interviewer is a powerful person in the eyes of the client. This being so, the private interview may give a client the illusion that the interviewer is the most powerful participant in decisions made about the client. In reality, the organization is a powerful force in an interview because it influences practitioner and client through its construction of the service domain.

SUBSTANCE OF COMMUNICATION

Regardless of skill and knowledge levels and the personal characteristics of the interviewer, the organizational context of the interview is important in determining substantive content. Often the organization shapes what is said by its rules and the content of its on-the-job training (Epstein 1980; Vinter 1969).

Health, human services, and educational programs are run by formal organizations that shape practices through their regulations, staffing patterns, reward systems, and public relations. These are components of the bureaucracy. They order the substance of communication and assign priority to practitioner intentions, plans, and decisions. The agency's substantive and priority requirements exert a powerful influence over the practitioner. The practitioner may like or dislike the system of rules and may approve or disapprove of them. Either way, the practitioner cannot avoid the influence. When the practitioner sits down to interview, all the bureaucratic baggage is there. What she says will, in large part, be what the agency authorities have mandated or influenced her to say. The words, phrases, and sentences will be individual but modified by agency policies and style.

Service agencies select staff who, according to their beliefs, have the education and experience most appropriate for the job. Regulations are constructed in accordance with agency opinion and the provisions of the law under which the agency is sanctioned. Organizations carefully monitor their public reputations in order to safeguard their status and position in the community, command appropriate client inflow, and protect their connections with funding sources upon whose good will their existences depend. What their staff members do with clients affects agency reputations.

Organizations rarely have the time and resources for monitoring individual interviews, but they can and do monitor interview results, reports, and outcomes. Although monitoring does not take place for each individual interview, evaluation of aggregate results influences individual practice. Shaping of interviews is indirect. Shaping of service provision is direct. In both instances the influence is strong and is felt even in the privacy of interviews.

If the client is to remain within the service delivery system, the problem of concern will have to be consistent with the types of problems that come under the agency's approved domain. The client will have to meet the official eligibility requirements. Interventions received by clients will be those which are part of the approved repertoire. The type of service will be dictated by organized resources such as short-term service, open-ended service, long-term care, short-term interim care, physiotherapy, remedial reading, job training, psychodynamic variety, and such types of counseling as behavioral and task-centered counseling.

RESOURCE AVAILABILITY

Interviewing styles and substance are affected by changing events inside an organization, by dealings with other services in the community, and by the state of the technology of intervention (Austin 1981). Human service organizations are interdependent, that is, they negotiate with one another, exchange resources, and develop agreements about privileges and responsibilities. At the service delivery level the practitioner is affected not only by resources available at his home base but by resources available from cooperating organizations. It will make considerable difference to the practitioner whether obtaining a homemaker—that is, someone who provides child care in the client's own home—involves a simple phone call or protracted and difficult negotiations. It will make a difference in assessment interviewing if the practitioner is certain that a client is in the right place and not better served by resources outside the agency or at another agency.

DIFFERENCES OF OPINION IN ORGANIZATIONS

A practitioner, especially if she works in a large organization, will know that there are differences of opinion and often conflict about goals, techniques, interviewing practices, and proper criteria for case intake, transferral, referral, and closing.

Practitioner interviewing will be affected by the practitioner's status, his length of time on the job, his performance evaluation, and the status of his supervisor in the hierarchy. Interview behavior will be affected by the interviewer's philosophy of service and his friendship coalitions with co-workers. Interviewers may believe in reality therapy, Gestalt therapy, humanism, or client-centered attitudes. They may see behaviorism as the most viable approach to intervention, or they may believe that underlying developmental and conflict problems cause human difficulties. The interest group to which a practitioner affiliates herself within a large organization will have a strong effect on how she uses interviewing techniques, what is selected for emphasis, what is ignored, and what priorities are assigned. Technology in human services is not neutral and will be inevitably colored by ideology.

Practice theories and guidelines

Practice theories are constructs based on an analysis of information about practice. They establish general principles intended to explain the information. Such theories aim to present a clear, well-rounded, and systematic view of the subject. Practice is a highly individualized and particular undertaking. Practice theories are never complete and tend to change, sometimes fairly rapidly, sometimes slowly. They are subject to continuous evaluation and revision, and they vary in range and emphasis.

Practice theories give rise to various guidelines, some of which are referred to as "models" or "approaches." These guidelines attempt to translate the theory into recommendations for conducting and regulating the helping process. Guidelines may also develop first in practice and later evolve into theory. Guidelines are characteristically subject to change. It is always appropriate and necessary that guidelines be adapted to particular circumstances. Such adaptations are made programmatically by organizations as they decide how they intend to implement the various practice theories. Adaptations are made continuously by practitioners as they exercise professional judgment on a case-by-case basis.

Certain general areas of practice theory and guidelines will determine how an interviewer thinks about the purpose and content of an interview. These areas are assessment, the professional relationship, and models of intervention. The following brief review will attempt to highlight ideas from practice theory and guidelines in order to suggest the background factors that affect the way an interviewer decides to communicate with an interviewee. The references at the end of the chapter provide suggestions for additional study.

Practice theories and guidelines affect interviewing in subtle ways. Neither psychology nor philosophy offers an exact explanation about how to relate theory and practice. The subject is immensely interesting but too large to cover in this book. For present purposes, it is sufficient to say that not all theories can be directly translated into action even when they are essential aids to understanding. Practical actions such as interviewing often derive directly from either past experiences (stored memories) or from present novel happenings. On reflection, however, we may explain the present more satisfactorily with the insights of a theory (Lobkowicz 1977).

Theories about assessment, relationship, and intervention help interviewers to understand some of the obscurities, ambiguities, and confusions that may beset them. We reflect on events and make decisions regarding the interview. Practice theory, although only a part of our activity, is influential in explaining what we have experienced and helpful in decisions about interviewing strategy.

ASSESSMENT

Practitioners form different impressions and images for each client. A problem is defined and a judgment made about its seriousness, that is, its intensity, frequency, and duration. From these impressions, images, and judgments, we make a tentative explanation (hypothesis) regarding the problem, the people, and the situations involved. These impressions and our explanations constitute the *assessment,* leading to the *intervention plan,* which is a judgment of what should be done and how we should act to reduce the problem.

Defining the problem and attempting to understand the people and their social situations lead to an idea of what needs to be changed, restored, or enhanced. A judgment can be made about how much change is necessary, desirable, and feasible. Available resources can be examined to determine their usefulness in effecting change. Available resources include practitioner knowledge, professional skills, concrete agency services, and client abilities and resources. The intervention plan is a guide to action. It specifies what can be done to reduce the problem, assist the client, and improve the situation.

Making an assessment requires information, standards, and rules. Clients and other persons involved in or knowledgeable about the problem are the major sources of assessment information. The standards and rules for assessment vary accoridng to the practice model being followed. Standards and rules are set forth by specific practice organizations and in the professional literature. Because assessment standards and rules are a highly technical and extensive subject, they will not be reviewed here. The reader is referred to specialized assessment references and also to sections on assessment contained in texts on the various treatment models (Francis and Munjas 1976; Sundberg 1977).

Diagnosis is a term whose origins are in the practice of medicine, including psychiatry, upon which the various helping professions draw heavily. The term diagnosis has acquired broad usage. In most respects it is synonymous with assessment. The major distinction between diagnosis and assessment is that diagnosis refers to the use of a classification system for *mental* diseases and dysfunctions of personal and social behaviors, attitudes, and emotions.

The assessment or diagnostic process has at least three major problems. First, the results of assessment have a low degree of reliability. Research in the subject has repeatedly revealed substantial differences in assessment results among practitioners in all of the disciplines. This state of affairs is explained by differences in educational background, theoretical persuasion, and assessor experience. Second, the present state of the art precludes accuracy of prediction about the probable course of a client problem. Third, the relationship of assessment results to intervention planning and selection is not always ideal. Planning and selection of interventions often depend on limitations in the knowledge and resources available. Preferred interventions are often unavailable, and substitutions that have to be made are often inadequate (Kendall 1975).

Despite these limitations, assessment is necessary. Assessment provides a working understanding of the client's predicament. It suggests what kind of interventions can be considered relevant and what kind are clearly inappropriate.

New assessment models and procedures are presently being researched and developed. These developments are attempts to organize and try out methods to gather information and make decisions. The revised 1980 *Diagnostic and Statistical Manual* (or DSM-III) of the American Psychiatric Association is one such effort at codification of the classification of mental diseases and social dysfunctions. Rapid assessment instruments are coming into wider use, such as brief standardized questionnaires that may facilitate assessment and monitor progress during intervention (Levitt and Reid 1981). Computer-assisted programs are being developed (Kendall 1975). Specialized assessment programs to guide interviewers are exemplified in a training manual for making decisions about child placement (Stein and Rzepnicki 1983). Other types of manuals that specify assessment procedures for a variety of situations are appearing (Rose 1981; Woody 1981). Techniques to assist in obtaining assessment information are described in Chapter 5.

ASSESSMENT AND PROBLEM DEFINITION

An assessment defines the problem. The definition becomes the focus or center of attention for intervention. However, defining the central problem is difficult. Ordinarily, the practitioner and client examine numerous problems with different parts. They must decide which problem or set of problems will become the focus for the work.

In the social sciences there is no single theory to define a social problem (Glick and Hebding 1980). In counseling practice, it is generally held that the problem as perceived by the client—the "presenting problem" or the "client's target problem"—is of crucial importance. At the same time, however, there may be a "mandated problem" identified by the court, police, or professional authorities that requires attention for the client to avoid adverse consequences. There may be a problem that is identified by professional opinion with which the client concurs or which the client accepts. However, professional opinion may be rejected or only partially accepted by clients (Epstein 1980).

To be defined as a problem, the condition must have been judged to be undesirable, unwanted, or deviant by the client, by a reputable sector of a profession, by the service organization, or by a practitioner, based on professional and personal knowledge, experience, and beliefs. A client's problem will be defined in accordance with the domain of the service organization where he has gone or been sent for help.

Some helping professionals tend to define problems as being primarily internal or intrapsychic. Others tend to see problems as being interpersonal or primarily existing in the client's relationships with other people. Still others view problems as being primarily situational. It is obvious that intervention plans will evolve differently depending on how the problem is defined (Proctor and Rosen 1983).

ASSESSMENT OF MENTAL ILLNESS: A SPECIALIZED TYPE

This brings us to consider specialized assessment in instances where mental illness is diagnosed, suspected, or defined as a problem. Although numerous types of staff handle mental illness and associated problems in many different types of organizations, the authority in that domain is exercised by psychiatrists. In a clinic or hospital run under medical authority, the specialized standard and rules for assessment will be established by the psychiatric staff. These rules will indicate the relevance of history and of ideational symptoms such as delusions and hallucinations, mood alterations, depression, and thought disorders. Assessment will consider social problems, physical health, and environmental stress, but it may emphasize exploration of the mental illness symptoms. Intervention planning and implementation will focus on control of the psychiatric symptoms, as well as the social and physical health situation (see Chapter 7).

ASSESSMENT IN OTHER SPECIALIZED SERVICES

For many specialized services, particular kinds of assessment are required by the experts in that field. The authorized view of the problem area that is the organization's domain will provide the central core of the assessment content. The interviewing techniques will be directed toward getting the information needed to fulfill the expectations of the specialty.

Intake interviewing is a specialized assessment procedure. Large organizations usually separate screening and assessment from intervention. There are separate units of staff for these functions. In bureaucracies that are large and vulnerable to public scrutiny, specialized intake units often control case inflow, assuring that eligibility decisions are fair, reasonably uniform, and in keeping with the agency's announced functions and funding levels.

ASSESSMENT: SUMMARY AND DEFINITION

The assessment is a formulation produced by combining the information acquired from interviewing and other sources. The assessment formulation outlines the nature and major characteristics of the problem, the persons most closely associated with it, the major circumstances, and an estimate of the problem's seriousness. The assessment process follows standards and rules established by the professions. Assessments may take a specialized form if prescribed by a particular field of practice, or a particular organization or unit. The problem that is the focus of an assessment is defined in various ways that depend on the practice model used and the beliefs and purposes that prevail in the organization.

THE PROFESSIONAL RELATIONSHIP AND INTERVIEWING

The professional relationship is composed of the thoughts, feelings, attitudes, perceptions, and interactional responses existing in the interpersonal process between the practitioner and the client. A relationship always exists when two or more people are together in any social endeavor. A relationship takes on a charged quality when people are communicating about intimate or significant matters, as is the case in human service work. The emotional charge in interactions is heavy when clients want something that they hope practitioners can provide, such as surcease of stress, food, money, a job, skill for acquiring a promotion, a husband, a wife, a divorce, a child placement, an education, better health, or parole from jail.

The establishment and maintenance of a positive working relationship in an interview is not a matter of a certain ordained selection of words, phrases, and sentences. It is a matter of the quality of speech, which is communicated by body motions, multichannel communication, and difficult-to-define spiritual characteristics. The "goodness" of a professional relationship is no small matter, since it is thought to influence the effectiveness of intervention. The research information we have suggests that a good client-practitioner relationship is an aid in conducting interventions (Orlinsky and Howard 1978).

Nevertheless, a specific, exact, and operational definition of a good professional relationship eludes those in the field. A good worker-client relationship is sometimes intuitively sensed without being specified. There are sets of beliefs among practitioners about the outstanding qualities that make up good practitioner behavior. The quality of empathy is high on the list of desirable attributes. Other qualities often referred to as basic are respect for the client, attentiveness, acceptance, and interest. Negative bias of the practitioner toward the client has been discussed as a problem in good relationship maintenance. This bias is often shown in pejorative remarks about the client such as "uncooperative," "manipulative," "unmotivated," and "resistant."

Two psychoanalytic terms are sometimes used in discussion of the professional relationship: *transference* and *countertransference*. Transference refers to the theory that people may tend to view a psychotherapist with the same or similar attitudes and expectations acquired in childhood in parent-child relationships. The therapist is perceived as having qualities and intentions like the original parents, although the therapist is different. "Countertransference" refers to the distorted reactions of a practitioner toward the client that probably come from early childhood conditioning and from acquired prejudices, biases, and intolerance (Levine 1961, pp. 232-237).

Another way to view relationships is as a combination of values, moral and ethical perspectives, and attitudinal and communication attributes (Shively 1961). Practitioners have an intuitive sense that their relationship with the client means something vital. A prominent expert puts it this way: "*Relationship* is a catalyst, an enabling dynamism in the support, nurture, and freeing of people's energies and motivations toward problem solving and the use of help . . . The emotional bond that unites two (or more) people around some shared concern is charged with enabling, facilitative powers toward both problem solving and goal attainment" (Perlman 1978, pp. 2-3).

There has been much research attempting to analyze the operational attributes of the practitioner-client relationship. Studies have attempted to define what qualities of speech, body motion, and spatial arrangement constitute a good relationship. This kind of research is difficult to conduct. It has depended mostly on laboratory studies rather than actual interviewing. The research problems of studying relationships are similar to the problems encountered in studying linguistic communication, discussed in Chapter 1. Pope (1979) published a comprehensive review of the research literature on relationships in interviewing. Another excellent review can be found in Parloff, Waskow, and Wolfe (1978).

From the standpoint of the interviewer, factors that seem to contribute to a good relationship are classes of attitudes and personal characteristics that facilitate the client's communication, that is, put the client in a frame of mind to talk to the practitioner. One of these factors is the practitioner's close attention to problems as they are perceived by the client (Mayer and Timms 1970; Sainsbury 1975). Another factor is the collection of attitudes that are combined under the term "empathy." In Chapter 1, being empathic was considered one of the regular lines of action in an interview.

Interviewer warmth facilitates communication and is closely related to empathy. It is thought to involve taking the client seriously, attempting to put oneself in the client's shoes, and being genuinely responsive to the client's concerns. Warmth has been analyzed repeatedly and is thought to be conveyed by a friendly tone of voice, a relaxed posture, leaning a bit forward toward the client, and sitting fairly close without invading the client's private space. Warmth is controlled by behavioral norms that are part of the usual repertoire of general adult social skills. An interviewer who knows he is regarded by others as too effusive should try to modify this behavior in an interview. A person who is normally aloof and distant should practice speech and postural qualities that increase verbal and gestural activity.

Indicating approval seems to be another way of communicating warmth. Approval is conveyed not only by phrases such as "that's good" but also by smiling, positive head nods, and spontaneous friendly gestures. Interviewer warmth may be reciprocated by the client, leading her to speaking more and to view the results of intervention in a positive light.

Genuineness is also a quality related to empathy and is regarded as desirable for interviewers to have. Genuineness in interviewing simply means being your best self, keeping in mind your appropriate status and purpose. Acting from a script is not necessary. Some clients are already conditioned to like or dislike certain kinds of people, so any one interviewer will match better with some clients than with others. These differences are to be respected and are basically unalterable. In a great many service delivery situations the client does not need to like the practitioner and vice versa, as long as respect and courtesy are evident. However, it is easier for all parties if there is a pleasant attraction. If there is unpleasantness or worse, special precautions are needed and will be discussed in a later section of this book (Chapter 10).

The relative status positions of interviewer and interviewee affect the relationship. An interviewer with high status may be perceived as possessing competence and experience, which may facilitate the interview. The relationship is experienced as "good" by the client. Competence can be shown by an inexperienced interviewer who has done her homework. Experience, however, is often judged by the chronological age and appearance of the interviewer. There is not very much a young interviewer can do about his age except wait a while. Research findings indicate a tendency on the part of clients to react less confidently to youth and to incompetence (Pope 1979). However, these are not at all necessarily the same thing. Experienced people can be incompetent, and young people can be competent. Clients make fairly individualized distinctions about these attributes.

Interviewer status also contains elements of dominance and power. Interviewers who are officers of the court may have great power over the client's fate. Dominance can be perceived by the client as a threat to his living circumstances or to his self-esteem. It can cut off or cut down the amount of confidence the client has in the practitioner. Status that is perceived by the client as "high" tends to make the interviewer attractive and facilitates communication. Good-looking offices and well-dressed staff members will communicate high status and facilitate good relationships, unless clients perceive them as threatening.

It can be concluded that the interpersonal climate that exists between a practitioner and a client is strongly experienced and important to the context of the interview. Although the research lacks definitiveness, studies of the subject make it clear that the relationship is not mysterious. Some of the factors associated with relationships have been touched upon. Other factors will be dealt with in later portions of this book, in which the special attributes of different types of clients are discussed.

Attentive listening, clear-headed observing, respect and tolerance, concentration on service provision, and problem solving are probably conducive, in the majority of instances, to the creation of a good relationship climate for interviewing.

MODELS OF INTERVENTIONS AND INTERVIEWING

The idea of models of intervention is a recently developed notion. It has resulted from the proliferation of intervention methods that have emerged over the last decade. The idea of models is a product of the attempts being made to develop technologies in the helping occupations. These are ways to organize input and identify results that are specific and possibly measurable, capable of being described, and replicable. There are models of intervention that have been in use for decades, although they were not originally named as models.

The main example of a model with a long history is psychodynamic psychotherapy and its many offshoots and versions. Because of its primary derivation from psychoanalysis and the complexity and ambiguity of its structure and components, psychodynamic psychotherapy was originally resistant to and difficult to study with research methods. However, in the last 20 years there has been a great deal of research in this model (Fisher and Greenberg 1977, 1978; Luborsky and Spence 1978; Smith, Glass, and Miller 1980). Its effectiveness has not been strongly established. However, none of the existing psychotherapies is found at present to be substantially better than any other, although they vary in efficiency and values. Research studies indicate that therapies that set time limits and have specific goals produce good outcomes and may be efficient (Budman 1981; Butcher and Koss 1978; Davanloo 1978; Epstein 1980; Reid 1978; Reid and Epstein 1972, 1977; Reid and Shyne 1969).

Many of the interventions practiced in the human services involve service delivery rather than psychotherapy. Service delivery can be divided into *soft* or *hard* services. The hard services are tangible, such as financial aid (money and food stamps), medical care, housing, or jobs. The soft services are those that emphasize counseling and are provided together with a tangible resource or as a substitute for a tangible service. Advice, expert opinion or instruction, consultation, reflection and deliberation, thinking, understanding, choosing, and deciding are examples of soft services.

Counseling and psychotherapy differ in intent and in their goals. Psychotherapy intends to change clients' minds, thoughts, ways of thinking, attitudes, and feeling reactions toward themselves and others. Psychotherapy needs a client's informed consent to undergo self-scrutiny in order to repair a personal deficiency. Counseling intends to provide clients with social skills they lack through individual and group encounters. The line dividing psychotherapy and counseling is ambiguous. The terms ar often used interchangeably.

The availability today of such a wide range of models of intervention presents problems of emphasis, selection, and acquiring expertise. From a practical standpoint, selections are often made according to decisions of particular organizations and leading staff members' opinions. Beyond that, the special interests of a practitioner or group of colleagues lead to the study and testing of models for adaptation to the organization and its service domain. Course work, in-service training seminars, and conferences often concentrate on dissemination of new or revised models.

A brief list of helping models in use today illustrates their variety and range:

Behavior modification
Cognitive therapy
Crisis intervention
Ecological models
Existential therapy
Family treatment
Generalist model
Gestalt therapy
Group treatment
Planned short-term treatment
Problem-solving approaches
Psychosocial or psychodynamic approaches
Rogerian therapy
Task-centered intervention

Each of these models identifies interview content somewhat differently. Each may define the focal problem differently. Ideally a practitioner with broad training would be in a position to conduct an extensive assessment and select the most promising model for an individual case. Still, in the average practice situation the opportunities for the exercise of such thorough assessment and selection of approaches may be limited by time and the need to act quickly. Often the choice of model is a practical matter determined by available knowledge and organizational desires and approval.

The psychodynamic psychotherapy model has been described in many texts and a multitude of journal articles over the past 50 years. The best way to approach this literature is to start with currrent work that is addressed to a particular problem field. Behavior modification, group treatment, and family treatment have a robust literature. The same advice is offered for dealing with that literature. Newer models are written up in a relatively small body of literature (Budman 1981; Epstein 1980; Germain and Gitterman 1980). There is a growing journal literature of brief statements of tested and untested procedures. They represent organized clinical thinking about ways to handle cases of a somewhat specific type.

For interviewing purposes, the importance of models is that they provide significant information for selecting interviewing techniques, for giving one emphasis rather than another, for putting some techniques in a priority position, and for allotting other techniques a subordinate position. Most practices today, whether delivering tangible resources, counseling, or psychotherapy, have an eclectic attitude toward available intervention models. They choose among ideas and frameworks found in the literature, or they choose according to habit, belief, and preference. Organizations and practitioners tend to develop their own models selected according to preference and judgment.

PURPOSE, GOALS, AND FOCUS OF INTERVIEWING

Practitioner decisions about the *purpose, goals,* and *focus* of interviews, made independently or by following the rules of the organization, influence the way the techniques are selected and emphasized. Purpose is the broadest and most encompassing of these terms. All three terms are often used interchangeably. However, some distinctions will be made in the present discussion.

PURPOSE

Purpose tends to be used to broadly describe what the intervention is for. For example, it can be stated that the purpose of a program is prevention of child placement through provision of family support. Another program has the purpose of rehabilitation of drug abusers. Another program intends to provide therapy for family relationship problems.

GOALS

Purpose is similar to organizational goals, which are intentions for the organization's whole colleciton of cases, or caseload. Organizational goals chart a direction for administration, stating what a whole program intends to accomplish. Organizational goals do not translate readily into individual case goals. However, it is unlikely that any individual case goal would contradict the general intention of the program's operation. Organization goals are put forward in broad terms, such as strengthening family life, reducing mental illness, educating children and youth, educating and training adults, rehabilitating the physically handicapped, and enhancing productive patient use of medical care.

Goals for a single case can be divided into professional, practitioner, and client goals. Professional goals are consensual opinions held by important groups and opinion makers within a particular helping profession. These opinions assert which intervention actions and results are considered good, effective, and valuable in the profession. However, professional goals vary depending on time and place, like any other expert opinion. Professional goals reflect the values that the profession strives for in carrying out its service ideology.

Personal practitioner goals are composed of the private opinions of practitioners. These are individual interpretations of professional goals and are influenced by one's own view of life.

Client goals represent what changes the client perceives as necessary, desirable, and wanted, and what he is willing and able to work on. Dissonance or lack of congruence between practitioner and client goals may set up conflict and possible struggle that will dispose a case to failure. Many clients are willing to seriously consider and often adopt professional suggestions about advisable goals.

FOCUS

Focus is the central point of attention and activity in any interview. It is the clear and sharply defined point of the discourse. Focus is not composed of any particular words, phrases, or sentences; it is a mental construct that organizes the work effort. Focusing in an interview is like focusing a camera. The practitioner must decide whether she wants everything clear and sharp, only the foreground clear and sharp, or the background sharp and the foreground blurry.

Client and practitioner characteristics and qualities

Client response to an interviewer is only partly a product of what words, phrases, and sentences the practitioner uses and what purposes, goals, and focus are employed. Clients' responses are conditioned by who they are and where they come from. Clients' responses are shaped by their expectations and their views of themselves, other people, and social institutions, arising from their ethnic background, culture, social class, personal traits, values, and circumstances.

Different types of mental and physical illness, handicaps, and background affect the manner in which a client presents herself. These conditions may affect the client's perception of the interviewer's appearance, demeanor, speech, and motions. Many different types of client behavior must be dealt with such as the ultrasuspiciousness of people afflicted with some forms of mental illness, the strained and laconic tension of some people who are frightened, and the halting speech of someone with a particular brain lesion. Ill and handicapped people have diverse personal backgrounds and attributes. If an interviewer plans to talk to a particular category of people, he should consult a text dealing with the group, take special courses, or obtain the necessary on-the-job training to establish familiarity with them. In other words, he should get good information on what to expect and how to interpret client attributes.

Dependency shown by the client may elicit rejecting responses from some interviewers. In fact, a folklore has been built up that uses the word "dependent" in a pejorative manner and suggests that dependency is pathological. However, a considerable amount of dependency is totally normal and appropriate—in life, as well as in an interview.

The worry that many practitioners have about client dependency is not warranted. The more helpless a person feels, the more he will need to be dependent. Faced with real deprivation such as poverty, lacking a natural social and kinship network, lacking employment prospects, facing massive insults to the body from illness and injury, losing crucial persons and things from one's environment, people are in fact dependent and are right when they reveal it. Interviewers are objectively limited in the amount of time, resources, and energy they have to give to others. It is important that they know what their limits are and draw the line where it belongs. Most clients understand this and will be helped by the support provided. An interviewer undermines the client with help only if she fails to attend to those things the client can do. To give unnecessary help is perceived as humiliating and demeaning and robs the other person of the satisfaction that comes from running one's own life. However, to avoid helping someone when they need help is a painful rejection.

Another interviewee attribute that strongly affects the conduct of an interview is the client's degree of anxiety and depression. On the whole, a moderate level of anxiety appears to stimulate talkativeness and effort. High anxiety is apparently counterproductive. Clients who are depressed tend to speak less, speak slowly, and seem unenergetic.

There are many other client attributes that strongly influence the interview. Some of these are the client's age, socioeconomic status and class, values and beliefs, and the degree to which the client is an involuntary participant. These factors are of such general importance that they will be discussed later in Chapters 7 through 10.

The individual characteristics of the practitioner influence the development of social interactions. The practitioner acquires a professional posture or professional "self" that is the result of knowledge, experience, and discipline. At the same time the practitioner is an individual with his own characteristics, and he should be. Developing a professional posture does not mean substituting a made-up self for one's real self; the personal and professional selves co-exist. Most of the relationship qualities discussed earlier in this chapter originate with the personal characteristics of the interviewer. Like the client, the practitioner has ideas about what to expect, what is preferred, and how she hopes to appear. These ideas are personal, derived from the practitioner's background, culture, values, and circumstances. The importance of self-awareness lies in appreciating that practitioner characteristics are present and affect the interview's social interactions.

Summary

An interview is contained within the helping process. It cannot be properly perceived separate from that process. It is somewhat arbitrary to study interviewing apart from general guidelines for counseling. Nevertheless, there is value in focusing upon interviewing processes by themselves, provided there is the understanding that they are an integral part of a larger process. The whole counseling field is too large for the scope of this book. Therefore selected processes relevant to interviewing have been briefly discussed.

The substance and style of an interview is affected by the organizational environment. The particular area or domain of the organization affects what an interviewer tends to emphasize. The fact that an organization is accountable to the public results in the interviewer being accountable to the organization, which limits the amount of privacy accorded to the interview. The particular requirements and viewpoint of the organization partly determine the substance of the interview. The availability of resources is basically determined by the organization.

There are numerous and various practice theories and guidelines that can be called upon to structure intervention strategies. These theories affect how an interviewer focuses the interview. After becoming acquainted with a variety of approaches, a practitioner evaluates them. Employing organizations also make evaluations, developing approved choices and adaptations to suit their needs.

The formal purposes of intervention and various levels of goals affect how an interviewer decides to focus discourse with clients. Individual deliberation leads to a judgment about interview focus. That focus is strongly affected by the client's characteristics and qualities. Clients vary not only according to their personal traits but also in terms of their culture, background, values and socioeconomic status. They vary in age, interests, and talents. Interviews, consequently, are shaped by clients in special ways.

The practitioner's own characteristics add another dimension to the whole social interaction. Being self-aware enables interviewers to sense how they are affecting the interviewing process.

REFERENCES

Austin, Michael J. *Supervisory Management for the Human Services.* Englewood Cliffs, N.J.: Prentice-Hall, 1981.

Budman, Simon H., ed. *Forms of Brief Therapy.* New York: Guilford Press, 1981.

Butcher, James N., and Koss, Mary P. "Research on Brief and Crisis-Oriented Psychotherapies." In *Handbook of Psychotherapy and Behavior Change,* edited by Sol L. Garfield and Allen E. Bergen. New York: John Wiley & Sons, Inc., 1978.

Davanloo, H., ed. *Basic Principles and Techniques in Short-Term Dynamic Psychotherapy.* New York: Spectrum Press, 1978.

Diagnostic and Statistical Manual of Mental Disorders (DSM-III). 3rd ed. Washington, D.C.: American Psychiatric Association, 1980.

Epstein, Laura. *Helping People.* St. Louis: C.V. Mosby Co., 1980.

Fisher, Seymour, and Greenberg, Roger P., eds. *The Scientific Evaluation of Freud's Theories and Therapy.* New York: Basic Books, Inc., 1977.

Fisher, Seymour, and Greenberg, Roger P., eds. *The Scientific Evaluationof Freud's Theories and Therapy.* New York: Basic Books, Inc., 1978.

Francis, Gloria M., and Munjas, Barbara A. *Manual of Socialpsychologic Assessment.* New York: Appleton-Century-Crofts, 1976.

Germain, Carel B., and Gitterman, Alex. *The Life Model of Social Work Practice.* New York: Columbia University Press, 1980.

Glick, Leonard, and Hebding, Daniele. *Introduction to Social Problems.* Reading, Mass.: Addison-Wesley Publishing Co., 1980.

Kendall, R.E. *The Role of Diagnosis in Psychiatry.* Oxford: Blackwell Scientific Publications, 1975.

Levine, Maurice. "Principles of Psychiatric Treatment." In *The Impact of Freudian Psychiatry,* edited by Franz Alexander and Helen Ross. Chicago: University of Chicago Press, 1961.

Levitt, John L., and Reid, William. "Rapid-Assessment Instruments for Practice." *Social Work Research and Abstracts* 17 (Spring 1981):13-20.

Lobkowicz, Nicholas. "On the History of Theory and Proxis." In *Political Theory and Proxis: New Perspectives,* edited by Terrence Ball, pp. 13-27. Minneapolis: University of Minneapolis Press, 1977.

Luborsky, Lester, and Spence, Donald P. "Quantitative Research on Psychoanalytic Therapy." In *Handbook of Psychotherapy and Behavior Change,* edited by Sol L.

Garfield and Allen E. Bergin, pp. 331-368. New York: John Wiley & Sons Inc., 1978.

Mayer, John E., and Timms, Noel. *The Client Speaks.* New York: Atherton Press, 1970.

Orlinsky, David E., and Howard, Kenneth A. "The Relation of Process to Outcome in Psychotherapy." In *Handbook of Psychotherapy and Behavior Change: An Empirical Analysis,* edited by Sol L. Garfield and Allen E. Bergin. New York: John Wiley & Sons, 1978.

Parloff, Morris B.; Waskow, Irene Elkin; and Wolfe, Barry E. "Research on Therapist Variables in Relation to Process and Outcome." In *Handbook of Psychotherapy and Behavior Change: An Empirical Analysis,* edited by Sol L. Garfield and Allen E. Bergin, pp. 233-282. New York: John Wiley & Sons, 1978.

Perlman, Helen. *Relationship, the Heart of Helping.* Chicago: University of Chicago Press, 1978.

Pope, Benjamin. *The Mental Health Interview.* New York: Pergamon Press, 1979.

Proctor, Enola, and Rosen, Aaron. "Problem Formulation and Its Relation to Treatment Planning." *Social Work Research and Abstracts* 19 (Fall 1983):22-27.

Reid, William J. *The Task Centered System.* New York: Columbia University Press, 1978.

Reid, William J., and Epstein, Laura. *Task Centered Casework.* New York: Columbia University Press, 1972.

Reid, William J., and Epstein, Laura, eds. *Task Centered Practice.* New York: Columbia University Press, 1977.

Reid, William J., and Hanrahan, Patricia. "Recent Evaluations of Social Work: Grounds for Optimism." *Social Work* 27 (July 1982):328-340.

Reid, William J., and Shyne, Ann W. *Brief and Extended Casework.* New York: Columbia University Press, 1969.

Rose, Sheldon D. "Assessment in Groups." *Social Work Research and Abstracts* 17 (Spring 1981):29-37.

Sainsbury, Eric. *Social Work with Families.* London: Routledge & Kegan Paul, 1975.

Shively, Mertaf. *An Analysis of the Construct "Relationship" as It Is Used in Social Work.* Ann Arbor, Mich., University Microfilms, Inc., 1961.

Smith, Mary Lee; Glass, Gene V.; and Miller, Thomas I. *The Benefits of Psychotherapy.* Baltimore: The Johns Hopkins University Press, 1980.

Stein, Theodore J., and Rzepnicki, Tina L. *Decision Making at Child Welfare Intake: A Handbook for Practitioners.* New York: Child Welfare League of America, 1983.

Sundberg, Norman D. *Assessment of Persons.* Englewood Cliffs, N.J.: Prentice-Hall, Inc., 1977.

Vinter, Robert D. "The Social Structure of Service" and "Analysis of Treatment Organizations." In *Perspectives on Social Welfare,* edited by Paul E. Weinberger, pp. 369-386 and pp. 428-443. New York: Macmillan Company, 1969.

Woody, Robert Henley, ed. *Encyclopedia of Clinical Assessment.* 2 vols. San Francisco: Jossey-Bass Publishers, 1981.

CHAPTER 4

Overview of basic techniques

Interviews have sense, structure, and sound. Thoughts and opinions are exchanged. The interview is an instrument for communicating information already processed in the participants' minds. In a series of related interviews over time the intervention will be implemented. An individual interview is a segment of the intervention. The parts of the interview are:

1. Information
2. Mode
3. Sequence
4. Dominant ideas
5. Pattern of discourse

A visual representation of interview structure is shown in Figure 3.

In an interview the practitioner and client seek and give information. The information is determined by their desires and goals. They inform one another of what is possible and feasible regarding events, happenings, attitudes, and feelings related to the client's problem. They give each other information about resources to deal with the problem, what can be done, what should be done, what obstacles are being encountered, and what results are being obtained. Interviewer and interviewee size each other up. Information is exchanged in a mode that is dyadic (one-to-one), in a family meeting, or in a group session. The interview proceeds in sequence from a beginning that sets the stage for the exchange, to a middle in which one or more themes are elaborated and developed, to an ending that ties up loose ends and completes the exchange for the time being.

The *sense* of an interview is what the interview means including ideas, attitudes, values, intentions, and feelings that are conveyed. The meaning is the product of the participants' mental beliefs, knowledge, prejudices, and persuasions. In order to come to a conclusion about an interview's meaning, the following are needed: a theory of human behavior, a belief about the value and appropriateness of the service preferred, and a model of intervention that is credible and convincing.

The *structure* of an interview is the arrangement of its parts. As shown in Figure 3, the interview's meaning relies on verbal and nonverbal discourse. The participants are interacting in an interview mode; they are with family members, or with a group of nonrelatives, or in a dyad with the practitioner. The interview is located in time and has a beginning, middle, and end. The interview is dominated by particular ideas such as the existence and overcoming of obstacles and the need for resource acquisition, social skills, and social and emotional supports. Relevant information is exchanged by the participants to facilitate desired intervention and problem solving.

Starting up	Familiarizing	←--→	Reducing strangeness Being secure Having self-confidence Perceiving the other person Putting at ease

First phase	Eliciting information	←--→	Get going Ask questions about relevant facts

	Explaining roles	←--→	Tell what you will do and why Explain what client ought to do and why

	Explaining problems, personal characteristics, and social context	←--→	Search out: ask, look around, suggest, consider What's the matter? What can/cannot be done? What's the other person like? What's going on at home? At work? At school? Are the social services right?

	Identifying problems
	Specifying problems
		←--→	Be open-minded
			Be respectful
			Be definite
			Be clear
			Define nature of problem
			Get specific about its features
			Draw a picture with a center
			    (specification)
			    and a near background (definition)

	Discuss priorities,
	goals,
	contracts
		←--→	Talk around and about
			    What acts done first would help most?
			    What should the results be, look like, feel like?
			    What exactly will be the agreement for work?

FIGURE 3   Map of basic interviewing techniques.

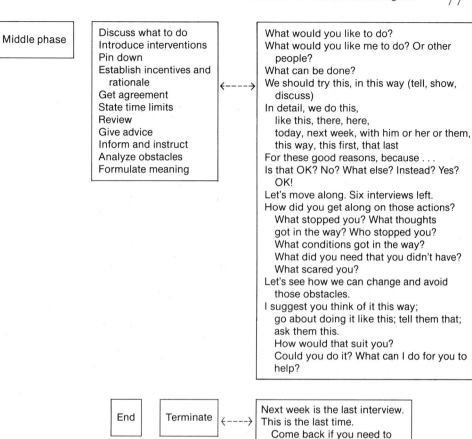

| Middle phase | Discuss what to do
Introduce interventions
Pin down
Establish incentives and
    rationale
Get agreement
State time limits
Review
Give advice
Inform and instruct
Analyze obstacles
Formulate meaning | ←----→ | What would you like to do?
What would you like me to do? Or other
    people?
What can be done?
We should try this, in this way (tell, show,
    discuss)
In detail, we do this,
    like this, there, here,
    today, next week, with him or her or them,
    this way, this first, that last
For these good reasons, because . . .
Is that OK? No? What else? Instead? Yes?
    OK!
Let's move along. Six interviews left.
How did you get along on those actions?
    What stopped you? What thoughts
    got in the way? Who stopped you?
    What conditions got in the way?
    What did you need that you didn't have?
    What scared you?
Let's see how we can change and avoid
    those obstacles.
I suggest you think of it this way;
    go about doing it like this; tell them that;
    ask them this.
    How would that suit you?
    Could you do it? What can I do for you to
    help? |

| End | Terminate | ←----→ | Next week is the last interview.
This is the last time.
    Come back if you need to
    We have accomplished these
        things
    We have not accomplished
        these things
    What you did
    What I did |

FIGURE 3, cont'd.   Map of basic interviewing techniques.

The *sound* of an interview is composed of speech that is augmented and modified by nonverbal communications. Speech in an interview is largely automatic, consisting of content and style acquired by the speaker through education, socialization, culture, and inborn physical and mental equipment. Professional speech is learned from models, books, course-work, and experience.

Information

GENERAL CHARACTERISTICS

Information theory deals with the characteristics, properties, and content of nonhuman electronic signals that are the physical embodiment of messages, or telecommunications. It has become commonplace to make analogies between mathematical propositions in information or communication theory and various social endeavors and enterprises.

When information theory is applied to social processes, it refers to knowledge in the form of interpreted and arranged news, facts, and data. This information is useful or useless, factual or imaginary, reliable or unreliable, precise or vague, and true or false (Cherry 1966, p. 228).

Information that is commonly conveyed in human services is communicated with interpretation (sense) and arrangement (structure). Because practitioners are always pressed for time and obey conventional rules in expressing themselves, interview information is transmitted in symbolic and condensed form. For example, when you say, "I just popped in to see how you are," you are condensing the content of your general knowledge about single mothers, a meeting on the subject recently attended, and a conference with your supervisor on a specific case. When you say, "Jack can't come back to this school anymore," you are condensing a lot of information about his grades, behavior, interaction with teachers, health, and much more. When you say, "You look terribly sad," you are condensing impressions based on personal experience with sadness or despair and impressions from what you have read in textbooks and seen on television.

Information generated in interviews is both overt and covert. Overt information is the open business of the transaction. Information available to and generated by the practitioner is secured from and conveyed to the client. This is done in order to assess the client and her situation; to negotiate an agreement on what is to be done; to teach, guide, advise, encourage, and explain to the client how to obtain and use the resources needed; and to help the client develop and use social skills that will enhance her life.

Covert information is the hidden or partly hidden business of the interview. Covert information is knowledge about the situation that is not openly shown and that may be masked, concealed, or disguised. Neither client nor practitioner ordinarily shows anger, although sometimes anger may be evident. Rarely does a practitioner show that she is afraid or wary of the client; and clients usually conceal these responses also. Practitioners try not to show dislike of or prejudice toward clients. Hidden elements are nearly always present in an interview. Also often hidden from awareness are thoughts and attitudes toward others that we may not even be aware of. Yet both client and practitioner may ferret out some of these covert bits of information by making inferences born of past experience. Information is thus exchanged about things unsaid and not overtly revealed.

WHAT IS INFORMATION FOR INTERVIEWING?

The information that a practitioner obtains from a client in human service interviewing should be related to the business of the application and intervention. It can be personal information but should be collected only if it is related to the business at hand. Information should not be sought to settle curiosity, except when curiosity is stimulated by a need to know something for work purposes. A definite understanding of the business that has brought the client and practitioner together must be arrived at in order to appraise the relevance of information.

The general business of human services or social welfare agencies is the supply and distribution of resources, social skills, and needed supports. Resources are supplies of goods (for example, food stamps) and arrangements (for example, foster home care). Social skills are aptitudes and abilities to deal with the dilemmas of living in the world with other people (for example, competent performance in the role of mother). Supports include resources and skills, but also intangible relationships and discussions that help to minimize stress of many kinds. Every human service agency, whether it is a school, employment agency, or medical clinic, stays in existence because it is sanctioned by law or custom to perform a defined, described, and authorized service (for example, rehabilitation of the injured and handicapped, assessment of degree and kind of illness, education of the young, and retraining of the unemployed). The information needed by the practitioner for dispensing a service in interviews is that which establishes the client's eligibility according to the program's rules, makes the problem clear, suggests feasible alternatives to design interventions, aids the client to use the service productively, and helps to monitor effects.

TYPES OF INFORMATION FOR INTERVIEWING

Information in interviewing can be classified according to the following subdivisions:

1. WHO: that is, the people who are parties to the encounter; their dominant traits, characteristics, roles, and status; their liabilities and talents; their opportunities and inequalities.

    For example: Mr. and Mrs. L. have requested marital counseling. Mr. L. is a reasonable and intelligent person who is subservient to his wife and resents that. He takes his responsibilities seriously but shows uncertainty about his success in husband-father roles. His income is erratic in his middle-management career. He seems to lack resolve although he is evidently flexible and imaginative. He is well educated but hampered by an unstable work record. Mrs. L. is bright, shrewd, emotional, and angry with her husband. She is well educated and a successful, experienced office manager.

2. WHAT: that is, the identity, nature, and importance of the problem.

For example: Mrs. L. is frightened about Mr. L.'s joblessness and his inability to get hired on a full-time regular job. Her income is not large enough to support the family (the couple and two daughters). She feels the stigma of being married to a man who is unambitious. Not only that, but her husband "puts her down." Mr. L. is doing freelance consulting that keeps him busy 1 or 2 days a week and brings home about the same money that he would earn on a steady job. But this income is uncertain and depends on luck. He enjoys his leisure. Both Mr. and Mrs. L. feel their marriage is in jeopardy.

3. WHERE: that is, at what position, in what direction, about what situation does the problem exist?

For example: Mr. and Mrs. L. are fighting and arguing with increasing frequency and intensity. They fight about sex, preparing and eating meals, and going out socially. They fight less about care of the children. They fight in the bedroom, kitchen, dining room, and car and sometimes in front of other people when they are out.

4. WHEN: that is, at or during what time or times does the problem occur?

For example: The fighting occurs whenever the L.'s are together, that is, home from work. Both feel happier and calmer when not together.

5. HOW: that is, in what manner or with what meaning does the problem exist, and what are its consequences?

For example: The problem causes Mr. and Mrs. L. continuous pain, although they are at least fond of one another and are comforted by their mutual dependence. The children appear to be accustomed to the situation. Mr. and Mrs. L. each wish that the other were not so abrasive and would make a behavioral change. They feel a wish to be rid of one another and yet they also fear separating and being alone.

6. CONTEXT: that is, the environment and conditions that throw light on the problem.

> *For example:* Mr. and Mrs. L. live a middle-class life and have interesting social and cultural activities (reading, theater, movies, dances, parties, and gossip). They like their children. They are partly estranged from their families because of old resentments and lack of mutual interests. They have a large circle of acquaintances but no intimate friends except each other. They live in a pleasant apartment where the rent is high and the amenities are good. Mrs. L. likes her job. Mr. L. likes his leisure and claims not to be worried about money. He thinks he might eventually start a business of his own. They are both extremely tense about the present high degree of conflict between them.

HOW IS INFORMATION SENT?

Speech, facial expressions, and body movement convey information directly. What to say, how to look, and how to sit or stand are primarily the products of inferences, rules, and habits. Inference is the process of arriving at a conclusion from judging some data, event, or observation. Inference is done by passing from one proposition believed to be true, at least tentatively, to another proposition thought to follow from the first.

Many, if not most, inferences are made automatically. Sometimes inferences are made with careful mental effort, but often the process is intuitive rather than logical or rational. Inference-making is likely to be erroneous. Inferences made without disciplined reference to reliable observations, actual experience, and respectable bodies of knowledge lead to unwarranted conclusions and irresponsible actions. In interviewing, inferences should originate as much as possible from verified knowledge and sober theories. Extremely fanciful and faddish notions should be avoided.

Interview mode or arrangements

Interviews are conducted in four modes, or arrangements of people. Cost, convenience, and preference dictate the mode (see Chapter 6).

The interview needs at least two persons, an interviewer and an interviewee. Often there are more. There may be more than one interviewer. There may be several interviewees, as in group and family interviewing.

Dual interviewing refers to an arrangement in which there is more than one interviewer, as in co-therapy or co-worker interviewing.

One-to-one or *individual interviewing* means one interviewer with one person.

Family interviewing means one or more interviewers with any collection of family members. If only the husband-wife or boyfriend-girlfriend dyad is present, this arrangement sometimes is called *couple interviewing*.

Group interviewing refers to one or more interviewees with any small group of persons who are not family, that is, the group members are unrelated.

Sequence

Interviews have a logical sequence from start to finish. An interview logically proceeds from start to middle to end. Separate interviews follow the same basic order as a series of interviews. Series, however, show variations depending on what has gone before and what is assumed will follow. All interviews, taken separately or in series, should have clear beginnings, middles, and ends. They can be constructed to move from becoming acquainted or reacquainted through various kinds of informing, explaining, identifying, discussing, and supporting — until the ending takes place.

In a single interview, the beginning contains greetings and sets the focus. The middle develops the focus. The end brings closure and a direction for the next interview, or direction for life experience if there will not be another interview. In a sequence of interviews the beginning stage consists of becoming acquainted and establishing the problem focus. The middle stage emphasizes assessment and planning and also moving into problem reduction work, which should consume most of the time. The ending stage involves summarization and direction for the future.

STARTING AT THE BEGINNING

Mrs. A., a 45-year-old black woman on welfare, has seven children, several of them with various handicaps. She is separated from her husband. She has had children in the day-care center over a period of several years. The youngest child is now in the center and has conduct problems. Mrs. A. is excitable and often seems suspicious. The case record says that 3 years ago she became exceedingly excited and was taken to a psychiatric clinic where a diagnosis of paranoia was made. She was hospitalized briefly. The planned and announced purpose of this interview, the first after a long time lapse, is to discuss and try to remedy her youngest child's bad conduct at the center. There is also a professional goal to attempt to stabilize a disorganized family.

Starting in the middle, a practitioner might say: "Let's see how the disorganization in your home is making Bobby misbehave in the day-care center."

Starting off to the side, the practitioner might say: "This is your hour. You may do with it as you like."

The plunge into the middle might have been caused by an assumption that a child misbehaves because of disorganized home conditions that ought to be addressed. There is reason to assume that this might be so. There might, however, be any number of alternative explanations for the child's present conduct that would require considerable additional information. His poor conduct might be the result of, for example, poor health, a disorganized classroom, or hostile peer relations. Without a normal beginning for the interview, the client might become fearful and misunderstood.

Starting off to the side might have been caused by the practitioner's false image of what he is there for. In the example given the practitioner is plunging ahead too fast and trying to delve too quickly into the client's inner feelings.

A good beginning for an interview is a greeting, followed by an explanation and discussion of the interview's purpose.

For example, a good beginning for the interview with Mrs. A. might be: "Hello. My name is Mr. E. You were asked to come in because Bobby is fighting a lot at the center, and we want to try to get him calmed down."

Subsequent interview beginnings might be: "How are you? Have you got something special to discuss today?" *or* "What's been happening about Bobby's problems at home?" *or* "Suppose I tell you what's been going on here at the center with Bobby this past week?"

STARTING UP PHASE

Figure 3 illustrates the starting up phase of the interview. The main technique in starting up an interview is familiarizing. The first interview in a sequence of interviews will use this technique heavily and perhaps exclusively under some circumstances. In most cases, however, a first interview that concentrates only on familiarizing is not sensible. Under normal circumstances a client is not present solely for the purpose of becoming acquainted with the practitioner. If a client is extremely fearful, however, time spent on familiarizing without directly relating to the client's problems could be useful. For example, time might be profitably spent playing cards or going to a baseball game with a shy child. Such circumstances occur, but they are unusual.

The purpose of familiarizing is to reduce the strangeness that is inevitable between practitioner and client, who have probably never seen each other before. If the parties are already acquainted it is still necessary to engage in bits of the familiarizing technique to reinforce the relationship. Later on, however, familiarizing techniques should occupy only a minor portion of interview time.

Because of powerful conventions in our society that inhibit strangers from talking openly to one another, it is particularly important for the practitioner to reduce the sense of strangeness in an interview. Practitioner anxiety about acceptance can create tension that reduces attentiveness to the client (see the example of the interview with Charles in Chapter 2). The familiarizing technique boosts practitioner self-confidence and helps free the practitioner's mind so that she can perceive, attend to, and listen to the client and put the him at ease. Chapter 5 will provide examples of familiarizing techniques in detail.

Familiarizing can be described briefly as ordinary strategies for conversing with strangers that have been learned by adulthood. These strategies include modulating voice tone, sitting or standing a moderate distance from the client, offering eye contact that shows interest but is not intrusive, and making appropriate conversation. Any of the common rules of good behavior, courtesy, and politeness are also part of familiarizing. Such things as inviting people to sit down, taking their coats, and making them as physically and mentally comfortable as possible mark the practitioner as a good host and also exemplify familiarizing techniques.

Sometimes practitioners have to interview in bad conditions in which no one is comfortable, there is much external noise, or people are running about. Practitioners have been known to interview in places where there are no chairs or there is water on the floor. Despite bad conditions, the practitioner should make the interviewee as comfortable as possible, considering the circumstances. You could, for example, be a practitioner in a setting with disaster victims and have to interview them in a tent in the rain and mud. Expressing regret about tension-producing or oppressive conditions puts people at ease or as much at ease as possible under the circumstances.

FIRST PHASE

As shown in Figure 3, the types of techniques most likely to be used in the first phase are eliciting information; explaining roles; exploring, identifying, specifying, and explaining problems; and discussing priorities, goals, and contracts.

ELICITING INFORMATION

The aim of the techniques in the first phase is to initiate the helping process. Practitioner and client want to start to get a job done. Most people, including the young, the elderly, the mentally defective, and the handicapped, have been socialized at an early age to understand that they must give information in order to get help. Clients usually accept the appropriateness of a practitioner requesting basic information. They know that the practitioner needs data from which to construct a helping experience for the client.

A client who is under stress of a fairly extreme kind may develop some impatience with the information-getting process. In this case the practitioner should explain why questions are being asked and why the information is necessary. A good rule is that if a client asks why we need to know something, we should be able to give a simple answer. If we can't think of any answer to the question, we probably should not be asking.

The organizing theme to guide the selection of words used to elicit information in an interview is *the need to know*. Given there is that need to know, two types of questions can be asked. One type is a direct question such as "What is _____?" *or* "Where is _____?" *or* "When was _____?" The other type is an indirect question that involves making a statement rather than asking a question.

The question is a sentence at the end of which the voice is raised. (This differs from a declarative statement in which the voice is dropped at the end, as if something is being asserted.) By raising his eyebrows, opening his eyes, and tilting his head, the practitioner says nonverbally, "I am saying this, but I want to know how it fits with you. Is it right? Is it wrong? Can you add to it, or would you subtract from it in order for the sense to be appropriate?" The implicit question is, "What more can you tell me about this?"

EXPLAINING ROLES

It must not be immediately assumed that the roles assigned to practitioner and client are clear. The interviewing techniques of role explanation involve telling the client what the practitioner will do and why and explaining what the client ought to do and why. These explanations should be verbal. It should never be assumed that any of this is understood until the client's words, actions, or facial expressions indicate that he does understand.

Having a meaningful interview requires that both client and practitioner give and receive information. Interviewers often feel constrained, embarrassed, or fearful about invading a client's privacy. Asking personal questions contradicts previous socialization about polite discourse and is frowned upon. However, the interview is a circumstance in which discourse is different from ordinary social conversation. Clients expect to be asked questions because they understand that they know much more about their situations than the practitioner does. In fact, the practitioner may know nothing. Clients will give information cooperatively if they see the relevance of questions to their problems. (See Chapter 10 for a discussion of unwilling clients.) Because relevance may not be immediately obvious, the practitioner should explain the purpose of questions in order to gain the client's cooperation. A good rule of thumb, already discussed above but worth repeating, is that the practitioner can ask anything if he can explain the question's relationship to the interviewer's focus. If he cannot explain the question in that light he should not ask it. If he *can* explain, then he may freely keep the discussion going and channel it so that the service may be started.

The client should know what the practitioner plans to do and why. It is unrealistic to expect clients to have respect for and faith in practitioner expertise and reliability just because they have an official position. It may even be difficult for a practitioner to get a clear idea of the exact nature of an agency's service, especially in large organizations. Clients have the same problem. Often an agency's name does not communicate what it does. Negative publicity raises doubts about an agency's reputation, or an exaggerated story in the press raises expectations that cannot be fulfilled. Clients may have incomplete or wrong impressions about what an agency can do. Agency policies are often in the process of changing. Information available to either the staff or the public may be incomplete or contradictory. These kinds of pressures create staff discomfort and uncertainty. Insofar as possible, it is advisable to provide clients with clear information about agency and practitioner capabilities and limitations and why they exist.

Clients may have little or no information about what they will have to do in their encounter with the agency, or they may have wrong information. These misunderstandings also need to be clarified in the first phase. Misunderstandings of this kind may not clear up with initial explanations; they may have to be dealt with periodically, sometimes for a few minutes during every interview session.

Some client misunderstandings of practitioner-client roles go deep and do not disappear with explanations. Sometimes the client feels deeply about some great inequality or disadvantage that is caused by structural problems in society such as racism, sexism, or ageism. Such problems will not go away on a case-by-case basis. It is to be expected that clients who feel such injuries deeply will not instantly recover from them, and problem topics will be raised in the interviews over and over again.

EXPLORING: IDENTIFYING, SPECIFYING, AND EXPLAINING PROBLEMS

The first phase puts a heavy emphasis on identifying, specifying, and explaining problems, client characteristics, and the social context. Assuming there has been modest success in overcoming initial strangeness and reasonable acquisition of information about roles, most of the first phase should be devoted to exploring: identifying, specifying, and explaining.

In normal practice, the problem that has to be attended to in an interview is the problem as it is perceived by the client ("target problem"). This is the problem that the client knows about, cares about, and wants to do something about. Concentrating on the problem as it is perceived by the client helps to motivate the client toward problem-solving action. A practitioner's effectiveness is related to working with the problem as it is identified by the client. Difficulty arises, however, because often the problem is mandated by an authority, and the client arrives with a prepackaged problem definition. These definitions may have been decided on by a judge, teacher, doctor, employer, or other authority. The problem may have been decided on by professionals within an agency or somewhere else.

Specifying the problem means eliciting information about the details of the problem as it is perceived in the present time. Through questions and discussion the practitioner obtains as much detail as possible about the exact nature of the problem, and also about when it occurs, with whom, where, what seems to provoke it, and its results or consequences.

Explaining the problem refers to discussion that has the effect of making problem situations plainer and more understandable, resulting in clarification about the nature of the problem and its meaning to the people involved.

In the first and second interviews of a sequence, there should be discussion to generate alternative ideas about what can and should be done. This leads to tentative decisions made with the client about priorities, goals, and an agreement on a plan.

DISCUSSING PRIORITIES, GOALS, AND CONTRACTS

The first phase will open up the subject of priorities, goals, and contracts. In some instances it is possible to arrive at moderately firm decisions about these subjects. More often the agreements are tentative. Priorities are made by judging what should be done and in what order. Goals become clearer as the participants visualize what can realistically be achieved in the time available for the intervention process. Agreements may be finalized in a written or verbal contract, which is a formulation that clarifies what is to be done, by whom it will be done, and why it will be done.

MIDDLE PHASE

Figure 3 illustrates the middle phase of the interview. In this phase the discussion focuses on review of the agreements made earlier, refining them, adding to them, subtracting from them, or making changes. Most important, the middle phase of a sequence of interviews is devoted to problem solving. What is done in the middle phase of a single interview depends on whether the interview occurs in the beginning, middle, or end portion of the whole intervention sequence and also depends somewhat on the model of practice being used.

An intervention sequence is a succession of related interviews plus intercurrent collateral contacts. These are the means by which changes in the problem or problem condition are organized, arranged, and effected. There are intervention sequences that are composed of 1 or 2 interviews only. Many intervention sequences last for about 3 months during which a series of interviews occurs. A certain number of cases are continued for long periods of time, depending on the purpose.

The separate interviews of the middle phase of an intervention sequence should concentrate on organizing the interventions, that is, on deciding and planning what should be done. After the first two interviews the middle period of the interviews can begin. Practitioner and client can review actions taken, find out what did and did not work, figure out what resources will be needed to support the actions, and arrange to get the resources if possible. This interview phase will provide the client with necessary encouragement from the practitioner, with advice and guidance on how to get desired actions to occur, with understanding of important people and processes in the client's life, with as much relief as possible from psychological pain, with learning skills to get the work done, and with reorganization of the intervention plan when necessary.

Ordinarily revision of the intervention strategy is needed if a plan has been tried several times and has failed or if new information alters the assessment, needs, and expectations. It is best to make alterations in gradual increments. An exception can be made if there is firm information that points in another direction and also suggests some other intervention strategy with strong credibility.

The middle of an intervention sequence or the middle phase of an interview will have one of two types of emphasis or a combination of these two types. The first type of emphasis is on increasing and expanding the client's understanding of herself and her world. This emphasis takes the form of client information about events, what feelings and ideas are aroused, what they mean, how closely they adhere to reality, and how they might be viewed and understood differently. The second type of emphasis tends toward a concentration on present conditions and action to alter a bad situation. The middle phase of the intervention sequence and the middle portion of individual interviews concentrate on review of actions, guidance, and alteration of plans and activities. Attention is paid to client feelings, attitudes, and actions, whichever emphasis is present. The difference is one of degree only.

The normal middle phase of an interview will emphasize mainly what to do, how to do it, what stands in the way, and how to get around obstacles. If we are in the first phase of a sequence, the middle phase of an individual interview will be primarily concerned with deciding what to do. As an interview sequence proceeds the emphasis will shift to identifying obstacles to action, including obstacles resulting from the way the client perceives and feels about the situation; and planning and checking on actions taken to overcome those obstacles.

The middle phase covers a large amount of content concerning the following subjects:

What to do

What the interventive actions should be

The timing of the actions, the persons who ought to be involved, and exactly what the actions will look and feel like

The incentives and rationale of the interventions, why they should be done, and what rewards should be expected

Being sure the client understands and agrees

How much time should be used

After the plan is set, reviewing what has taken place and revising if needed

Giving advice and encouragement and demonstrating how to practice the interventions outside the interview

Finding out what the drawbacks are, or what is stopping the client

Planning actions to minimize the effects of obstacles; this is done by the practitioner and client

END PHASE

Figure 3 illustrates the end phase of the interview. The end phase of an interview involves winding down and briefly indicating where it would be advisable to start next time. If there is to be no next time because the work is over, the client should be directed toward things in his future that are encouraging or problems that need to be watched for. New matters have a tendency to crop up as an interview is winding down. Unless these are of extraordinary importance they should be noted for attention at the next interview and not discussed under pressure.

The matter of new issues coming up on the way to the exit causes practitioners to become anxious. Trying to understand and deal with new issues under duress can be fatal. It is surprising how often client anxiety about an issue seems to vanish by the time the next interview comes along. Some clients show a tendency to become perturbed if the whole sequence is ending. At the end of the last interview their whole panorama of problems seems to come back, perhaps worse than at the start. This should not be taken by the practitioner as a sign to immediately recontract and start all over, nor is it a sign that the practitioner has failed. Ordinarily the client is reacting to the loss of support that the practitioner has provided. This reaction will pass. The practitioner should rely on the fact that she has done as much as possible under the circumstances—and should let go.

Dominant ideas in interviewing

The themes of an interview, that is, the subjects or topics of an interview, follow:

1. *Resources:* physical and material aids and arrangements that can be obtained to reduce a problem, such as:

cash benefits	employment bureaus
food stamps	medical clinics
foster homes	hospitals
institutions	tutors
schools	housing
bodily aids for the disabled	

2. *Skills:* developed aptitudes for learning and action, such as:
   appraising other people
   appraising one's personal world
   appraising oneself
   dealing with relatives and friends
   dealing with strangers
   dealing with authorities
   dealing with dangers, ambiguity, and uncertainty
   dealing with sex and sexual partners
   dealing with dependents
   dealing with one's own anger and the anger of others

dealing with love and friendship
working
studying
problem solving
staying or becoming healthy
understanding norms of expected behavior
making decisions
making changes relating to self, others, and environment
other individually determined skills

3. *Support:* the quality of interaction in which the practitioner enables the client to endure problems and take necessary risks to make changes; support involves:

being responsive, empathic, concerned, interested, accepting, realistically reassuring, and encouraging; offering good advice; expressing the above verbally and in attitude

making relevant suggestions and giving guidance on how to follow them; comforting a client who is distraught

4. *Obstacles:* behaviors, relationships, and physical and social barriers that impede problem reduction, such as:

lack of resources
lack of skills
lack of information
fears
strong dysfunctional habits
attitudes and values at variance with norms
lack of friends, family, or social group
negative attitudes in the community, such as discrimination

EXAMPLE

The dominant ideas in the interview with Mr. and Mrs. L. were as follows:

Mr. and Mrs. L. possessed excellent resources that could be put to use in problem solving, except that their income was too low or too uncertain because of Mr. L.'s irregular employment. Their level of social skills was high except when dealing with one another, with their anger, and with uncertainty. Therefore Mr. L.'s employment—or lack of it—and their anger and uncertainty about the future were dominant themes. The practitioner's support was continuous.

At the early stage shown in the example of Mr. and Mrs. L. the practitioner would not yet know what obstacles to emphasize because these would emerge only after an intervention plan was formulated and reasonable action steps were decided on and started. Obstacles show up as clients start to act on their problems and run into difficulties carrying out the action. These difficulties are usually caused by conditions that impede problem reduction and are discovered in the process of problem solving. Some large obstacles can be anticipated, such as those that call for a high degree of change or for resources that are very difficult to obtain. In such instances the dominant ideas for the interview are how to break down change into manageable increments, how to reduce expectations, and how to substitute obtainable resources for those that are too difficult to secure.

Pattern of discourse

The various parts of the interview are held together by the pattern of discourse, which represents the totality of communication processes that are occurring (see Chapter 1). The pattern of discourse is composed of all the speech, body motions, facial expressions, visual interactions, and spatial behaviors that are characteristic of the client and the interviewer. It includes the influences on communication of the organizational context, as well as pertinent beliefs, attitudes, values, and cultural characteristics of both interviewer and interviewee. Pattern of discourse is a complex entity to identify and visualize. Nevertheless, its presence is real and is perceived as an active process.

Summary

This chapter has provided a quick overview of basic interviewing techniques. The next chapter will cover the same topics but in more detail. A Map of Basic Interviewing Techniques was presented that can be used as an organizing tool for studying Chapter 5.

Interviews have certain meanings that give them a particular importance to the client and are related to the concerns and problems that originally caused the client to obtain service. The most prominent aspects of an interview are the way it sounds and what the participants say and hear. This is communicated by the speech that occurs.

Interview structure can be perceived as the result of combining the information exchanged; the mode of the interview, whether it is a dyadic arrangement with one practitioner or a family or group session arrangement; the sequence of the interview, that is, the beginning, middle, and end; the dominant ideas that pervade the interview; and the wide and general pattern of discourse.

REFERENCE

Cherry, Colin. *On Human Communication.* Cambridge: The M.I.T. Press, 1966.

CHAPTER 5

Analysis of techniques

In this chapter interviewing techniques will be discussed in detail. Each section of the Map of Basic Interviewing Techniques from Chapter 4 will be considered in close-up.

Techniques are described in chronological order, from the start, through the middle, to the ending. This order is ideal because it conforms to the perception that events progress over time from start to finish. Ordinarily this order exists to such an extent that people can get on with their business.

However, the order is flexible and can be changed if necessary. The interviewer may select from the techniques, omitting those that are not necessary for understanding. If the information is already known or is unimportant a technique need not be used. However, if the information arrests the interviewer's attention, he can decide to rearrange the chronology in order to concentrate efforts.

Decisions on the specific timing of techniques are formed from a combination of observations, conclusions, and "hunches," often made on a split-second basis. These decisions are informed by multichannel communication processes that affect the practitioner's sense of client information, feelings, and expressions.

Starting up

The starting-up phase shown below is the phase in which the initial encounter (or the beginning of a renewed encounter) takes place. The participants begin to define the situation and assess one another.

FAMILIARIZING

The familiarizing technique is used at point zero, that is, the absolute start, of the interaction. Client and practitioner are meeting for the first time, never before having set eyes on one another.

This point is fraught with tension. The client may be a supplicant, asking, imploring, or perhaps entreating the practitioner for life supplies — money, caring, or surcease of pain. Full of pride and resentment, clients may pour out entreaties that sound like demands, commands, threats, or complaints. Having learned to disguise pain and need, applicants may exhort an interviewer humbly. A really scared or shy client may

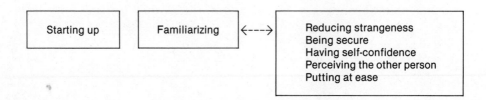

just be numb. A more sophisticated client may adopt a demeanor of rationality, which is the preferred demeanor in our culture. A street-wise client may size up the interviewer and put on an ingratiating attitude. The client is likely to be in the down position. The practitioner is in an up position; she has professional status and the backing of a powerful organization. The organization often has a monopoly on the services the client is seeking. Sometimes there are no available services on the market for a fee. Sometimes the fees in the marketplace are beyond the ability of poor and middle-class clients to pay.

The quality of strangeness encountered in interviewing results from a perception that the interview experience deviates from other usual or expected experiences. Confrontation with strangeness may be disarming and surprising. We may take protective cover if we interpret a strange event as peculiar or bizarre. Fear of the stranger and the strange context is a common denominator that afflicts both client and practitioner in these circumstances. The practitioner's knowledge, experience, and supports should help to control fear and enhance personal security.

Conventional social communications reduce the client's tension, which results from strangeness, and put the client at ease. Techniques for helping a client to be more at ease are greeting, or extending a welcome; reducing strangeness by demonstrating basic knowledge of the problem of concern; and sitting at ease and expressing or displaying warmth, empathy, and genuineness.

Techniques	Examples
Greeting	1. Hello. Good day. Come in, please.
Extended greeting	2. Please sit down. You can put your coat there. Are you cold? Shall I shut the window? The weather is fierce.
Reducing strangeness	3. The intake department says you need day care for your daughter. I understand you are a single mother and have just started work.
Perceiving the other person	4. Yes? O.K. Then would you describe the kind of arrangements you are looking for?
Putting at ease: Developing security by having client explain her situation in her way.	5. No? I haven't got it right? Tell me about it, please.

Greeting and welcoming activities include:

Hosting — asking the client to come in and be seated comfortably and expressing pleasure at meeting her; extending other greetings.

Physical arrangements, or *proxemics* — making reasonably comfortable arrangements for seating with a moderate distance between client and practitioner. Coffee, ash trays, and decent ventilation should be provided if possible. These arrangements can convey that the client is welcome.

Straightforward, businesslike, and friendly demeanor — having this is necessary for most client-practitioner relationships. Keep facial expressions appropriate, try to take turns smoothly, keep the body relaxed, maintain an interested tone. This attitude will ordinarily allow a proper degree of empathy to start to flow. However, if a barrier becomes evident between practitioner and client, the practitioner should try to determine whether his attitude is biased, or too much or too little is being expected from the client, or the client and practitioner have brought distorted attitudes to the interview that should be studied so that a normal relationship can emerge, or the client and practitioner are focusing on different matters.

To reduce strangeness and enhance security and self-confidence, it is advisable for a practitioner to acquire basic knowledge about the major characteristics of the client group that will be seen. Practitioners can reduce strangeness by demonstrating knowledge of the problem of concern.

Human services organizations tend to specialize in a sector of the population. The organization usually has access to experts who are knowledgeable about that category of the population. Literature and short courses offered in in-service training and continuing education help to familiarize a practitioner with the special group of persons that constitutes the clientele. What needs to be known are the socioeconomic conditions ordinarily found in the population group, the characteristics of the general range of problems usually identified, and the estimated value of the several major types of interventions thought to be effective with those problems.

Warmth, genuineness, and empathy are ordinarily shown by maintaining a serious demeanor and close attentiveness when listening. The client thereby perceives that there is a commitment to him. Understanding can be shown by a moderate amount of eye contact and by leaning toward the client without getting too close. Encouraging remarks help the client express her ideas and attitudes. Practitioners should maintain a natural spontaneity to reduce alienation that may be the result of the practitioner's status and power (Pope 1979).

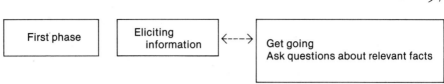

First phase

The first phase (shown above) proceeds in increments to assess the situation, to define it in more detail, and to propose priorities, goals, and contracts. At the start there is a tacit agreement about purpose and goals; it becomes more explicit as the phase proceeds and merges with the middle phase.

ELICITING INFORMATION

Information is elicited directly and indirectly. The only way to get information directly is to ask questions. Practitioners need not have inhibitions about asking clients questions as long as they are germane and well-intentioned. However, they should try not to ask clients "why" questions. "What" questions should be asked instead. "Why" questions might be answered with "I don't know" or with some unfounded hypothesis from television psychology. The resulting discussion might sound like the script of a play and have limited value in an assessment or intervention effort.

"What" questions tend to produce useful information that describes and may even explain a piece of the problem.

For example:

Question	Answer
"Why did you feel that way?"	"I really don't know." *(Silence)*
"What did you do there?"	"I started to be very down."
"What happens to you when you get down?"	"My guts get in a boil."
"Then what?"	"I had to go to eat something. Some people can't eat when they are blue. I gorge myself and get overweight . . ."

Sometimes practitioners fear that their questions will hurt or anger clients. This is sometimes the case, although not frequently. If it is anticipated that a question will be hurtful, a verbal explanation should be given about the question's purpose. The practitioner should say that she is *not* asking the question in order to criticize, scold, invade the client's privacy, or satisfy idle curiosity. She should stress that questions are a way for client information to be transferred to the practitioner and that this information can then be used by the practitioner to understand, think, and plan how to help intelligently. If the question is too hurtful, the practitioner should express regret and perhaps apologize. For example, the practitioner should say, "I am sorry that question hurt you", *or* "I did not realize how painful that was. I am sorry. Tell me how I made you feel."

Another reason to avoid "why" questions is that they are often perceived as scolding. "Why did you do that?" is often used in social conversation as a prelude to criticism. It means not "why" but "you should not have done that." People in our society place a high value on being in control and understanding why they behave as they do, often without realizing how little is known about causality in human behavior. Even when reasonable inferences can be made about causality they are often of little practical use. It is far better in the usual practice situation for the practitioner to know details of specific events so that he can pick out what should and could be changed and make practical plans to change it.

Even when confining themselves to "what" questions practitioners still need a framework to understand which questions are relevant. There is no universal guideline for judging relevance. Common sense should be respected as a good guide in defining information that will assist in making sense out of a problem. The best rule is: if you do not understand what the client says or means, ask him.

Intervention methods are derived from models of practice that, among other things, recommend guidelines for assessment (see Chapter 3). These assessment guidelines identify relevant content for circumstances often encountered in practice. In order to enhance the relevance of questions, it is advisable to consult current assessment models in a particular field of human service work. In general most assessment models advise that relevant questions are those that (1) obtain basic identifying information; (2) produce a clear and understandable picture of the present problem; (3) elicit a general picture of the client's social context and a reasonably specific notion of client capabilities, resources, supports, and liabilities; and (4) give a reasonably clear idea of what the client wants to happen and what she can do to make it happen. Sample questions to elicit information follow:

"It would help me to know where you work and what you do."

"I am trying to see why you can't get any rest at home—what is your apartment like?

"What kinds of things do you like to do?"

"Are you strapped for money?"

"Does anyone help you out?"

"What kinds of things get in your way?"

Indirect means for eliciting information include certain kinds of statements and observations. Reliance on direct questions exclusively is perceived by most people as "cross-examination;" it may seem that the practitioner has the client in a witness box. That type of relationship is fearful or potentially fearful for the client and should understandably be avoided. However, the direct question in an interview can be used any time there is a need for starting the flow of information, moving a topic along, or getting something pinned down, especially if there is little time.

Statements that substitute for questions keep the discourse flowing without undue leading of the client. The practitioner should avoid strong leading because she needs to know what is on the client's mind, not how much her mind can influence the client's. Statements that are question substitutes are of several types. We can say that we would like to know more about a topic. This allows the client to select what she is going to say in a way that makes sense to her. We can also comment on what the client has just said: for example, "That remark your mother-in-law made must have cut you to the quick," or "That must have been awful." Such comments not only elicit information but also support the client.

As important as verbal communications are, information can also be elicited nonverbally by observing the client. The practitioner can observe the client's face and posture for emotions that seem to be associated with certain topics. Information can be gained from clarity or unclarity of speech and from the amount of reality orientation the client has. Body motions, head motions, speech patterns, and spatial arrangements convey information about tenseness, openness, anger, and other attitudes. A client sitting on the edge of her seat, ready to flee, gives the practitioner an indication of her fear. Settling comfortably into a chair suggests being ready to work. Nodding vigorously suggests agreement. Looking grim suggests fear or anger. Failing to speak intelligently or talking too fast suggests tension and confusion.

EXPLAINING ROLES

It is unwise to assume that a client knows what a human service consists of or what a practitioner does. Therefore it is necessary to communicate information that explicitly conveys what the practitioner intends to do and can do. Explaining roles is briefly illustrated below.

Most clients are under a great deal of stress. The functions of various

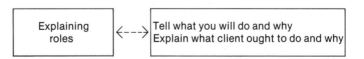

social programs are often incompletely presented in the media. Common knowledge of programs, passed on verbally from person to person, is affected by group influences. A picture may be painted that is distorted, out-of-date, and confused. Many occupations are represented among the personnel of the human services agencies. Each occupation has a particular style, background, status, and type of education. Clients may not understand these differences.

From an ethical standpoint clients need to understand what will be attempted or done because under normal circumstances they have a right to give or withhold informed consent to the arrangements. Only in special circumstances, in which a practitioner operates from a strong authoritative position to stop or prevent harm, can the necessity of informed consent be avoided. Furthermore, only a consenting person can behave cooperatively.

Clients have expectations that affect how they perform their roles. They may be resource seekers, trying to obtain such things as employment or job training, funds, child care, care of aged parents, medical care, or schooling for children. Clients may be seeking information and skills to manage their personal affairs, emotional reactions, close relationships, and uncertainties. Clients may be seeking relief from extreme hardships such as poverty, discrimination, serious illness, or dangerous social hazards.

A client's hopes and expectations are affected by whether or not he perceives that the practitioner can, at least in part, provide what is wanted. Incongruence between practitioner and client expectations is a major source of strain (Blizinsky and Reid 1980; Pope 1979, p. 324). To bring expectations into congruence it is advisable to elicit information from the client about who did the referral and what the client knows about the agency and its activities. Is the client optimistic, pessimistic, or uncertain about his reception? How long has she had to wait? It might also be necessary for the practitioner to comment on the correctness or incorrectness of the client's understanding of what the agency does, to express regrets for tensions that may have been caused by wrong information or insensitive handling, to explain what the agency can and cannot do in relation to the problem, to detail the agency's resources and staff availability, and to clarify agency limitations as well as possibilities.

It is necessary to tell the client what work will be done, where it will be done, how often the practitioner will be seen, what the client will be expected to do, and about how long all this will take.

Most clients understand clear explanations of these matters. However, such explanations need to be repeated if understanding seems to be uncertain in later interviews. Time used to speak about these role descriptions is well spent and contributes to good outcomes.

EXPLAINING THE PROBLEM CIRCUMSTANCES

In the first phase of the interview, explaining the problem circumstances is an integral part of the assessment process. The process of defining the situation proceeds and is elaborated on along with the process of clarifying images that the participants develop about one another. From these processes agreements on focus are made, usually in increments.

These explanations involve getting and understanding information about the client's problems, personal characteristics, and social context, which is illustrated below. In many intervention models these discussions are called *exploration*. In order to search out information in the interview, the practitioner's major activities should be asking questions, observing nonverbal behaviors, suggesting explanations to the client to see how they fit, and discussing with the client what has emerged and what needs to be thought about in the future.

The inquiry, which is made up of questions, statements that substitute for questions, suggestions, and content for consideration, is determined by general questions or lines of investigation. There are many variations on the question, *"What is the matter?"* For example:

What is wrong as you understand it?

What trouble is the problem causing?

How important is that trouble?

Is it dangerous? Occasionally? Always? Is it only a nuisance?

To what degree is it a problem?

When does it happen?

What seems to bring it on?

What happens afterward?

What other people get involved in the problem?

What are they like?

What do they think about you?

What do they do to you, for you, or with you?

What kinds of things go on at home, at work, or at school that set your mood, help you out, hurt you, or deprive and hamper you?

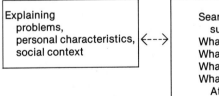

What do you think can be done or ought to be done?

Are the services you have already received satisfactory? In what way "yes"; in what way "no"?

What can be done, cannot be done, or ought to be done?

The answers to these questions have easily understood meaning on paper. However, nearly all responses are further colored by the client's personal characteristics, whether he is intelligent, moody, pessimistic, timid, easily frightened, extremely fearful, clear-thinking, lacking in self-confidence, anxious, suspicious, excitable, withdrawn, or lacking in affect.

The interviewer gets impressions of these traits from observations in the interview, from nonverbal cues, and sometimes from other people who get involved in the intervention program. It is also possible to get such information from personality inventories, although for ordinary purposes the interview observations suffice.

In cases where the client is hard to understand it may be useful to collaborate with experts who can shed light on what obscure personality traits mean, especially when these traits might indicate the existence of mental illness.

IDENTIFYING AND SPECIFYING PROBLEMS

Identifying and specifying problems in the first phase allow practitioner and client to get closer to agreement on priorities, goals, and a contract (see illustration below). These communications begin to pave the way for the intervention program. Later these communications serve to evaluate progress and show what revisions have to be made in an intervention plan.

From explanation-seeking discourse the interview moves to identifying and specifying. Time may not permit going this far in a first interview. Such discussions may carry over into the second interview and come up repeatedly thereafter.

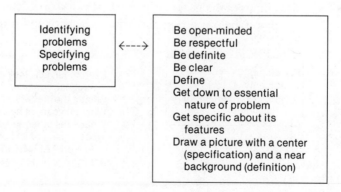

```
┌─────────────────┐        ┌──────────────────────────┐
│   Identifying   │        │ Be open-minded           │
│    problems     │ <---> │ Be respectful            │
│   Specifying    │        │ Be definite              │
│    problems     │        │ Be clear                 │
│                 │        │ Define                   │
└─────────────────┘        │ Get down to essential    │
                           │   nature of problem      │
                           │ Get specific about its   │
                           │   features               │
                           │ Draw a picture with a center │
                           │   (specification) and a near │
                           │   background (definition)    │
                           └──────────────────────────┘
```

Explaining is making a problem plain and intelligible. *Identifying* is an exposition of the essential character of a problem, or its objective reality. *Specifying* a problem means naming it and stating it explicitly and in detail. For problem-solving purposes, the specification is what counts most, because it names what the practitioner can and should intervene on. Human thinking tends to be roundabout, so it is rare to get right to a specification. People go through phases or stages to get to specifics. The pattern of discourse becomes complex and involved. Usually we return to the explanation again after the specification is made and find that we now have a better explanation, that is, one that fits the known facts more closely.

EXAMPLE

Mr. S. is a 35-year-old man, overly tied to his mother. He has just been laid off his steelworker's job. In the interview he emphasizes that he has been rejected by his girl friend, Miss O. He acts unconcerned about being unemployed. He does not want to discuss job prospects. He says he wants help to improve his relationship with Miss O.

Mr. S. is a union steward and is an expert on the employment situation in his trade. The stress of his unemployment has brought him forcibly to confront the fact that at 35 he ought to emancipate himself from his mother and get married. He cannot understand why his girl friend has lost faith in him and become cool and distant. He has increased his attention to her without the desired results. The problem is identified as conflict with the girl friend. Mr. S. specifies the problem as Miss O.'s drawing away from him, not accepting dates, and refusing to talk about marriage.

Miss O. seems to be drawing away from involvement with a jobless man. Mr. S. may have been keeping up his courage by making light of the unemployment problem. He might want her closer so she can help him keep up his courage. The practitioner wants to carefully examine whether Mr. S. ought to consider his joblessness as a problem.

In going from an explaining discussion, as illustrated above, to the identifying and specifying discourse, the questions and statements take on certain different qualities. We go from questions such as, "What is the matter?" to questions about naming, stating, and describing in detail what is bothersome, painful, or destructive. The practitioner needs to create an unpressured climate that respects a view of circumstances as the client sees them.

The possible communication lines between the practitioner and Mr. S. in the previous example might be:

So you see the problem as your needing help with your girl friend's coldness.

Tell me the details about how she shows this coldness.

How is her attitude different now from earlier?

What is she doing all this for, do you suppose?

The practitioner's statements have to be definite and clear in order to encourage the client to be specific:

Am I hearing you right?

Is your job situation under control?

You know what to do?

But your girl friend is a mystery to you?

Give me an example.

Another example, please?

What did she say?

What did you say?

Then what happened?

How did that make you feel?

Can you put yourself in her place?

How might she have felt?

What do you suppose she is afraid of?

Have you discussed all this with your mother?

What does she tell you?

Defining the problem is fixing its context and essentials:

So — the essential thing is that you want to get married, and she wants to have less to do with you?

Until you lost your job she was interested in you as a date, but she never allowed you to get really close? Now she is more distant?

Because you are worried about your job future you would like very much to have the support of closeness with her? And she says no?

DISCUSSING PRIORITIES, GOALS, AND CONTRACTS

To make any helping process work it is necessary to establish *priorities, goals,* and a *contract,* which is an agreement on what is to be done and how to do it. This process is illustrated on the opposite page.

There are several ways to decide on *priorities.* Each way has values and drawbacks:

1. Priority may be assigned to the problem that is identified by the client as being of highest interest (Epstein 1980). This choice contains a

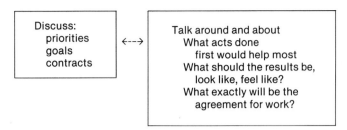

high probability of success because it is congruent with client motivation. However, it is possible that the client's decision is peripheral, which poses questions about the appropriatenes of proceeding.

2. Priority may be assigned to the problem as it is identified by professional judgment. This judgment is more or less significant depending on the strength of the knowledge it is based on. Professional recommendation is especially needed in cases where the client is unable to develop appropriate and feasible ideas about priorities. Professional recommendation may be needed where legal or police authorities require that the client work on a particular problem. Without some degree of client agreement, however, it is not likely that much progress can be made.

3. Setting priorities may be postponed for a short or long time, during which the participants explore questions from a number of different perspectives. A tentative posture on priorities is appropriate when an issue is obscure. The client's commitment may be ambiguous, or the client may be perceived as needing more time to become secure in the helping situation. The difficulty of this position is that the impetus for work may be slowed, causing the helping process to become inefficient.

The guidelines of the helping model that is being used can assist in decision making. This phase begins with discursive discussion. We may circle around the subject to start with, exploring what the client thinks and believes would help most, what she thinks should be done first, and what should follow. The intervention model the practitioner follows and his own experience and knowledge about similar problems indicate what should be done.

The practitioner shares his opinion with the client. If the practitioner thinks the client's formulation is mistaken, he should try to convince the client to make a change. That is done through discussion, exploration, explanation, and clarification. The practitioner's attempts to influence the client may fail if the client considers the practitioner's opinion to be wrong or if the professional opinion contradicts strongly held beliefs and values of the client.

Some intervention models may view the client's reluctance to be influenced by the practitioner as resistance. Considerable discussion and interaction would be required to unearth the hypothetical causes of client inability to accept the professional person's view. Starting up such a discussion prolongs the time needed to reach a working agreement. A more rapid accommodation of views may be achieved by accepting the client's formulation after a reasonable amount of discussion, provided that the client's view does not contain any unethical components. The idea is to achieve some gains for the client, even if they are modest.

Most people do not easily change their minds about what they want. However, good results are still obtainable. If the practitioner is unable to convince the client to follow a recommendation, she can concentrate on developing a program of work that is congruent with the client's stated concerns.

The major communication to facilitate reaching an agreement on what is to be done is this: What acts, if done first, will help most?

In Mr. S.'s case he wanted two priorities arranged in this order:

1. The practitioner should talk to Miss O. to appeal to her to change her attitude.
2. The practitioner should show Mr. S. how to talk and behave to have more influence with Miss O.

This is an example of a common occurrence when priorities are discussed. The first priority (that the practitioner should talk to Miss O.) is impossible for the practitioner to do. The second priority is possible, but the practitioner disagrees with it because the idea is too narrow and oversimplified. This means that the practitioner has to take issue with the client, knowing that the client may be distressed by that disagreement.

To put the refusal in a positive light the practitioner ought to say: "You and I could talk with Miss O. together, provided she is willing to come here for such a conference."

The client should be told the reason for the practitioner's inability to comply with the request: it is not out of unwillingness to help but out of the practitioner's knowledge that there is no way to call in Miss O. for a talk without being extremely rude. It is fairly certain that she will respond negatively to such a call, making things worse for Mr. S. However, if he wants to ask Miss O. to come and she agrees, the practitioner will discuss the interpersonal problems they have together.

How he should go about asking her to come can then be rehearsed. Mr. S. and the practitioner can rehearse when and where to broach the subject, what should be said, what attitude should be projected, what should be done if she says no, and what should be done if she perhaps says yes. If all this seems too difficult for Mr. S., the practitioner should propose that the second priority—helping Mr. S. learn some interpersonal skills that might be more effective—should be made first priority.

The practitioner may choose to explain that he has reservations about both these priorities. The problem is composed of more complicated factors that are not directly touched on by Mr. S.'s suggestions. It is not clear what the couple mean to one another or what Miss O.'s reservations are. They could have something to do with Mr. S.'s personality and unemployment, or with Miss O.'s hang-ups about marriage, or maybe even with her desire to marry someone else.

When the priorities have been decided, the *goals* should be discussed (see Chapter 4). The practitioner should elicit from the client an image of what the results of the intervention program should be, for example, what they should look like or feel like. Mr. S. should be asked to describe his idea of a successful ending: what he should be able to do, to have, or to feel.

A minority of clients may be reluctant to make plans and goals. Problems relating to this will be discussed in Chapter 9. However, most clients are capable of pursuing a reasonable program if they understand it and if it is in line with their interests as they see them.

A *contract* is a formal or informal agreement to identify what will be worked on. Contracts in interviews are not legally binding but have moral weight. Some agencies ask for written contracts as a means of control and for the sake of accountability. Some prefer the greater flexibility of a verbal and informal contract (Maluccio and Marlow 1974).

Contracts cover the following subjects:
1. Major priority problems
2. Specific goals
3. Activities the client will undertake
4. Activities the practitioner will undertake
5. Duration of intervention (approximately how long the process is expected to last)
6. Scheduling for interviews
7. People who will participate

SUMMARY OF THE FIRST PHASE

The first phase contains problem identification, specification, and goal setting. These are the initial steps in the problem-solving process. This process assumes that problems are best handled if they are as clear and specific as possible. The first phase calls for reducing strangeness between client and interviewer and beginning a relatively secure interpersonal engagement. To this are added the processes of eliciting basic information; explaining roles; and explaining problems, personal characteristics, and social context. Identification and specification of problems follows, leading to a focus for the work. The result is a contract that makes the goal more firm.

The communications and social interactions of the first phase start with greetings and are followed by turn taking when asking and answering questions and elaborating on ideas. Questions may be direct, or they may be indirect (as in statements implying a need for more information). Knowledge of the client is obtained through speech augmented by body motions, facial expressions, and other nonverbal messages.

Middle phase

The middle phase, which is shown below, advances the problem-solving process. Ideas and plans are generated and choices are made and revised about actions that may alleviate the problem. The middle phase moves into *implementation,* that is, putting the plan in action, observing its effects, revising it as necessary, and preparing for termination.

Interventions are actions that lead to change in the client's problems

| Middle phase | Discuss
    what to do
Introduce
    interventions
Pin down ←---→
Establish incentives
    and rationale
Get agreement
State time limits
Review
Give advice
Analyze obstacles
Encourage
Give guidance | What would you like to do?
What would you like me to do? Or other people?
What can be done?
We should try this, in this way (tell, show, discuss)
In detail, we do this, like this, there, here, today, next week, with him or her or them, this way, this first, that last
For these good reasons, because . . .
Is that OK? No? What else? Instead? Yes? OK!
Let's move along. Six interviews left
How did you get along on those actions? What stopped you? What thoughts got in the way? Who stopped you? What conditions got in the way? What did you need that you didn't have? What scared you?
Let's see how we can change and avoid those obstacles.
I suggest you think of it this way; go about doing it like this; tell them that; ask them this. How would that suit you? Could you do it? What can I do for you to help? |

and circumstances. Judgments are formed about which interventions are realistic, proper, and acceptable to clients. Parallel judgments are formed by clients. Differences in the judgments of clients and practitioners can be explained by disparities in their knowledge, values, life-styles, and aspirations.

The middle phase of intervention is highly individualized according to type of problem, client, and organizational purposes. This phase also varies depending on the recommendations contained in the particular model guidelines that are being followed. Decisions are made in the middle phase about what techniques to emphasize, what to omit, and what to add. Decisions may be made about the preferred order for using techniques. These decisions cannot be prescribed for all cases because they are made according to individual professional judgments. The basic middle-phase communication techniques reviewed here are building blocks from which more complex individualized communications can be constructed.

DISCUSSING WHAT TO DO

Interviews in the middle phase frequently begin with a review of what is being done, what the plan is, and what has transpired since the last contact. By the third interview practitioner and client have probably just finished making a plan and reaching an agreement or contract. The interview begins with a brief resume of the plan to fix it in mind. Then the following questions might be asked: "What would you like to do now?" *or* "What would you like me to do?" *or* "What can be done?" If client and practitioner are past the third interview there should be a brief review of the status of the work, followed by a discussion of obstacles (pp. 117-118).

The interventions, or changes in them, should be introduced by speech conventions such as "We could try this," or "I would suggest _____," or "Have you thought about this?"

As the client waits for the practitioner to continue or starts to respond, the practitioner's speech tells, shows, and discusses. The practitioner didactically describes and explains the intervention.

The practitioner can describe the desired intervention plan to the client. She can discuss aspects with the client that are not well understood or are misunderstood, unclear, or anxiety producing. The thought that governs selection of the practitioner's speech is this: the purpose of the middle phase is to get results, to effect change, and to give help that is wanted. The whole aim of intervention is to reduce the problem by overcoming obstacles that stand in the way of potentially helpful activities.

INTRODUCING INTERVENTIONS

NAMING THE INTERVENTION

We name the intervention so that it can be known, clarified in thought, and understood to have meaning.

For example:

We are starting this program to expand your family's means to help one another.

What we are doing is rescheduling your play time.

These activities are the preliminaries to job retraining.

These are exercises to improve the flexibility of your wrist after your cast is taken off.

These are medications for cutting down muscle contractions.

Naming the intervention usually involves phrases that reflect the intervention's purpose.

DESCRIBING THE INTERVENTION

Describing the intervention means recounting and tracing the outline of the intervention. For example, the interviewer might tell the client, "The preliminaries to getting job retraining are checking what jobs will be available in the near future and finding out what training programs there are, what they cost, who will pay for them, how they match your interests and abilities, and how they might help your future income and advancement."

EXPLAINING THE INTERVENTION

The practitioner should make the activities of the intervention as plain and intelligible as possible. Explanations might include: who does what, in what order, with what alternatives, with what timing, and with what purpose. For example, the practitioner might say, "You should go to union headquarters and the state employment office. Get what information they have about job market prospects for the near future. Ask about the location and conditions for existing and planned retraining courses. Then you need to decide if they appeal to you. Talk it over with the union steward, your friends in the same boat, your wife, and me."

Details are put into this explanation to match with individual circumstances.

PINNING DOWN

It is advisable to fix the major ideas of the intervention in the mind. Thus they can be held onto, pictured clearly, and firmly perceived. This involves describing interventions of immediate interest in words and phrases.

Pinning down means discussing and giving information in detail. The practitioner should say that this or that should be done, like this, in this manner, there or here, today or next week or after such and such, or before that, with her or him or them, this way, with this first and that last.

There is often a fear that going into such detail is boring or redundant. If the practitioner goes into unnecessary detail the client will show impatience. He will sigh, turn his head away, wrinkle up his brow, show displeasure, tap his foot, or twist up his body in the chair. Whether or not too much detail is being discussed can be checked out simply by asking the client.

Impatience with detail may not be a problem for some clients. Rather, they may be distressed by clear picturing of distasteful things that need to be done. If discomfort emerges, the practitioner has an opportunity to discuss it as an obstacle to overcome so that the client can get what she wants. For example:

> **P:** Considering all that we have talked about, it seems to me that we are going to have to discuss your husband's illness with him directly.
>
> **G:** Oh no!
>
> **P:** Let me explain. You and I do not really understand what is wrong with him or how sick he is. We don't know what the clinic is doing or how he is reacting.
>
> **G:** That's true . . . But he won't come here. I don't even know if he's strong enough.
>
> **P:** Then I could come to your apartment and see you there together.
>
> **G:** But he will have a fit if he finds out I told anybody about this. He'll take it out on me. I can't stand that!
>
> **P:** Do you feel you wronged him by asking us to help?
>
> **G:** Not really—but maybe.
>
> **P:** What is wrong about it?

ESTABLISHING INCENTIVES AND RATIONALE

In order to do something novel that may be unpleasant, frightening, or full of ambiguity, human beings need to have a compelling reason and some confidence in a reward. The actions have to be worth the trouble.

The purpose of problem-solving work is to reduce a problem so that it becomes less frequent, less intense, or of shorter duration. The client needs incentives and an acceptable rationale to undertake problem solving. The rationale is a foundation of thoughts and values, based partly on experience, that justifies what is about to be embarked on. To impart strength of will to a client in proceeding with an intervention that may be uncomfortable, discussion should be held to determine what is in it for the client, what improvement is expected, and why the proposed activities are good and reasonable.

The incentives and rationale can usually be identified by starting with the target problem and picturing the conditions that can be expected when that problem is reduced. The basic incentive is to obtain the goal: the job; the diminution of tension; the satisfaction of a desired relationship with another person; the resources to house, feed, and shelter oneself and one's family; self-respect and a sense of well-being; or the skills for building self-confidence, meeting the right people, having the necessities of life, or developing a desired life-style.

It is best for the practitioner to phrase his part of the discussion in plain, straightforward terms that are familiar to the client. Examples of such formulations are:

> Suppose you were to go through with these activities—what would you expect to get out of them?
>
> Do you think you would get those things?
>
> What difference would it make to you?
>
> Is the effort worth it, do you think?
>
> Is this program we have worked out reasonable to you?
>
> Well—I think it's reasonable, because you said you wanted this to happen.
>
> I think it's reasonable because most people feel that.
>
> I think it's reasonable because most people do not do that, and they stay out of trouble.
>
> It seems you are too dependent on your mother; it would be better if you weren't.
>
> You would like to be your own boss and you can be.

GETTING AGREEMENT

Often agreement is routinely reached throughout the discussion. Everything indicates that the client understands and accepts the program. Practitioners get confirmations of agreement when clients make positive facial expressions, nod, maintain eye contact, or move in closer.

It is not advisable, however, to take agreement for granted; it should be checked out in a verbal exchange. For example, the practitioner should ask:

> Is this all right?
>
> Are we going too fast?
>
> What reservations do you have?
>
> Shall we continue this?

Clients respond to such phrases mostly with head shakes or brief phrases such as: "OK," "No," or "I don't know." These are the signals that put closure on the discussion. If the client's answer is "OK," it is safe to proceed. An uncertain response is a signal to discuss more to get agreement. The likelihood of a client acting successfully on an intervention with which he disagrees is slight.

STATING TIME LIMITS

All intervention programs have time limits, although they may not be explicit. Some programs are limited by circumstances. For example, the time limits for a schooling or training program are set and publicly known from the beginning of the program.

Many interventions, however, do not dictate a specific ending time. In order for organizations to control costs, assign staff, and plan operations, it is still necessary to know approximately how much time will be used. There have to be planned endings so that the client can apportion his time, energy, and interests.

Except for programs with obvious limits there are no established criteria for the optimum time necessary to find a job, recover or gain self-esteem, improve interpersonal skills, or get a child back from foster care. More and more agencies are making administrative recommendations about length of time to be provided for cases. In situations where agencies are responsible for long-term care such as foster home placement or institutional living for frail or sick elderly people, the long term is not an intervention as much as it is caretaking. Direct intervention takes place within the time allotted for caretaking work and can be limited.

The best time to bring up and discuss time limits is during the starting-up phase of an intervention program. This is also the time to advise a client about the allotted time for individual interviews. Sometimes a client asks right away, "How long will this take?" Whether she asks or not, the practitioner should introduce the subject by saying, "I want to tell you about how much time we will have for this work." The practitioner then goes on to say that it is the agency's recommendation that they use five interviews (or six, or eight, or twelve, as the case may be) over a period of two months (or three or four) to get the job done. The practitioner should add that these numbers can be reduced if the work goes fast, or they can be increased if necessary. The client should also be advised that he can come back at a later time if there is further need.

If an agency operates without time limits, this should be stated and the criteria for termination given. Most clients find such plain statements about time limits reasonable and welcome.

Once the statements of time limits have been made by the practitioner, clients usually keep track of the time. However, some clients may forget and should be regularly reminded of how much time is left. It has been a frequent observation of all types of clinicians that setting time limits provides an atmosphere that spurs activity.

REVIEWING

It is advisable to review at every interview or at least at every other one. The review examines the problem condition at the start, identifies the major interventions attempted and their results, and confirms or changes the anticipated content for the remaining sessions. The review should be initiated right after the greetings or an inquiry about what is new. The review permits taking stock, or measuring results, so that practitioner and client can accelerate, slow down, or change a program that is not working.

The phrasing to elicit the review might be, for example, "Let's look at what has been going on here. When we started we agreed that we would concentrate on your finding a job as the first priority. Second, we would try to work on a better relationship between you and your wife. In the three weeks spent working on these problems we have almost totally concentrated on the problem with your wife and have paid little attention to the job problem. That's how I see it. What do you think?"

The client replied that the problem with his wife did seem to be taking precedence. The practitioner asked for an assessment of progress with the marital conflicts. According to the client these conflicts were abating; he gave details. The practitioner asked if he preferred putting the job problem aside so that the most concentration would still be on his marital situation. No, he said, the job problem was uppermost. His savings were getting low. Soon he would have to confront going on welfare if he did not get organized to find a job. From that point, most of the interview time was spent on the priority problem of job hunting. The review thus obviously served to keep the intervention process from failing.

GIVING ADVICE

Clients of all sorts seek advice. Many different kinds of people—those who are exceptionally dependent or ambivalent, or those who characteristically have a hard time making up their minds or feeling self-confident, but also well-organized and responsible people—all know from experience the value of a capable person's advice. Someone who is reliable can often throw light on a matter and provide assistance that people cannot provide for themselves.

Most people do not wish to project themselves as domineering or to make unwarranted intrusions into the lives of others. It used to be thought that advice given by a practitioner would encourage a dependent relationship that was unrealistic and might be harmful to the client. Although there is probably some truth to fears that giving advice can be domineering or weaken the client, much new insight into this subject has been uncovered. As a result of research into advice giving and data from practitioners who give a good deal of advice it appears that fear is not necessarily justified. There is much to be gained from a reasonable amount of advice giving (Davis 1975; Reid and Shapiro 1969).

Surveys of client opinion show that clients sincerely seek advice and feel dissatisfied if they fail to get it. Clients do not necessarily follow advice exactly; however, they use it as a jumping off place and to get started. They reorganize the advice in a way that feels right and makes the most sense to them. The advice triggers a process in which the client develops his own advice. That trigger is what the client really wants.

> Mr. A. was receiving counseling for a marital problem. He and his wife had been drawing apart. She had developed open resentment about his long work hours that made him fatigued on evenings and weekends. Mr. and Mrs. A. had no time together, had stopped going out socially altogether, and had virtually stopped conversing except to say things like, "Where are the car keys?" After 25 years of a full and often happy home life, her distancing and his shyness about discussing it with her were causing Mr. A. extreme distress. He was blaming everything on "women's liberation."
>
> Among other things, it was decided that Mr. A. must court his wife. He must "date" his wife, starting by taking her to an elegant place to dine. Mr. A. had been actively leading the discussion to make these decisions with the practitioner supporting him. Now, contemplating his first date with his wife, this capable, middle-aged, intelligent, and strong businessman asked the practitioner: "Where should I take her?"
>
> Stumped, the practitioner thought about where she would like to go if she were his wife. She suggested a chic Chinese restaurant.
>
> Next time she found out that Chinese food was not to the A.'s liking. However, Mr. A. had taken his wife to a Bavarian restaurant in the suburbs that plays loud oom-pah music; they danced the evening away and had a great time to start off their reconciliation.

There are rules about advice giving. The practitioner should not give advice if it is motivated by the urge to make the client do something because the practitioner likes it. Advice should not be given unless the practitioner has exchanged enough ideas with the client for them to decide together what should be done. Also before giving advice the practitioner should observe the nonverbal cues that communicate a client's genuine and deep fear of going it alone. (This was the case with Mr. A.)

Most particularly a practitioner should not give advice when she does not know what the client should do. The practitioner should say straight out that she does not know and why she does not know. She can say that she will think about it, consult an expert, or read up on the subject so that she might give good advice later. Or she can refer the client to a good, reliable source that can be expected to have the necessary information.

A practitioner almost never knows what a client should do about major life decisions such as having a baby, giving up a child for adoption, getting married, leaving a spouse, changing jobs, or retiring. The practitioner and the client know that the pros and cons of such decisions involve predictions that are unreliable. A client who asks for advice about these major decisions is really asking to discuss the pros and cons in detail before taking the final leap into a decision. Practitioners are, however, free to give good advice, if they have it, about sub-parts to such questions. They can certainly give reasonable advice about a good restaurant or a good hour of the day for broaching a question to a spouse, employer, or landlord. They can with sureness advise clients on such issues as disciplining children, planning and conducting weighty discussions with important people, or finding the best available resources for their problems.

The strongest form of advice is that shown in the illustration with Mr. and Mrs. A. "I think you should do this" was the advice that was communicated. Less force is exerted by stating the advice as a suggestion: "It seems to me that if it suits you it would be good to do this or think this." The weakest form of advising is to put emphasis behind one alternative that the client has already considered: "Of the several things you are thinking about, doing this seems the most promising." Strong advice should probably be reserved for putting a quick end to indecision that is pressing, highly anxiety producing, and only temporarily important.

GIVING GUIDANCE/ANTICIPATING OBSTACLES

Some purposes of the middle phase are to accomplish target problem reduction, solve problems, and plan to overcome barriers that stand in the way. The type of change that is usually sought in human services is change in the complement of resources that can be brought to bear on a problem or change in the quantity and quality of social skills that an individual, family, or group possesses to improve well-being or quality of life.

Most of the interviewing techniques in this phase are those that teach, enlighten, and influence clients so that they can accomplish their goals. Giving guidance and its related process of anticipating obstacles are chief vehicles for problem reduction.

In the middle part of an interview the emphasis is on pinning down the intervention program. Later in the series the emphasis will be on getting the problem reduction actions to take place. The middle phase becomes a process of education and reeducation. Giving useful guidance can help to identify and avoid obstacles. It is a means for increasing the efficiency of the whole process to save missteps. Guidance is leading a person through unfamiliar terrain and aiding her to reach a destination. The major communication in giving guidance is: Let me show you *what, how,* and *in what manner.*

After this introduction the practitioner initiates discourse in which he directs the client in ways to put into effect the mutually planned steps of action. Clarifying — for example, who to talk to or what to say — may be in order. Giving thought to what something means, how something feels, or what to do with emotional reactions may also be necessary.

Speech used in guidance can be either direct or indirect. Direct speech is didactic, that is, instructive. Indirect speech consists of statements that confirm and emphasize the idea being discussed.

Guiding statements contain a great deal of information that informs clients where to go, how to get there, who to see, what to say, and what to do if an anticipated obstacle occurs. These instructional guides can be specific to the point of dotting every "i" and crossing every "t" if necessary. An example of this kind of guidance follows.

> The client, Miss D., is a chronically mentally ill young adult. She has recently been released from a 6-week stay in a state mental hospital. She lives at home with her parents in impoverished circumstances. She is attending an outpatient clinic regularly for checkups on her reaction to medication and for help in making an adjustment in the community. She wants to get a job so she can have income and feel like "a real person," not sick and dependent. She is characteristically a frightened and shy person. She never seems to know the right thing to say to another person to get a desired response. The clinic has secured a reservation for her in a sheltered workplace located downtown. To get there she needs to take a 20-minute ride on public transportation from her home.
>
> Miss D. is given the information about the reservation. She is told what kind of work is involved and that she can expect

helpful supervision. Her remarks suggest that she does not feel comfortable going downtown or seeing strangers at the workplace office.

In order to assure that Miss D. gets to the office she has to be instructed which way to walk from her house to get on the right bus. She has to be coached on such subjects as: what the sign on the bus will say so she knows she has the right one, how much fare and which correct change she needs to have ready, what will be the most comfortable place on the bus to sit if she has a choice, what will be the best place to stand if the bus has no seats, what sign to look for to know where she has to get off, where to go for coffee after the bus trip to get herself together for the interview, and the name of the person she will be interviewing with at the workplace office.

The practitioner and Miss D. rehearse what to say in greeting the interviewer at the workplace. The practitioner suggests things the employment interviewer might say and questions that might be asked and rehearses answers with Miss D.

In addition to or as a substitute for didactic instruction there is rehearsal. The practitioner acts out the role of a person whom the client deals with. That other person may be a son, daughter, spouse, or friend or a teacher, doctor, lawyer, judge, or other authority. Such rehearsals give the client an opportunity to practice, to fix ideas in mind, to gain experience, and to obtain constructive criticism and suggestions on how to put his best foot forward.

The process of guidance is not complete unless the practitioner speaks about difficulties that can be expected and prepares the client for them to some extent. It is also necessary to alert clients that something untoward, unexpected, or adverse might happen and to tell them how to conduct themselves in that case.

There is great variation among clients in how much guidance they will need. It can, however, be assumed that practitioners will have to give verbal instruction and guided rehearsal to nearly everyone to a greater or lesser degree. Guidance should always be considered when a client is about to undertake a novel action for the first time and is anxious about doing well. Any client with a marked lack of experience or a mental impairment, such as Miss D., will need maximum instruction.

GIVING ENCOURAGEMENT

Giving encouragement fosters hope and inspires self-confidence. Encouraging statements can be important and powerful even when they are small words and phrases such as "un-huh," "oh yes," "that's right," or "go on," as long as they are uttered in an emphatic way.

In conventional speech the previous common phrases convey a friendly and approving spirit. A fearful person may further benefit from hearing sentences that convey approval from the practitioner, such as:

That's pretty good.

Well done.

Good thought.

You're on the right track.

Encouragement can be furthered by statements that explain why the client's thought or deed is exemplary and why the practitioner thinks that the client can do even more. For example, the practitioner might say:

> That was quite courageous of you to speak up in the meeting. It's probably fairly safe for you to do that again. Your supervisor was taken aback, but she responded politely and was interested. You did not get fired on the spot. That could happen, but it is unlikely. In fact it rarely happens even though people are always fantasizing about it. You were right, you know. Your fellow workers supported you. Of course they won't always do that; you have to decide whether something is worth the risk.

Encouragement is cognitive in the sense that it conveys information to the client. It is also affective in the sense that it conveys the practitioner's friendliness and caring.

ANALYZING AND OVERCOMING OBSTACLES

The obstacles of concern in an interview are barriers to client attempts to carry out planned actions in real life. These obstacles exist in several areas. Some are in the mind of the client. They may be attitudes and mind sets that make the client fearful, usually to an unrealistic degree. They may be adverse beliefs originating in the client's personality and life-style. Unless these mental obstacles are of recent origin they are difficult to change. If they are of recent origin it is worthwhile to approach them by rational discussion, in which a practitioner points out the way the belief or attitude conflicts with known reality. Two examples of practitioner responses follow.

> I thought your son had been cooperative in helping you until recently. What makes you change your mind about him now? What happened?
>
> I understand that most of the companies in your area of

work are disorganized and pay poorly. Stories about that are written up in newspapers. What is going on that makes you think you are being personally singled out for humiliation?

Mental obstacles of long duration can be addressed directly if the client is willing and the practitioner has advanced skills. Faced with chronic mental attitudes the practitioner might find it advisable to concentrate first on conditions that are more changeable such as improvements in the environment, in living arrangements, in recreational outlets, and in skills to minimize conflicts with other people.

A major obstacle to intervention activity is the presence of hostile other people who have negative attitudes toward the client because of race, religion, sex, age, or ethnic characteristics. Prejudice, discrimination, and unprovoked random attack exist in society and are often misinterpreted as personal. A client may believe that she is responsible for a problem when in reality she is being victimized. Also, friends and relatives may not give anticipated closeness and support. They may be jealous, hostile, contemptuous, or enraged with the client because of their own problems. The client may live under financial and social restraints that in fact limit her ability to act in desirable ways and conduct life in a normal fashion.

It is necessary to find out what particular obstacle or set of obstacles is preventing the client from taking a planned action. Then the practitioner and client should make a special plan to cut down the negative effect of the obstacle and develop ways to help the client avoid it, confront it if necessary, get over it, or go around it. There is no way that is always preferable; for example, there is no virtue in facing up to something if it is ultimately better to avoid it. What matters is to hit upon a plan that will get the client over or around the obstacle so that the problem-reduction plan can take place.

The way to identify the obstacle is to review what the client has (and has not) done about it. The client may have put the action into effect and succeeded, or tried it out and failed, or not done it at all.

In case of failure or nonperformance, what needs to be asked is: "Tell me exactly what you did . . . and then what happened? . . . and then what did you do?" Thus we can draw out a specific picture of what events took place and how the client felt about them. With this information a judgment can be made about the location of the obstacle and what it consists of. Then client and practitioner can approach the problem in a different way.

If the client is a nonperformer, the highest likelihoods are that she was frightened or that the plan was too hard, too easy, too unrealistic, or too vague. If nonperformance seems to be due to fear, the practitioner should make encouraging comments, give advice, establish incentives and a rationale, give didactic instruction, ask questions, and make comments that help the client express her fears so they can be viewed realistically. Then the intervention can be planned again to see if it will work next time.

If the intervention plan was inappropriate, it should be immediately revised, using the same techniques discussed earlier for establishing a plan initially. For example:

> Mrs. T. must find an apartment to move into because very soon she will be evicted from her present quarters. She has an ill husband and two small children. Her present landlord refuses to accept welfare rent payments. Mrs. T. is not accustomed to taking action to meet and negotiate with businesspeople, and she is afraid. Her husband is housebound and cannot go out to negotiate with prospective apartment agents.
>
> Preparing for the action the interviewer has discovered Mrs. T.'s fears of being looked down on by building superintendents and her tendency to become ashamed and withdrawn. The interviewer has been encouraging and supportive, but Mrs. T. remains fearful.
>
> The interviewer rehearses with her the best time of day to go out apartment hunting, plans for child care in her absence, what clothes she should wear to make herself feel her best, what she should say to the building agent, and what questions she should ask.
>
> At the next interview Mrs. T. says she did not go apartment hunting.

P: You were planning to go Wednesday?
Mrs. T.: Yes.
P: Well, let's go over what stood in your way.
Mrs. T.: You know, you know. I just can't.
P: I do know already how scared this makes you. But let's start from the top. You were going to leave the house at 10 AM. Please go over what happened and what you were thinking from the time you got up until 10 AM.

> Mrs. T. then reconstructed the early morning. Her husband was mad because of being laid up. The kids made a mess over breakfast. All she had was a gulp of coffee. The current landlord pounded on the front door and yelled that they would have to appear in court next week.
>
> The interviewer turns to Mr. T. and asks him if he could do

all the household chores tomorrow and let Mrs. T. concentrate totally on getting herself together to go out to face building agents. Although grumpy about it, Mr. T. says he can and he will.

SUMMARY OF THE MIDDLE PHASE

Interviewing in the middle phase can be carried out using the following basic problem-solving outline:

1. Identifying the problem
2. Generating various solutions
3. Deciding on preferred and alternative actions
4. Implementing the plan
5. Revising the plan as necessary
6. Terminating
7. Evaluating the results

The process of problem identification receives central attention in the initial phase. The rest of the steps are part of the middle phase. The basic responsibility of the interviewer is to bring expert knowledge to bear on helping the client select and accept activities and ideas likely to lead to a feasible amount of problem alleviation. The practitioner then needs to assist the client in finding out how to accomplish the development of new ideas and actions.

Clients need their own individualized programs to achieve results. Among the interviewing techniques that can be used are explaining interventions clearly, pinning interventions down, establishing incentives and a rationale for activities, getting agreement, advising as needed, giving guidance, reviewing, analyzing obstacles, and planning their removal.

Having a structure for the middle phase provides a useful framework and minimizes drift and ambiguity. Nevertheless, it is likely that developments will proceed in a halting and uneven manner. Many unforeseeable problems tend to occur, necessitating flexibility and revisions in the plan. Most clients experience uncertainty about what they are doing. They develop new fears. Unplanned events occur in the family and neighborhood that upset plans. New thoughts emerge that seem to call for unspecified revisions.

It is not uncommon for clients to need more problem exploration and revised specification. Time often needs to be spent on exploration rather than direct problem-solving activities. These struggles in the middle phase are part and parcel of an expected process. As much as possible it is advisable to persistently focus on the central problem-solving process while being flexible enough to sensitively attend to client concerns and reactions.

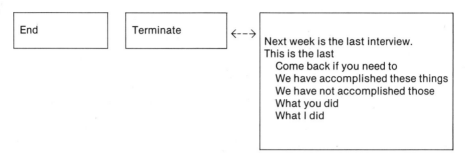

Termination

The termination interview, illustrated above, is a review of what has taken place in the intervention. The purpose is to fix events in mind so they may be called on in the future to guide in problem solving. There are five communications in a termination interview: (1) "This is what we accomplished," (2) "This is what we did not accomplish," (3) "This is what you did," (4) "This is what I did," and (5) "Come back if you need to."

There are some problems that may occur at termination. Some clients fail to show up for the final interview, apparently because the work is over and they have no interest in a summary. Some clients may develop separation anxiety and feel upset by the ending, preferring to avoid it. Practitioners may also feel distress over ending a sequence of interviews. On the one hand they may criticize themselves for things they now wish they had done differently. Or they may have become genuinely fond of certain clients and hate to see them go. Sometimes a practitioner is proud of a client's accomplishments and of her own work and does not want the experience to end. The practitioner's feelings are important but not part of the client's situation, and they ought to be controlled. However, it is no cause for undue concern unless the practitioner allows her own feelings to engulf the client. Termination decisions are made according to the intervention model and agency policy.

CASE EXAMPLE: EMANCIPATING A TEENAGER (Taylor and Rooney 1982)

P is the practitioner; C is the client, a 16-year-old young woman. She is a ward of the court who has moved out of a foster home and into a boarding house; that is, "independent living" is being attempted.

In this audiotape script all of the body, eye, and head movements are missing and have to be imagined.

PATTERN OF DISCOURSE

There are 87 statements in this interview, distributed evenly between practitioner and client. The general pattern is logical and orderly. There are greetings at the start, and there is a closing greeting. These greetings are straightforward and unencumbered by extraneous matter.

The practitioner's speech throughout is clear. Both the practitioner and the client display the ordinary circumlocutions of verbal speech. Their words and phrases are often ungrammatical. Thoughts run together without clear ends and beginnings and are hard to punctuate on paper. Sometimes beginnings and endings of sentences are somewhat vague (see Interchanges 30, 47, 52, 53, and 54). However, the interviewer and client seem to be attentive. They are listening to each other and getting each other's meaning. The farewell clearly communicates the relationship between the two and indicates what has changed. Client and practitioner will not be meeting regularly any more, but they will see each other in court. The practitioner will help the client with the uncertainties of that experience.

Turns are taken smoothly in this interview, perhaps more smoothly than usual. There appear to be no interruptions or simultaneous talk. That is not necessarily always the case. There are some discontinuous interchanges (such as Interchanges 49, 50, 53, and 54). Although the interviewer is not at all coercive, she leads the client strongly through a planned set of subjects that was established at the start of the interview (in Interchange 3).

This interview reveals much use of adjacency pairing of interchanges. The client seems to respect the conventions of turn taking and responding to the focus or inquiry of the interviewer.

The client's verbal style in this interview is the frank, bold speech of a teenager. However, the practitioner does not use teen language; she respects her own style. She is somewhat formal and uses rather intellectual language. She keeps her role distinct, but this does not interfere with the genuineness of her communication.

Interchanges	*Comments on interchanges*
1. **P:** Hi, Misty.	1, 2. Greeting and familiarizing
2. **C:** Hello.	
3. **P:** This is our eighth session of the contract that we contracted to have, which means that today's our last time to get together. So it's the proper time for us to review how we have done on the problems that you identified in the first session and see how close you are to the goal that you set at that time.	3. Reviewing

Interchanges	*Comments on interchanges*
When we first started getting together, you said that your goal was to get off supervision and achieve independent living. The problems you wanted to work on at that time were three: first, you wanted to—you were tired of people telling you what to do. Second, you wanted to be able to stay at your aunt's until you had your own place. And the third problem was to continue seeing your boyfriend, but you didn't want to be fighting him all the time and you wanted to improve that relationship. How do you think you did on reducing these problems? How about number one: you were tired of people telling you what to do?	
4. **C:** I think I've begun. There is nobody telling me how to run my life and it makes me a little bit more at ease, and as far as me taking charge really of my own life—I don't know, nobody's really commented about it, you know, they haven't said that I've done that bad and so I don't know, I like not having people telling me how to do this and how to do that.	4. Turn taking; adjacency pairs
5. **P:** To me it seems you are a lot more relaxed and a lot happier today than you were eight sessions ago.	5. Giving information
6. **C:** Yeah.	6. Turn taking
7. **P:** I can remember you were so tight and angry that day that it was all you could do to stay in the same room with your aunt and me and talk about what you wanted to do.	7. Reviewing
8. **C:** Yeah.	8. Turn taking
9. **P:** You have a court hearing coming up. You want to ask the judge to grant you independent living and terminate your supervision. What are you going to say to him as far as things that you have undertaken in the last eight sessions—ways you could demonstrate to him that you have become more responsible?	9. Giving information Eliciting information
10. **C:** Well I'm living on my own right now. I	10. Giving information *Continued.*

Interchanges	Comments on interchanges
haven't done nothing that I could get caught by the cops. Ah, I've checked into schooling even though I don't have to, but I have, and I have been out looking for a job, have been out looking for a place to stay, and I do have proof there. I don't know, I think I'm capable of taking care of my life more than anybody else is, because I know what I want and nobody else knows what I want, besides my freedom.	
11. **P:** You . . . you did not want to work on your drinking or your drug use as a problem when we identified the problem, even though that had been something that other people had identified as a problem. Looking back on the past 8 sessions, which was probably about 2 1/2 months time, what has happened in that area of your life? And how would you express that to the judge?	11. Eliciting information Guiding
12. **C:** I could almost say I quit, cause I — my drug and my alcohol use — I've realized I can't be using it as a cop-out towards my problems and I haven't, and it's made a lot of difference, and you know I didn't have to go through any treatment or any drug center to realize how I was using it, that I was going to hurt myself sooner or later. I don't know, I think I've done pretty damn good compared to what I was eight weeks ago, eight sessions ago, because before I was really into drugs. I wasn't using them a lot, but I was using them as a cop-out and not as a socializer and it makes a difference, when you do it.	12. Explaining problem
13. **P:** When you were upset was when you would go looking for some drugs or something to drink?	13. Eliciting information Reviewing
14. **C:** Yeah.	14. Turn taking
15. **P:** Thinking about the relationship with your boyfriend, you wanted to reduce the fighting between you and him. How has that gone? How much were you fighting at the time when we first started talking?	15. Eliciting information Reviewing

Interchanges	*Comments on interchanges*
16. **C:** About six or seven days we were fighting, and now we are down to about once a week, yeah, if that. We just sit and talk about our problems. We're not screaming at each other or yelling at each other, we aren't mad at each other, you know, and it makes a difference cause now we're more—I guess it was pressure on both ends, when my life was going and his too, and at first I didn't really realize how my life was ruining and affecting his and now I do, because what I do does affect him, and what he does affects me, but I think we accomplished a lot, because we are sitting down talking about it now. Arguing with each other, you do this, and you do that, and we're not arguing with each other, you do this, you do that, we're not bossing each other, we ask each other will you do or will you not do that, you know, and it makes a difference cause when he tells me "Do this," I'll turn around and do the opposite damn thing. I've already been that way, done that with my parents, my aunt, foster homes. People tell me to do something, it don't work. If they ask me to do something, it will probably work. Yeah, depends on what it is.	16. Explaining problem
17. **P:** When you were trying to work on this problem with Dan, did you say to him that it was a problem to you and you were working on it or did you just start changing without his being aware of what you were doing? How did you approach that?	17. Eliciting information
18. **C:** I told him that we gotta stop arguing, fighting, and hitting each other, on each other, cause it's more of a childish behavior than it is responsible and I guess we both made an agreement that we would sit down and talk about it and it helped, and another thing that's helped with this, we're not out partying every night and then we aren't	18. Explaining problem, personal characteristics, and social context

Continued.

Interchanges	*Comments on interchanges*
seeing the people that started our problems. Yeah, we kinda, like he was living with his brother, brother didn't like me, ah, now he's out of his brother's place. My aunt didn't like him, I'm out of her place and that made a lot of difference, a tremendous difference because they all think we're not going out together anymore.	
19. **P:** Ah.	19. Turn taking, conventional expression
20. **C:** That's what we heard through the grapevine. It's kind of cute, cause here we are all lovey-dovey and they think we're hating each other. Hunh. It's kind of gigglish about the whole matter.	20. Explaining problem
21. **P:** Well, I can imagine that before too long somebody will catch on to what's happening. The only thing that we really — that you really had for that problem was that you were going to talk to him about that. I think the task was in relationship to your aunt. You were going to ask him to stop hassling her and barging in.	21. Reviewing
22. **C:** I got them both in the same room, and then I kinda mentioned it and the truth came out. He did approach her one time. Otherwise she approached him, and that's another thing, I'm, I don't like people to lie — the truth will come out sooner or later and that's when I stopped lying. I stopped lying to myself and I stopped lying to everybody else because it will catch up with you. Telling the truth will catch up with them, to the people you lied to sooner or later. Yeah. *(Pause —silence)*	22. Reviewing
23. **C:** Now like when some guys think we're breaking up, you know, that's kind of like a little gag, you know, we're just pulling their leg, cause they just — they lay off more if they don't think we're going out, so then that's the same way uptown, if you go and ask about me, people been asking about	23. Explaining problem

Interchanges	*Comments on interchanges*

me because I don't go up there with him anymore. You know, I was up there Monday, no Friday, with him. I don't wanta go up there, because that's where all the talk starts again, yeah, and he went uptown, he was uptown yesterday afternoon and people were coming up to him asking for me. "You guys still going out? Where she living at? What's her phone number?" Dan said, "I don't know and I don't care" and dropped it. It kind of cracks me up, you know, then because I don't have to listen to it, it seemed like every time I went out, "Where's Dan? How's Dan? You and Dan been in a fight?" "You Dan" this and "You Dan" that. It got to be a drag, yeah, and then when my aunt — "Where's she, you and her fighting again?" They got a big mouth, I get so sick and tired of hearing those people's problems and too, and mine ain't none of their business, unless I ask them, you know.

24. **P:** Thinking of the future, this is the last time that we will be getting together other than at the court hearing, although if a crisis comes up, or if you need some information, you know where I am, and certainly will expect you to call and we can talk things over on the phone at least, but how are you going to keep things going along at the — in the direction that you seem to feel is the right one for you?

24. Terminating

25. **C:** I don't know, in the daytime I got a lot of time by myself and I can think about it then, about what I think is right, and so far my judgment hasn't been bad, so lately I just been doing whatever my first intentions to do, whatever comes to my mind the first time. I go ahead and do it and if people don't like it, well, that's their problem, if I felt that it was right and I'm satis-

25. Explaining problem, personal characteristics, and social context

Continued.

	Interchanges	*Comments on interchanges*

fied with what I've done, you know, I'm pleased out of it, you know, cause I guess the main thing right now, I got to please myself and stop worrying about other people and how to please them, cause some of the things I do Dan doesn't approve of, but he accepts them because that's me, and that's my first, that's what my mind tells me to do and that is what I am going to do, you know, and he just accepts that. Sometimes I don't like what he does, but then again that's Dan and I can't stop that. You know, I ain't going to change him, cause that's not right either.

26. **P:** So it sounds like you have developed an attitude along with a way of deciding what you are going to do, developed an attitude that you have to rely on your own judgment first of all, and that you're going to allow some people that same right, that they are going to have to be able to determine their life and you're not going to be telling other people what to do either.

26. Guiding

27. **C:** Right.

27. Turn taking; adjacency pair

28. **P:** Ah.

28. Turn taking; adjacency pair

29. **C:** I'm just trying to mind my own business and hoping everybody else will mind theirs. You know, cause I don't like people meddling. I hate it. Unless they have to be in it, I don't want them to be in. I figure that's my problem. I got myself into it and sure enough, I'll get myself out of it.

29. Reviewing

30. **P:** Thinking specifically about how we went about deciding what the problems were that you wanted to work on and what you were going to do from session to session, is there anything that you've learned from the process itself that you think could be helpful to you when you're on your own, from here on, when a problem comes up, say, you don't have any money or —

30. Eliciting information; directing to the future

Interchanges	Comments on interchanges
31. **C:** Just take whatever, you know, one step at a time. Before, you know, I was trying to do them all at once. That's impossible. It's like living in pure hell, trying to work out every problem in the same day; and now, I just like take on one problem and when that's done, I'll work on another one, you know. It's—I guess I have to take my time and gotta know what I'm doing in order to get it done, and before I didn't know what I was doing. Hunh. I didn't, sometimes I didn't know what my problem was, but once I realized my problem, I just work on it that day or put it in between other things and work on it. Yeah, because before I guess I was really working on all my problems at once, and it got to where I had a battle. I didn't know where to turn, and I just sat down one day, and you know, I got to work them out, one at a time, so it makes a difference.	31. Explaining problem; reviewing; explaining roles
32. **P:** It does, doesn't it? It can be very helpful to me too to think about being helpful to you in a more simplified way, not trying to do everything, but identifying the most three problems that were important to you and then doing a little bit at a time, like you said.	32. Explaining roles
33. **C:** Yeah.	33. Turn taking
34. **P:** And making plans. I notice that little notebook you brought today. I don't know what kind of lists you are going to use it for, but I've noticed you are doing that.	34. Explaining roles
35. **C:** Apartments, and little this and that notes I have to write to myself when I want to do something. Think about them ahead, and go do something else and I'll forget about them. Dan took my other one cause he likes writing out things he has to do. He asked if he could take the other one, and I said sure, I'll get another one.	35. Giving information
36. **P:** I also think that its very useful to keep track of what you're doing because then you	36. Giving information

Continued.

Interchanges	*Comments on interchanges*
have a record of what you have accomplished.	
37. **C:** Yeah.	37. Turn taking
38. **P:** Sometimes, it's when problems seem overwhelming, your memory of what you have done in the past or how much you've been able to do gets very distorted, and you feel like you've never accomplished anything and you've not been accomplishing much in resolving your previous problems. But I think you know from the sheets that we kept how many things you have followed through on.	38. Reviewing
39. **C:** Yeah.	39. Turn taking
40. **P:** In terms of looking for jobs, contacting school, which was a task you hadn't thought you wanted to do, but you ended up doing. On your own you've done a lot of tasks around finding an apartment.	40. Reviewing
41. **C:** Financial wise, budgeting. I am so different lately.	41. Giving information
42. **P:** Yes you are.	42. Encouraging
43. **C:** *(Laughs)*	43. Turn taking
44. **P:** As far as being tight with your money, is that what you are saying?	44. Eliciting information
45. **C:** Yeah.	45. Turn taking
46. **P:** I've noticed that.	46. Turn taking
47. **C:** Dan says I'm probably about the tightest person he knows, because if he asked me for dollars, it's like, you what, but Dan *(laughs)*, sooner or later I will give it to him you know, but it's just that when I go to grocery store I try to find the best deal, like when I got some soup and crackers, I sat there, there was about 15 brands of crackers and I figured out which one would probably be the best, what has more quality and taste, and is cheap. You know, that ain't one of the highest ones, yeah, because I got that for 69 cents and some of them were 80 and 99 cents, and that had more in them than the rest of them, so I might as	47. Explaining personal traits and social context

Interchanges	Comments on interchanges
well get that bag. My soup, I'm picky on, I got to have my certain kind of soup. It's always beef noodle.	
48. **P:** One thing that comes to mind, at the time you did follow through on, but you might be more interested in it now, is the class on independent living skills. The kinds of things they cover are establishing credit, what to look for in a lease, how to open a charge account or a checking account, taxes, a lot of the business, financial aspects of being on your own.	48. Giving information
49. **C:** Yeah, they said I could go to school.	49. Turn taking
50. **P:** Legal issues?	50. Eliciting information
51. **C:** They said I could go to school for checking, balancing, and taxes, and all that stuff, she said at school.	51. Giving information
52. **P:** What if you do have questions about things like your rights as tenant, or . . .	52. Eliciting information
53. **C:** I'd probably call that office for the apartments. They got a new office open. It's for something like do you have certain rights on your apartment and . . .	53. Giving information
54. **P:** Tenants' Union.	54. Giving information
55. **C:** Yeah. I'd probably call there and ask them.	55. Giving information
56. **P:** Um hum.	56. Turn taking
57. **C:** Otherwise I'd check in somewhere else, I don't know where.	57. Giving information
58. **P:** There's a number down at the City-County Building called Info and	58. Giving information
59. **C:** Yeah, I got that.	59. Turn taking
60. **P:** Do you have that?	60. Eliciting information
61. **C:** They have, I called them myself, because they have suggestions about where to get more information for all different kinds of resources in the community and questions you might have.	61. Giving information
62. **P:** I think that you can anticipate that there are going to be problems that are going to come up and I don't know what you think they might be. I imagine you and Dan	62. Analyzing possible obstacles

Continued.

	Comments on
Interchanges	*interchanges*

might break up, or might be evicted from an apartment, have no place to go. I don't know. What are the kinds of problems that you think you are going to be encountering?

63. **C:** Hum, getting a job. That's so hard right now. The students are coming back, it's almost impossible. I suppose they are so scarce, 'cause on the — I guess I'm like my dad, I don't like to use somebody else's money. Put it that way. I don't know. There's going to be probably a lot of things, me going out with different guys, Dan going out with the guys, going out with girls.

63. Analyzing possible obstacles

64. **P:** How do you think you might deal with those things when they come up?

64. Eliciting information

65. **C:** I'll talk them out, if it has to do with him, if it has to do with just me alone, I'll have to sit down and think it over myself, or call my friends. He always helps me out. I got to depend on him quite a bit. He always gives me a little advice if I call and ask. He's kinda like a little brain. He's got the big head. I don't know.

65. Analyzing obstacles

66. **P:** Well, to summarize, I have real positive feelings about the work that you've done in the past 2 1/2 months, to get yourself to the point where you are now, and to be ready to go to the judge and tell him that you feel you are ready to try independent living, and that you have shown me that you are ready to try independent living.

66. Reviewing; encouraging

67. **C:** The worst I can do is fail, and have to start all over. I always put it at the highest point, and then I look at the lowest point. The worst you can do is fail.

67. Turn taking; formulating meaning

68. **P:** And what would you do if you failed?

68. Eliciting information; analyzing obstacles

69. **C:** Get up and start all over again. There isn't much you can do. You have to get up and redo it all over.

69. Giving information; analyzing obstacles

70. **P:** Think of a new plan?

70. Guiding

Interchanges	Comments on interchanges
71. **C:** Yeah, go a different way, I don't know.	71. Turn taking
72. **P:** Well, I think you have seen what it is to be in a foster home or group home, you have known what it is to be with your family, you have known what it is to be on your own, and I think you have an idea of what your choices are and what the problems are so deal with each one, so I think you will be able to make a new plan on the basis of what you've already tried.	72. Analyzing obstacles
73. **C:** Yeah, what turned out and what didn't.	73. Turn taking
74. **P:** Right.	74. Turn taking
75. **C:** *(Laughs)* No, no, I don't.	75. Turn taking
76. **P:** I think that you have shown a lot of, a lot of progress both in your approach to solving your problem, not running away, but sticking with them and taking your time too.	76. Reviewing
77. **C:** I just realized that.	77. Explaining role '
78. **P:** And deciding what to do.	78. Explaining role.
79. **C:** Running away don't get no way, besides causing more problems. That's not what you need. Dad says, you get yourself in it, you always got yourself out of it sooner or later. You just got to look at it a certain way.	79. Reviewing; formulating meaning
80. **P:** Right. So I congratulate you on the good work you've done, and I know that you have a lot of hard work ahead of you, but I . . .	80. Reviewing; encouraging
81. **C:** Um hum.	81. Turn taking
82. **P:** But I feel that you are going to be equal to it.	82. Encouraging
83. **C:** As long as I got your phone number, I can call you.	83. Explaining role
84. **P:** I'm glad to know that you feel that you can. I don't think you'll have to very much, if at all. I do believe that.	84. Explaining role
85. **C:** There probably will be one or two times that I will need a little advice or help.	85. Explaining role
86. **P:** I'll be glad to give it. So congratulations, and I'll see you in court.	86. Turn taking; closing greeting
87. **C:** Okay.	87. Closing greeting

Special issue: self-disclosure and personal interactions

Self-disclosure refers to the matter of the practitioner revealing personal information to the client. This is an uncertain area. Because of the paucity of empirical evidence on this subject it is customary in mainstream practice to keep practitioner self-disclosure to a minimum. The client is either paying for the service directly or is being subsidized by public funds. Because of the business aspect of the encounter the client surely has a right to know that the practitioner has the proper professional qualifications. The practitioner is obliged to reveal this kind of information. Ordinarily the client can obtain the necessary knowledge by checking the qualifications and reputation of both practitioner and organization before coming. If the practitioner is an employee of a reputable helping organization, it is normally taken for granted that he is a reputable professional. The practitioner's qualifications are attested to by the agency.

However, a client may want to know more. Clients often want to know whether a practitioner has had the kind of experience that will make her understand the problem at hand. These client concerns are legitimate and indicate proper interest in getting good service. The practitioner is obliged to answer such questions in a straightforward manner without feeling insecure or defensive about being checked on. When an organization hires a staff member or takes on an intern or student, that person has already been checked and double-checked by agency and school officials who have judged her adequate. Therefore there is no reason for the practitioner to be threatened or suspicious of such client inquiries.

Some clients may want to know personal details and may ask such questions as: "Are you married?" "Do you have children?" "Where do you live?" On occasion they may invite the practitioner out socially.

Social invitations probably come from a lack of knowledge about the norms of appropriate behavior or from a wish to convert the practitioner into a personal friend. Some clients have been reared to believe that giving a present or giving food in a social encounter is the proper way to show esteem, respect, and trust. Invitations and gifts should normally be turned down politely and diplomatically so that the client does not confuse the transaction with a social relationship. It is best not to make a big production of such a refusal but simply to say something like: "That would be nice but I could not do it" *or* "Thank you, but I cannot accept this." The practitioner should try to avoid giving the client the idea that it would be distasteful for them to be together socially.

However, the practitioner occasionally runs into a client who presses for a social relationship and does not get the right idea from a simple, straightforward explanation. This is a situation in which the client needs an explicit explanation from the practitioner. The practitioner should explain that the client is making a mistake about the relationship and then should discuss what the client needs so there can be clarification of appropriate routes to that end.

Refusing offers of food becomes difficult when interviewing in a client's home. It is natural for someone to offer a guest coffee, fresh bakery goods, or dinner. About all that can be said about this is that, in a client's home, the practitioner can be on a diet or partake of the goodies frugally.

On termination of interviewing clients may offer a gift. If the gift is an inexpensive token or something the client has made, the practitioner can take it and say thanks. If the gift is a big one, the practitioner can say thanks and give it back politely.

To avoid mix-ups of working transactions with personal considerations, most experienced practitioners advise caution about practitioner self-disclosure. Give the client information about yourself that is legitimate and needs to be understood, but no more.

REFERENCES

Blizinsky, Marlin H., and Reid, William J. "Problem Focus and Change in a Brief Treatment Model." *Social Work* 25 (March 1980):89-93.

Davis, Inger P. "Advice-Giving in Parent Counselling." *Social Casework* 56 (June 1975):343-347.

Epstein, Laura. *Helping People: The Task-Centered Approach*. St. Louis: The C.V. Mosby Co., 1980.

Maluccio, Anthony D., and Marlow, Wilma D. "The Case for the Contract." *Social Work* 19 (January 1974):28-36.

Pope, Benjamin. *The Mental Health Interview*. New York: Pergamon Press, 1979.

Reid, William J. *The Task Centered System*. New York: Columbia University Press, 1978.

Reid, William J., and Shapiro, Barbara. "Client Reaction to Advice." *Social Service Review* 43 (June 1969):165-173.

Taylor, Nancy, and Rooney, Ronald. Private communication, 1982.

CHAPTER 6

Interviewing individuals, groups, and families

Interviewing takes place in one of three modes, or arrangements: individual, family, or group. In the individual mode a single person is the unit receiving attention. Usually the individual person with a social problem has close relatives or companions who are involved and participate in the problem. If it seems advisable for these significant others to take part in an interview or in several interviews, the individual mode can become the family mode. The whole interviewing process may be transferred into the family mode. The client may or may not also continue to be seen individually as circumstances dictate. Interviewing may be transferred into the group mode if the client joins with unrelated persons for a collective problem-solving effort.

Choice of arrangements

Whether it is advisable to choose a family or group arrangement rather than an individual mode is a question of judgment and expediency. The combined personal and professional preferences of the agency, practitioner, and client determine what form is used. Family interventions are of interest as shown by the development of a large, growing literature and by conferences and special training courses devoted to the subject. There are widespread concerns in our society about the security of the family as a social institution, and there is a widespread perception of substantial unhappiness, dissatisfaction, and turmoil in family life. This may in part account for the current interest in family interviewing.

Persons can be seen individually by choice even if other people are involved in the problem. The client may prefer to assume individual responsibility, or the practitioner may believe that one-to-one interviewing is preferable. Widows, widowers, people who have never married, and people whose families are in a distant location are examples of clients for whom the individual mode would be natural. Persons who are institutionalized in medical, correctional, educational, or substitute-care facilities are often interviewed alone because of the impracticality of involving others.

There are no hard-and-fast rules about what modes are best. There is a pervasive impression among many clinicians that involving families is a more powerful intervention strategy than concentrating on one individual alone. The indications for treatment of marital couples, family treatment, or group treatment constitute a complex technical subject and are influenced by value considerations. Also influential are emerging research findings that favor such strategies as the involvement of couples in reducing marital problems and the involvement of family members in therapy to alleviate children's behavioral problems (Gurman and Kniskern 1981). Family interventions appear as a powerful strategy for preventing placement in a foster home or for returning a child from foster care to his own home (Fanshel and Shinn 1978; Magazino 1983). In an extensive review of the research literature, Bednar and Kaul (1978, p. 792) indicate that group psychotherapy can be effective in helping people achieve more positive evaluation of themselves and others.

At the present stage of development there is no certainty about making a choice between the group or the individual mode. According to Middleman (1978, p. 17):

> There has been no empirical demonstration that group or individual services are more effective with respect to the problem, sex, age, or developmental needs of the clients. There is some evidence that groups might be a preferred approach for adolescents or populations whose main needs are in the area of social competence. No criteria for service choices presently exist. The choice of a preferred context for service for particular individuals should be negotiated client by client according to what seems preferred/familiar to the client.

It could be added that the preference and familiarity of the practitioner and the agency also needs to be respected.

Individual mode

An interview is usually initiated when one person comes on her own; is referred or sent; or is sought out by a practitioner whose function is to "reach out," that is, to find those in the community who might benefit from services.

The individual mode is serviceable and needs no special construction.

Both research and practical evidence indicate that individual interviews are often successful, get the job done, and satisfy many clients.

Interviewing techniques have evolved largely from extensive experience with the individual mode. Conversational stratagems in the individual mode mainly take into consideration two actors, which limits the field of interaction to readily manageable proportions.

A sense of intimacy and interpersonal closeness can be found in the one-to-one interviewing situation, primarily because one of the participants is the service provider and the other participant is in need. This relationship raises complex issues concerning power, attraction, and the willingness of one person to respect and legitimate the other. The course may not be smooth. Conflicts, disagreements, and misunderstandings may occur. The practitioner should recognize that this kind of intimacy and its problems are inherent in the situation.

Most of this book deals with individual arrangements. Briefer descriptions will be given for the group and family mode arrangements. References at the end of this chapter indicate sources for further study.

Group mode

Although the individual mode is predominant, a good deal of interviewing takes place in groups. No figures are available to indicate how much interviewing is done in groups, but common observation suggests that the mode is popular.

A group is a collection of unrelated persons who have some explicit connection to one another that makes them interdependent. A committee, for example, is a group in which individuals are connected by responsibility for some matter; committee members depend on one another for investigating, considering, deciding on, and reporting on a subject. Groups consisting of parents, children, or couples are formed in human services organizations. People taking similar medication or facing similar illnesses, struggling in the midst of similar crises, confronting similar personal and social problems, or seeking increased competence in social skills are typical examples of those who might constitute a group.

In human services work, interviews are conducted in small groups of approximately three to nine people. Small groups are considered to be a way to achieve socialization of the individual, to educate, and to change aspects of personality such as self-image, attitudes, and behaviors (Hartford 1972, p. 61). Large groups are characterized by macrosystems group processes, which make them different from small groups. In a large group one person leads, lectures, and has limited question-and-answer discussion, but this person does not interview.

Groups may be effective in solving problems if group members can accommodate differences of opinion about the facts and values of various alternative solutions. However, groups may also be a barrier to problem solving and can interfere with the individual's ability to change and accomplish personal objectives. Plentiful research has not yet clarified questions about which of the two types of problem solving—group or individual—is superior. Group phenomena have proved difficult to identify, describe, and interpret. It remains necessary for practitioners to depend on their own practice experience to develop a feel for what makes sense for a group at a particular time (Luft 1970).

A group is an extremely complex phenomenon. It possesses the characteristics of all the individuals in the group, plus qualities and dynamics of the collective entity. The group is more than just the sum of its members. The group has a *program,* that is, a goal with a plan for its achievement. The group program is similar to the goals, priorities, and intervention strategy described earlier for the individual case. The group program is public because it is openly shared among members. The program may be shared with significant others; this is the case, for example, in a group whose members are striving to maintain a drug-free life-style.

TYPES OF GROUPS

Small groups are used for a wide variety of purposes. Informational groups give and interpret sets of facts, helping participants to obtain and understand knowledge. Other groups emphasize personal change and improvements in social relationships. Still others concentrate on problem solving.

Examples of different types of groups abound in the literature, as do theoretical discussions of approaches considered applicable to different populations and problems. Rose has published considerable work depicting increasing adaptive behavior and decreasing maladaptive behavior in children (1972); parent training, assertiveness training, weight control, and improvement of marital couple communication (1977); and problem solving with the elderly, training children in classroom behaviors, and social skills training for fourth- and fifth-grade boys (1980). Garvin (1981) not only summarizes the present state of the art but also describes groups used for reducing anomie, enhancing role attainment, obtaining social control, or arranging alternative role attainment. A great many of the problems that are dealt with in individual treatment are also inherently appropriate to deal with in groups. Readers interested in group work for purposes of psychotherapy in the psychodynamic perspective can find an abundant body of literature (Yalom 1975). Encounter groups have also been carefully studied (Lieberman, Yalom, and Miles 1975).

GROUP COMPOSITION

A group is constructed by selecting certain people to participate. Most experts lean toward obtaining a moderate degree of homogeneity among the members, but there are no strict rules about how much homogeneity is best. For example, it is thought best to keep the ages, occupations, or problems of group members within a similar bracket, but there are many exceptions to the rule. Some people do not merge into a group experience and should not be forced.

PHASES OF THE GROUP

Groups go through fairly predictable phases. The following description of group phases is adapted from Hartford (1972).

CONVENING

It is during this phase that the group first comes together. Before the group's actual first meeting, the activities are administrative: making the decision to organize a group, outlining its purpose and program or potential program, announcing the formation of the group, and recruiting members.

The beginning session or sessions comprise the "starting-up," or familiarizing, phase. During this time there should be discussion to clarify the group's purpose, introductions of all participants to one another, and opportunities for group members to share their points of view about the group's purpose and procedures. Ordinarily the interviewer, or *group leader,* is active in initiating these techniques and promoting discussion, sometimes to a great degree. Drawing out those who seem passive and limiting those who are overly aggressive are additional responsibilities of the group leader.

GROUP FORMATION

Convening leads to group formation, that is, to getting organized. The leader needs to help group members determine what they want to do, how they want to do it, and what kinds of relationships they want with other people in the group. There is no exact counterpart for this phase in individual interviewing.

INTEGRATION, DISINTEGRATION, CONFLICT, AND REORGANIZATION

It is common for group morale to undergo changes as soon as group formation and organization are well under way. After about the second, third, or fourth session the group atmosphere can get "stormy." People may start to quarrel, object, become uncomfortable, or absent themselves. People may start to have second thoughts about "belonging" and question the purposes and value of attending and participating. Occasionally this phase does not occur; however, it usually does. After this period of conflict, it is common for the group to reorganize and proceed satisfactorily. However, from time to time, groups do not "jell" after this phase.

The leader's activities during this phase should focus on interpreting and, if necessary, confronting the group with the existence and nature of the conflicts that have erupted. Because the group undertaking is changing at this point, the original planning and composition may be faulty. The leader explains the naturalness of the process and helps the group to rework and perhaps redefine its structure and purpose.

GROUP COHESION

Group cohesion acts as a kind of glue to keep a group together, resulting in a sense of "we-ness." Democratically led groups tend to have greater cohesion, although strong cohesion may also develop when a group rebels against an autocratic leader. Because it often develops during processes of reorganization following the original disintegration phase, group cohesion usually becomes a powerful force. The group starts to act as if it had a life of its own as powerful as, or more powerful than, the leader.

Some groups are *open-ended,* that is, the people in attendance come and go. In these groups members are present to obtain information or some kind of limited input regarding an action. They do not want or need to commit their time and interest to an ongoing process. When participants come and go, group cohesion is weak. Therefore it is mainly the leader's responsibility to establish program continuity. Dropouts, new participants, and unexplained absences may cause the regular attendees to become uncomfortable. They may act as if they have been left "in the lurch" by dropouts and may ignore new participants because they feel imposed on. The group may generally be worried about absenteeism. It is always necessary in open-ended groups for the leader to explain and interpret the comings and goings of group members and to encourage discussion of concerns felt regarding departures and arrivals. Groups that become used to open-endedness take it as a matter of course. There is no exact counterpart to this phase in the dyadic mode.

GROUP MAINTENANCE

In the group maintenance phase the norms and expectations of behavior within the group are established. The group is preoccupied with accomplishing its work. Subgroups will have formed naturally, and friendships will have developed. The leader's position will have become set, often in a less than central role; that is, the leader may become an enabler and troubleshooter rather than a director. Natural leadership will have surfaced from within the group itself. Natural leaders in the group should be expected and welcomed; they can assist the formal leader. However, if there are several natural leaders in the group and they are oppositional, an atmosphere of conflict will result.

TERMINATION

The group may end by contract, that is, the group's duration may have been set at the beginning. This means that everyone knows the time parameters and can act accordingly. Another possibility is that the termination time can be negotiated during the course of group meetings, depending on particular circumstances. People may become attached to or dependent on the group and feel distressed by the ending. Open discussion of such distress is called for. Some members will continue to see people from the group socially.

The interconnections between individual, family, and group modes are illustrated by the following example from a medical clinic:

> The practitioner was a physiotherapist whose specialty was restoration of hand and wrist handicaps resulting from a variety of fractures. The established practice called for the therapist to see a particular patient individually the first and second time. She assessed the problem, patient motivation, and the patient's physical capacity for rehabilitation. Ongoing treatment consisted of guided exercises that were tailored to fit the patient's limitations.
>
> The ongoing exercise program was conducted in groups. The individual patients were of different ages and of both sexes. Each person had a fracture and healing process that were different from any other person's. What the patients had in common was their hand or wrist handicap. In the group were teachers, professors, students, factory workers, and businesspeople. None of them could use their hands properly, and all wanted to recover as much as possible. Some patients came to the group alone. Others came with spouses, friends, or parents. The relatives sat with the group of patients, learning how to help them and coaching not only their relatives but other patients also. The therapist interacted with them all. Modeling, encouraging, explaining, and analyzing obstacles and developing means for overcoming them, she comforted people as well as instructed them. Furthermore, the patients helped other patients. Since

the relatives and friends helped everyone, some of the work
was taken off the shoulders of the therapist herself.

This example indicates how a problem-solving focus can lead to a
combined use of modes. What governed the success of the program was
taking advantage of any and all available opportunities for problem reduction.

LEADERSHIP STYLES AND COMMUNICATION QUALITIES

There is a general consensus that the practitioner's ability to relate and
communicate in a one-to-one interviewing mode is equally applicable to
interviewing in the group mode (see Chapter 4). It is also frequently said
that a group interviewer needs to be more outgoing and "free and easy"
than an individual interviewer. However, this idea is speculative. One area
of group leadership that has been studied suggests that a democratic
leadership style is preferable to an autocratic or authoritarian one. Autocratic leadership has a corrosive effect, setting up communication barriers
of all kinds. Democratic leadership tends to promote a desirable openness
and friendliness and helps group members develop their abilities (Luft
1970, pp. 44-45).

COMMUNICATION IN GROUP INTERVENTION

General techniques for use throughout the group phases, as adapted
from Middleman (1978), are:

SCANNING

Scanning is a nonverbal technique that involves taking in the whole
group with your eyes. Scanning gives the interviewer feedback from which
to make a general estimate of what is going on in the group. Visually, it
resembles the sweeping eye movements (looking forward, backward, and
from side-to-side) that a motorist makes when driving a car. Being as
unobtrusive as possible, the practitioner should frequently survey all
group members, noting where they are sitting, where they move to, their
obvious facial expressions, and their overt body movements. Agreement,
disagreement, comfort, discomfort, impending conflict, and signaling for a
turn can all be handled because of practitioner knowledge gained from
scanning.

REACHING FOR A FEELING LINK

Reaching for a feeling link is done after a group member or leader has
made a statement that expresses how he feels about something. For example:

A parent of a hospitalized child has just said that he always feels put down when the doctor gives a curt explanation of some medical procedure. The group leader says: "Anybody else? Who else feels that way? No one? It would be a normal response." There is a pause; then a mother signals that she wants to speak up. The group leader acknowledges this by saying, "Yes?"

The practitioner tries to bring together those group members who feel the same to promote reassurance, encouragement, and the eliciting of information. The interviewer encourages any enlightening or comforting responses that group members might have for one another. This sharing and mutual support are considered valuable, helpful products of group interaction. Reaching for a feeling link makes the rewards of group interaction visible and obvious to the participants.

REACHING FOR AN INFORMATION LINK

Reaching for an information link is a communication practice that is similar to reaching for a feeling link because both practices are used to obtain information. The quality of the information sought is different, however. In this technique the practitioner elicits responses from participants about an opinion that is voiced by a group member. The practitioner has two purposes. The first is to encourage the sharing experience, which is thought to be enlightening and encouraging in itself. The second purpose is to encourage the discussion of an idea that might be important in stimulating participants to consider their own situations.

The kinds of comments that elicit an information link are: "Who agrees or disagrees?" "What do you think about that?" "Who has noticed that?" or "Who has done that?"

AMPLIFYING SUBTLE MESSAGES

Amplifying subtle messages means calling the group's attention to verbal or nonverbal activities in the session that seem relevant to the subject at hand but have not been noticed or commented on by participants. The purpose of this technique is to enable the group to consider an important matter that is being neglected or to mobilize the group to help a particular member. For example, the practitioner might say, "I'm noticing that John isn't taking part at all"; *or* "Maybe we should stop and spend some time on that throwaway comment Esther just made"; *or* "It seems to me that several of you have been saying the same thing in different ways, and maybe we have hit on a core to some of your problems."

TONING DOWN

The technique of toning down involves restating a highly emotional speech or interpreting a body motion to clarify meaning and cut down on possibly harmful effects. For example:

> In a group of mothers of hospitalized children, a woman says in a crescendo that doctors are killing her baby and she has got to stop them! The others go into shock; they sit up straight and are silent, their eyes round with distress. The practitioner tones this down to manageable proportions by saying, "Mrs. B. is terribly upset because she just found out her son is critically ill. She is under an awful lot of stress at the moment." The others relax and start comforting Mrs. B. instead of hurting her by isolating themselves from her.

Another example of toning down follows.

> John turns on Mary and says, "You make me sick! I'm not going to let you needle me!" The practitioner says, "We have already talked about our tendency to make a bad example of John. Obviously he feels pretty bad about it. What do you think we should do about how John feels? How do others of you, including Mary, feel about what's happening to John?"

Toning down is a way to protect members from being hurt and to help the ones doing the hurting to handle the guilt that follows. It is a good way to handle conflict that may break out. However, the leader sometimes believes that conflict ought to be made public and perhaps even escalated. This belief can be put into practice. However, it is a two-edged sword and should normally be avoided unless a special case warrants it.

REDIRECTING

Redirecting refers to the practitioner's efforts to help group members clarify their intentions toward one another. Sometimes, one group member gives a message to another but clearly means it for a third person. Normally, the leader would initiate straightening out this mixed message to prevent conflict escalation and hurt. For example:

> After John accuses Mary of needling him, the interviewer says, "John, did you mean Mary? She's the quietest one here."

COMMUNICATION EMPHASES ACCORDING TO PHASE

Group processes are exceedingly complex because of the number of people involved and their interactions, the combined effects of which are numerous. The processes quickly tend to overlap and become obscure and confused. Group processes have been subjected to a great deal of study but, like the subject of linguistics, they have so far evaded firmly established theory and empirical certainty. Group phenomena are inherently very difficult to identify and clarify. Our perceptions of them are constantly altered by the fast pace of practice and by continual molding of technique in the hands of inventive practitioners.

The absence of firmly defined and verified techniques should not turn practitioners away from group interviewing, although many practitioners feel anxious about jumping into group discourse because they have to rely so much on their own intuition and common sense. However, some practitioners have a talent for group interviewing and should definitely use it.

It may be helpful to make some suggestions outlining emphases in using interviewing techniques with groups. Such a guide is found in Figure 4.

General: all phases	
Scanning	Eye/head sweeps to collect nonverbal messages
Reaching for feeling link	Who else feels that way? To share, support, assess
Reaching for information link	Who agrees/disagrees? What do you think? Who noticed? Who has done that? To share, support, assess
Amplify	Let's look at that more Stop and consider Go over that again/more To develop focus

FIGURE 4   Interviewing outline: small groups.

Continued.

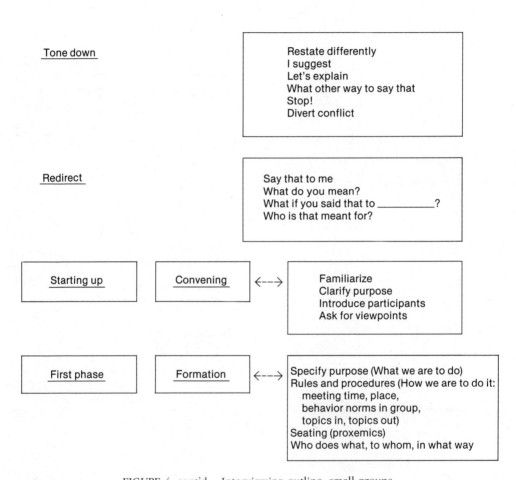

Tone down

> Restate differently
> I suggest
> Let's explain
> What other way to say that
> Stop!
> Divert conflict

Redirect

> Say that to me
> What do you mean?
> What if you said that to _____?
> Who is that meant for?

Starting up → Convening ←--→
> Familiarize
> Clarify purpose
> Introduce participants
> Ask for viewpoints

First phase → Formation ←--→
> Specify purpose (What we are to do)
> Rules and procedures (How we are to do it:
>   meeting time, place,
>   behavior norms in group,
>   topics in, topics out)
> Seating (proxemics)
> Who does what, to whom, in what way

FIGURE 4, cont'd.   Interviewing outline: small groups.

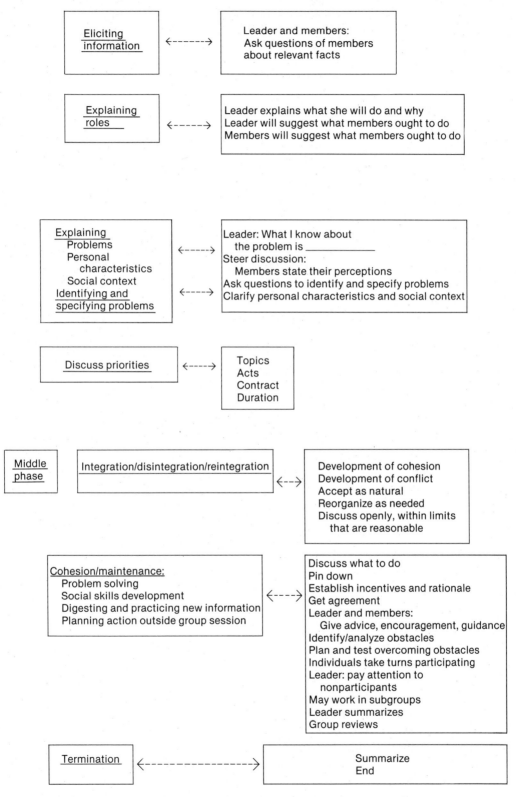

FIGURE 4, cont'd.   Interviewing outline: small groups.

ASSESSMENT

Often before a group is formed the practitioner will have conducted one or two individual interviews with a prospective member to arrive at a personal assessment, environmental assessment, and picture of the problem to be focused on. Any standard assessment procedure may be used for these purposes (see Chapter 3).

A preliminary individual interview helps the practitioner gauge how the person will fit into the proposed group. Additionally, a person's previous experience in a similar type of group is a useful guide if such information is available.

Assessment is carried out in the early phases of a group and is probably refined throughout the whole time that the group meets. A member's behavior in group sessions offers immediate and visible evidence of his personal characteristics, which can be noted by other members as well as the leader. In the natural course of meetings group members often elicit enough relevant information to identify and specify problems and social context that the need for questioning by the interviewer is considerably lessened. Practitioners may train members in what kind of information to seek, if this seems desirable.

OVERLOADING

An interviewer in the group mode may be the recipient of so much stimulation that he may become unable to observe accurately, listen closely, think about what is going on, or identify the important actors in the group. This is most likely to occur with a group of teenagers or unruly children. In an overreactive group there is probably a lot of noise (if members fail to obey the conventions), constant speaking out of turn, interruptions, yelling, and running around. A group of this kind may do better with two interviewers. Two sets of eyes can do more scanning. The interview partners can consult and can break the group into subgroups. Another option is for one interviewer to observe and keep track of physical activity while the other moves ahead with the discussion. However, there may be a tendency for one of the interviewers to blame the other for disorder, which is an unfair thing to do. It is essential for both interviewers to be, if not friendly, at least tolerant and forgiving of one another.

Sometimes an interviewer feels overloaded even if the session is orderly. This happens when more things are going on in the room than the interviewer can process. With so many actors involved, it is not at all uncommon for the flow of discussion to be hard to understand.

Unruliness must never be allowed to get to the point of hitting, punching, overthrowing furniture, or strong verbal attacks. Under such duress the interviewer must be authoritative and must signal the group to stop the behavior. It is best to get open and verbal agreements from the members in advance on such topics as rules of behavior, taking turns, rudeness, running around, and yelling. It is well worth the time to get these rules worked out in the early group sessions and to repeat them as necessary. If this is done, the chances are great that the more disciplined group members will help the leader to keep a reasonable amount of order.

SCAPEGOATING

Scapegoating refers to a situation in which the group gets together to "dump on" one of the members in a consistent way. A member is picked on to be derided, provoked, and ridiculed. The interviewer must stop this. The best way is to call the group's attention to what they are doing, to point out the unfairness, and to support the person chosen as the target for the group's nastiness. Sometimes people selected as scapegoats are, in a sense, "asking for it;" they may behave in a way that is generally not likable. However, sometimes the scapegoat does not realize that she is provoking attack. It is advisable to take this type of person aside and help her contain the behavior that provokes the group. Also, she should be helped to formulate words and actions to stop the others when they begin scapegoating.

POWER POLITICS

If there is conflict in the group or potential rewards for participation, the interviewer may sometimes be perceived as siding with one faction or the other. Those who side with the interviewer will be perceived as the party in power. The others may form a loose and shifting alliance that might be perceived as attacking, undermining, or manipulating the leader. Groups tend to become political if there is some reward or turf to fight over. The struggle may involve the affection or favors of the interviewer. This is a good reason for the interviewer to show neutrality in her relationships and not have favorites or show obvious preference for some members over others.

However, both individual group members and groups as a whole can get inaccurate perceptions about whom the interviewer favors. These erroneous perceptions need to be discussed. Sometimes misunderstandings can be corrected and sometimes not. If the interviewer in reality has access to resources that everyone wants but that are in limited supply, political divisiveness may develop between the "haves" and the "have-nots." Some groups do not work properly when this occurs. Open and honest discussion can go quite a distance toward healing a group's political divisions.

CO-LEADERSHIP

There are no definite criteria for deciding on either co-leadership or solo leadership of groups. The decision is a matter of judgment. Various factors that influence a practitioner about leading alone or in partnership are discussed in the following paragraphs. The choice between solo or dual leadership is based on the practitioner's consideration of possible effects of co-leadership, taking into account preferences, feasibility, and specific group states.

There are some potentially beneficial conditions thought to stem from co-leadership (Galinsky and Schopler 1980). Group members can learn from observing the leaders publicly resolve differences or conflicts between them. They may dislike one of the leaders but relate well to the other. The co-leaders may devise different roles, one of them being aggressive and confrontational in style while the other is more passive and supportive. Another division of labor may occur if one leader takes primary responsibility for administering and maintaining the group while the other concentrates on following development and carrying out tasks. Still another possible division is for one leader to concentrate on developing and monitoring interventions while the other observes and corrects directions that are unproductive.

Because of gender and position of authority, co-leaders may represent significant other people who pose problems for group members in real life. If the co-leaders are of opposite sexes, group members may find it feasible to work out feelings with them particular to their relationships with men or women. Members may reveal and resolve feelings they have about the leaders themselves when there is one male and one female co-leader. These ideas are conjectural but are often perceived as interactional effects of co-leadership.

The group may be easier to manage if there are two leaders. If a group is unruly or disruptive, two workers may find it better to divide up the tasks of controlling conflict and misbehavior. Furthermore, the power of leaders to be helpful may be enhanced when there are two experts in problem-solving instead of one.

Co-leadership may be advantageous for training practitioners who are new to group processes. It may decrease a new practitioner's anxiety and minimize emotional impact if the group members are exceptionally distressed.

On the negative side it must be noted that co-leadership is expensive. Two salaries instead of one are paid for leading the group. Also, the two leaders must meet to plan ahead, and they must review at the end of each session. Whereas one leader would use a brief time for preparation and review, co-leaders' meetings are more time-consuming because of the necessity for collaborative work and premeeting and postmeeting conferences.

Disagreement between co-leaders can slow down and complicate the processes of leadership. Areas of possible conflict include disagreements about theoretical perspective, such as pursuit of active solutions to current concrete problems versus pursuit of clarification of underlying problems; disagreements about pursuit of practical goals; and disagreements about pursuit of developmental and growth objectives. Leadership conflicts can arise over characteristics of personal style, sexual tensions, competition, or domination. Leaders who have to hide antagonism toward a partner are likely to take it out on group members in the form of scapegoating, ridiculing, or criticizing unfairly. If conflict is high, group members may be drawn into it.

AN EXAMPLE: TECHNIQUES IN ACTION

YAG was the name given to the Young Adult Group, which was composed of six people of both sexes between the ages of 18 and 25. All had been outpatients of a community psychiatric clinic. They were all unmarried and had experienced difficulty finding and holding jobs and connecting with suitable mates.

The members' names and ages were: George, 18; Tom, 25; Karen, 20; Andy, 20; Harold, 21; and Sally, 19.

Convening

When I arrived in the interviewing room, George was there. The rest of the young adults arrived within the next 10 minutes except for Sally who never arrived. Thus the meeting was composed of four men and one woman.

While the group was assembling, George asked me who was in the group and I told him. I repeated the names when the others had come in. They all knew each other either from the neighborhood or from having met at the clinic. Everyone was talking at once, milling around, speaking to one other, and occasionally speaking to me. Everyone was greeting everyone else and mentioning the weather. In a loud voice that everyone could hear, Tom told me that there was too much noise and confusion and he could not handle that pressure. It became quiet. Several of them made comments such as, "We are all in the same boat." I said that we had to get organized and everyone started nodding assent. I said that I knew from their files that they all had had difficulties in handling pressure, and that was a problem we might well be able to cut down on. They were interested.

Reaching for information links

I asked them to each take a turn to tell what pressures gave them the most trouble. Karen explained that she got confused when she heard a lot of people talking at once. Andy said he got pressured from having a lot of things to do and didn't know how in the world to get them all done at the same time. Harold said he did that to himself, too. He said, "Nobody is supposed to do everything at once. They should go at it one by one and get something finished." Harold said that when he started to feel overwhelmed he went out and fooled around until he collected himself. George said he thought that was a good idea. He wished he could do it. I said "What else? Let's get a good picture of what pressures you all feel."

Identifying problems

They all started 'taking turns listing all the different things that made them tense and what they did or did not do about them. I said it sounded as if they were talking about two kinds of pressures; one kind came from outside, that is, things other people were demanding of them. The other kind was a buildup of feeling distressed. They all agreed.

Introducing priorities

I asked them if they preferred working on pressure problems that came from inside or ones that come from people and things on the outside. They all said they wanted to do both. Because our time was up, I said we would pick up at the same point next time; we would try to pin down what pressures we wanted to do something about, what else we wanted to take up, and what we wanted to get straight about how we should do our work.

Formation

At the second interview, George and Tom came in first. George started talking immediately, angrily asking me what this group was supposed to do, anyway. Tom sat attentively, waiting to hear. However, right away the rest of the group filed in and sat down. Sally, who had been absent at the first meeting, was present this time and was introduced to the group.

I told the group what George had said and that I thought it was a fine place to start. George looked angry. The rest sat expectantly looking at me.

Explaining role

I said it might have been desirable to discuss this subject at our first meeting, but then everybody had had the subject of pressure on their minds. Also, everybody had been getting acquainted so no one had interrupted anyone else.

Specifying purpose

I said that the group was put together for young people having difficulty with jobs and friends. The clinic thought group members might make progess if they discussed and worked on problems in a group.

Tom said, "There are other patients in the clinic with problems like ours, but they aren't here."

Reaching for information/feeling link

I asked the group if they believed Tom was right. Each group member took a turn to briefly describe what his or her work or vocational training difficulties were and to tell something about satisfaction and dissatisfaction with boyfriends, girlfriends, and other friends. Nobody addressed Tom's question.

Explaining problems

George said his parents didn't understand him. Tom turned angrily on George, asking him how he knew his parents didn't understand him. Tom said, "Parents know you since you were a kid, and they're sure to understand you." George shook his head and said, "No, my parents never even understood me as a kid."

Karen said, "George can be right. My parents always acted as if they knew me but I am sure they didn't. But anyway, what's that got to do with our being here? Why bellyache about our parents when we have more important things to do, such as getting jobs or getting started on some kind of vocation?"

Sally stood up and made an angry speech. She said, "It's unfair to say your parents let you down. They give you a lot, and they have a right to expect thanks." She sat down. George piped up, "I don't think I owe my parents anything. I didn't ask to be brought into this world. They did that on their own. You shouldn't put strings on what you give."

*Identifying problems, discussing priorities,
and amplifying*

I said, "We are getting caught up in problems and opinions
about parents. It seems like a subject that most of you are
interested in. However, the original idea for this group was to
find some solutions to problems about jobs and friends, especially friends of the opposite sex. What do you think? What kind
of priorities do all of you want to follow?" Then I said, "Before I
forget, I would like to go back to Tom's question about who is
included in this group, since there *are* other young adults attending the clinic who are not here. Does anyone want to comment on that?"

Scanning

The group members started shifting around in their seats,
looking at one another, and throwing questioning glances at
me. I observed that they seemed to be looking for allies to share
their discomfort.

Explaining roles

Tom spoke up. He said, "I'm not sure why this group of
people has been picked to meet. We aren't the only ones with
job and friend problems." He said he suspected that I was
putting them on. He said, "There must be some other reason
we are thrown together, for what I don't know." Everybody was
looking at me.

I said, "The clinic director has given me your names. Six is
a good round number for a group. I really don't know exactly
what kind of a selection process has gone on in the director's
mind, and honestly, I have not thought to question it because I
trust the director's judgment. I don't know who or how many
have been excluded or if anyone has been excluded, and if so,
why."

Discussing priorities

Harold spoke up and said to Tom, "Don't be a sorehead.
Getting a job and straightening out the mess with my girlfriend
are the two most important things to me. I want to go ahead and
work on those things." Andy spoke up and said, "Bitching about
our parents is a popular subject for rapping but it's a side issue.
I want to get help about what kind of job training I should get."

After everyone had a chance to speak, with some group
members speaking several times, there was a consensus that

jobs were the number one problem. Second in importance were problems with friends.

Eliciting information

Tom was still angry, however, and no one really understood what he was angry about. I asked him if he would tell us but he just slumped into his chair, shook his head, and said, "No."

Discussing priorities

I said that it looked like most of us were prepared to work on problems with jobs and friends. I said we could meet eight times on a weekly basis. At the end of the eight-week period we could consider the merit in continuing, and we could decide on the work to be done if we continued. These plans seemed to be all right with them.

Setting a purpose, rules, and procedures

I suggested that each group member tell us about his or her vocational education, job experiences, and what ideas they had about the type of work they would like to get into. If they didn't know about future plans, that was OK too, and they should be frank about that. I said that, if they wanted, I could arrange an extra session or bring a speaker to our regular session who would outline the available training and job-seeking services in the area.

George and Tom, both of whom seemed distressed to some extent by being in the group, were sitting next to each other on my left. Because their problems seemed less integral to the concerns of the whole group, I asked the person on my right to start the discussion, leaving Tom and George for last. We discussed the problems of three group members at this meeting: Harold, Andy, and Sally.

Explaining problems and eliciting information

What emerged was that all three of the young people had left high school in either freshman or sophomore year. They were totally lacking in job skills. They had existed on handouts from their parents and on odd jobs such as baby-sitting and housecleaning. Sally and Harold had teamed up with some others and gone hitchhiking, depending on shelters for runaways. All three of them had used drugs but not seriously. Harold was so defeated at 21 that he believed it was out of the question for him to acquire job skills or get a decent job. He didn't even know what a decent job for him might be. Sally thought nursing or social work were good occupations, and she wondered if she could get into either one. Andy was now waiting on customers at McDonald's, had heard that the company sometimes offered good careers, and vaguely wondered about that. All three, in one way or another, indicated that they lacked the nerve to approach authorities about job possibilities. Andy said, "I think of myself now as a piece of garbage that's good for nothing."

Guiding

To keep the meeting from ending on such a depressed note I said, "It's clear that Andy, Harold, and Sally have real problems, probably somewhat like others in the group who have not yet explained themselves." I said that youth unemployment was a serious problem in the present economy and that there were large numbers of young people around with similar predicaments. I said that there were some ways to get a handle on job problems for youth, mainly in the area of decision making about goals and allocating time for getting the necessary job training. I said that in the meetings to come we would work out a sort of road map that would show group members what things they could and should do to get started.

Disintegration/reintegration

At the third meeting things started to disintegrate. George and Tom took over and said that the three who had talked at the last meeting were a bunch of fools. The two young men said that society had no use for young people; if the laid-off auto workers and steelworkers were done for, if banks were failing, and if the environment was being laid to waste, how could some silly group talk do *anything!*

Pinning down and establishing incentives and a rationale

Sally took them on, asking them, "What's in your heads? If you could dream, what would you like to do?" If George and Tom had ever considered that question, they weren't talking now. However, it really seemed they had given the subject no thought. Sally pressed them, and then so did Andy and Harold. George either could not dream or had forgotten how. Tom, however, announced that being a doctor was something he would like because doctors make a good income, live a good life, and are attractive to women. Karen said, "I'm getting disgusted. This is wasting my time. I want to get on with some practical ideas. George and Tom are just out of line."

Toning down

I said that we should expect our group, like any other group, to have some wide differences in outlook, but it was likely we could all learn something useful from one another. After a while the group calmed down, and everyone talked about job problems, ideas, and past experiences.

Integration, disintegration, and reintegration

After everyone had spoken, Karen said, "I think most of us are feeling that the doors to good jobs are closed to us. It will take lots of effort to get a door to open a little. I'm not used to thinking about putting in effort, but maybe I can. I don't know."

Discussing priorities: topics and acts

Harold said, "There's only one thing to do that I can see and that is to start some place, even if it's a small place." He said he thought the group members were all a bunch of bums who were not educated for anything and the first thing to do was to get some more education.

At the end there was a consensus, with George and Tom expressing reservations, that a career counselor from the community college should speak at the next session, as I had proposed. Everyone wanted to know what kinds of training were available and where training might lead.

Maintenance/cohesion

At the fourth meeting the group listened to Jack C., the career counselor from the community college. Everyone was present except Tom. Mr. C. outlined the various available educational options for young adults who had not finished high school. Everyone in the group fit this category except for the absent Tom, who had graduated from high school. Mr. C. outlined available job training programs at the college and through several other organizations. He also reported on the current government estimates of occupations expected to be the best employment bets in the near future. It was an informative session. At the end everyone made an appointment with Mr. C. to individually discuss the possibility of fitting into different programs. No pressure was put on anyone to enroll in a program or make a premature decision. The idea was to get reliable information to be used in decision making.

Conflict and toning down

Tom came to the fifth session. Everyone was angry at him for his absence at the last meeting. Tom sulked and refused to explain himself. People started ganging up on him. I said I thought they ought to stop, that Tom had a right to come or not, and that he surely must have his reasons.

Karen, Sally, and Andy had already had their appointments with Mr. C. Karen and Sally were both serious about enrolling in preprofessional social work courses. They told the group how they had sized up their personal qualifications for work that would relate to child care in institutions, day care, and service provision for welfare clients. The group questioned Karen and Sally a lot and ended up thinking such plans could be good ones for the young women.

The group discussion turned to Andy, but he had a more difficult situation. Andy could not visualize himself going back to school. It emerged that Andy had a talent for photography. He had a cheap camera and a room that he used as a darkroom at home. Andy had brought his portfolio to the meeting and showed everybody his work, which was good. People were impressed and Andy was beaming but embarrassed. There were photography courses offered at the college, but Mr. C. had advised him that it would be very difficult to get a job, especially a good job that paid decently. You had to be exceptionally good to break into that field, and no one knew if Andy was good enough. Still that was the only career suggestion at the college that interested Andy at all. He hated thinking about grubbing his life away, but he was very afraid to strike out on a career in photography.

I said, "Andy needs time, and we can discuss his decision at the next meeting along with reports from the rest of you who will have seen Mr. C. by that time." I gave Tom the phone number he could call to get an appointment if he wanted it. I said very little at this meeting because everyone was so busy working on various issues.

Continued problem solving

At the sixth session we heard the rest of the reports on meetings with Mr. C. By this time Andy was getting rather excited about going all out to pursue a photography career. No one else had made any firm decisions yet.

Explaining problems

Early in the meeting Tom took the floor. He said, "All this talk seems unreal to me. I'm the oldest in the group. I have been out of school already for 7 years. I worked in construction with my father and brothers until the industry went bust. My parents are on welfare and I am in their grant." He spoke of the terrible boredom and humiliation he had felt washing windows, mowing lawns, and shoveling snow, all for pocket money. Once he had had a girlfriend whom he planned to marry, but after a while they drifted apart. He could not take girls on dates. He had no male friends. He said, "The only friends — sort of — I have are you guys here, and you're not friends." He got into drugs, but that disgusted him and his father raised hell with him. His life was a waste. He walked the streets and spent endless time at the lake just looking at it. He said, "I wanted to die and tried to cut my wrists, but I couldn't even do that right." That was how he had ended up in psychotherapy at the clinic.

Sally said to Tom, "You're all alone. It's terrible. I know because I'm the same way. Even though I think that a social work education would be sensible for me, I don't have the steam to start because I am so dragged down by being so alone." Again, I had little to say except to encourage their discussion because the group members were well into analysis of their problems.

Everyone in the group was isolated from intimate relationships with other people. Andy thought he might be gay but he didn't even know. Sometimes various group members would join some neighborhood people in activities, usually involving drugs or booze. They had all had unsatisfactory sex. Tom thought he might be a father, but he wasn't sure and he was upset about it. Karen, by now the group's natural leader, said, "It's no wonder people here can't think straight about jobs when they really aren't even living and are so lonely they are eaten up by it."

Cohesion

Karen said she was glad she had gotten into this group by accident or luck. She felt closer to her group than to any other people. She said she thought she was starting to love the group members — even Tom a little, although he was so aloof. Everyone became embarrassed at this.

Problem solving, action planning, and analyzing obstacles

I said that along with working on job problems we ought to think seriously of a program to lessen their loneliness a bit. I said, "In general, loneliness is a common problem for adults, especially those without a lot of predetermined activity and those who are detached from relationships with family, work, and school that would require interaction. One of the major adult developmental tasks is to find activities that force you to do things with other people. By mixing you increase your chances of meeting people you will like and get support from."

Karen said, "What should we do? We can't marry this group. We can't stay together forever." I said that one of the good side effects of a group like this was possibly finding a friend or two in the group itself. "But also," I said, "it's possible to plan for social activities just like you plan for job training activities."

Sally then pointed out, "You can't just go up to somebody and say 'Let me be your friend.' Especially with boys; they think you're a hooker. I'm shy. I don't know what to say."

Guiding

I said, "We have two more sessions to go. We could start next time by going around in a circle so each one could tell us what problems they have with friends and mates. Then for a start we can identify what kinds of social skills are needed to learn to increase friendships. We can also talk about good places to go to practice social skills. These plans will help, but they won't automatically relieve loneliness. A good part of such relief is settling on things to do with your thoughts and time when you are alone, because everybody is alone a lot of the time throughout life."

At the start of the seventh session I asked for a review of the job situation. Karen, Sally, and Andy had enrolled at the community college and would start at the beginning of the semester. Everyone, even Tom, applauded. Harold and George were not present. We talked about why they hadn't come — maybe they were so undecided that they felt funny about coming, or maybe they had colds.

Pinning down problems

I said, "I think we should move along and try to get a specific picture of problems that you think you have with your social lives."

Individual turn taking and a leader summary

After each group member had given a statement, I made a summary. I said that what they had mentioned as problems could be made into a list of things they did not know how to do well: starting conversations; possessing good posture, eye contact, and facial expressions of a nonabrasive and nonprovoking type; giving and receiving compliments; controlling negative thoughts and negative self-statements; giving or receiving criticism; and listening to others. I said these were all essential beginning social skills and were a good place to start. I said the list did not include problems with close and intimate relationships but that we ought to start at the beginning.

Planning to overcome obstacles

Tom said, "You mean we can study how to do these things!" I said we could and that there were programs available that had pretty good track records (Monti, Corriveau, and Curran 1982). This did not mean that everyone would become a perfect sure-fire success story, but many *would* get a lot of help. This prospect definitely excited Tom, who said, "My God! If that's true, I'll come twice a week or every day." It was obvious that the others were also interested.

Planning the duration

I said that the program took a minimum of 10 weeks. I said it consisted of discussion to enable the group to understand the basic ideas of the social skills involved, to get a picture of them, to practice the skills in the sessions and in real-life situations, and to get feedback. I said that, although I would be the instructor, all of us together would reflect on skills, model activities, and assist others. I said we would have to decide to extend the weekly sessions, starting next week for 10 more weeks. Time could also be partly used to monitor how we were all doing with the job training project. There was really little question at this time — the group wanted to continue and agreed to start the social skills program the next week.

SUMMARY: GROUP MODE

It is common to interview groups of people brought together for discussion of some common purpose or problem. Groups are complex entities, containing the characteristics of all the individuals plus the features of each particular group's dynamics.

Groups appear to go through phases that constitute a beginning, middle, and end. Group processes influence the individual group members and often exert a beneficial effect on problem solving.

Group communication consists of many of the same elements that individual communication consists of. There are, however, additional elements of communication that are derived only from the interaction of group members.

Group interviews may involve special problems such as overloading, scapegoating, or power politics. Co-leadership can either be a problem or an advantage.

Family interviewing

Family interviewing can be instrumental in providing services, practical problem solving, and therapy. Famiy members may also be seen individually either for a series of sessions or intermittently. For example, a married couple may be interviewed together, that is, *conjointly,* while other family members may also attend sessions but only from time to time.

Service delivery and problem-solving family interviews can be used for a variety of purposes, such as to assess the situation, to decide on priorities and duration, to divide problem-solving activities among family members to increase the impact of interventions, and to create flexibility in goal attainment actions. Case management may be facilitated by family interviews, allowing the practitioner to coordinate services and monitor them to assure efficiency and effectiveness.

FAMILY INTERVIEWING IN CONNECTION WITH THE USE OF SERVICES

For the most part problems come to the attention of service organizations because an individual seeks help. When the service organization judges that family involvement might be useful, the family is approached and asked to participate. There are many opportunities for family interviewing in the human services system. Services and systems whose clients might benefit from family interviewing are described here.

UNEMPLOYMENT SERVICES

Family interviews may be supportive to families that find themselves dealing for the first time with the trauma of unemployment. Interviewing husband and wife, if they are willing, may help to assess need, identify problems, and secure a realistic grasp of what the agency can do and cannot do and why. The shock is severe when people have lost earnings, career, and position in the family and community. Plant closings and mass layoffs result in severe doubts about ever again resuming a valued place in social life. Also, the eventual running out of unemployment compensation and health insurance can induce depression and cause marital conflict to erupt. Interviewing both husband and wife, where feasible, helps to provide assistance and alleviate some stress.

HOSPITAL AND HEALTH SERVICES

When someone becomes ill, family members often accompany the patient to clinic or hospital, visit the hospitalized person, and are on hand at discharge. When diagnoses are explained, when treatment is planned and instituted, and when discharge is prepared for and arranged, families are always part of the process, even when the identified patient lives alone. Money problems always escalate when there is illness, even if there is insurance coverage. The life of everyone in the family is dislocated, often severely, in cases of serious illness. There is good reason to interview families to instruct, explain, demonstrate, discuss, and plan to get maximum benefit with the least possible stress.

MENTAL HEALTH SERVICES

In our society it has become commonplace to accept mental illness or distress as a family affair. However, in the area of mental disturbance, mild or severe, it is also true that high levels of privacy are culturally approved. The involvement of others in the assessment and treatment of mental problems is often unwanted by patients and therapists. However, some families will respond to proposals for family interviews despite reservations. And others are able to participate in treatment regimens that fully involve them as copatients. The growth of the family treatment movement is an expression of the ability of some families to become partners with the identified patient in the treatment.

HOUSING SERVICES

Family interviewing is often advisable for establishing eligibility for subsidized housing, for clarifying eligibility, and for acquainting tenants with rules and procedures.

CHILD WELFARE SERVICES

It is now believed that human services programs operating on behalf of the health and social well-being of children should involve families. Family interviews are therefore recommended to address all the stages of a child-welfare problem case: preventive services installed in the home; preplacement; child placement in foster homes, group homes, or institutions; and discharge from foster care.

SERVICES FOR THE AGED

Although some older people have lost or become estranged from relatives, most of them have families. Most older people are capable and self-sufficient. However, when they *do* have problems they will usually be ones involving loneliness, loss, grief, or ill health. In such problem areas families may provide effective support if they can become involved.

EDUCATIONAL SYSTEMS

Family interviewing may help when educational decisions affecting children are being made. The crucial social problem that human services professionals deal with in schools is the need to help children and youth get maximum benefits from the education offered. Children have no control over luck or the socioeconomic status of their parents, but they *can* improve their chances for success in life by becoming educated. What helps students "make it" in school is a combination of their own characteristics, the capability of the school, and the quality of support from the family. Family interviewing can help organize the psychological and social environment for greatest effectiveness.

CORRECTIONS AND THE JUVENILE JUSTICE SYSTEM

This is an area of human services that is in a state of uncertainty regarding goals and methods. Laws, court procedures, and values are in flux, and so are the functions and practices of human services occupations in corrections and juvenile justice. Where children and youth are concerned, there is no question about the advisability and necessity of working with families of children and youth who are entangled in these systems.

OTHER POSSIBILITIES

The preceding situations give an idea of the extent of the opportunities for family interviewing but do not exhaust all the possibilities. However, the existence of one of these situations does not always dictate that family interviewing must take place. Some families are not willing. Young adults often prefer individual attention and should "go it alone," independent of their families. The list of situations can be used as a guideline regarding a range of family involvement possibilities. Judgment should be exercised so that available opportunities are not lost.

EXAMPLE: FAMILY INTERVIEWING FOR PROVIDING SERVICES AND PROBLEM SOLVING

Mr. M., at 45 years of age, was a successful insurance executive for a large company. He supervised a department of 30 people. Despite his high-pressure job he was satisfied in his work. His income was high. He thoroughly enjoyed the challenge to his wits and skills provided by expanding sales, planning marketing programs, and "beating the competition." He enjoyed the camaraderie with co-workers. Also, he liked being the boss.

Mr. M. was married to a neat and capable woman. The

couple seemed to care about each other. Mrs. M. kept an attractive household for him, entertained well, and had a satisfactory job as a librarian. Mr. and Mrs. M. had two children: Don, aged 15, and Betty, aged 12. Both were fine children.

Driving home from work one night, Mr. M. suffered an aneurysm. He lost control of his car and skidded off the road into a ditch.

While Mr. M. was in the hospital, Mrs. M. had to get a leave of absence from her job to reorganize the family finances, take special care of the upset children, and attend to her husband. When Mr. M. was ready to be discharged from the hospital after 6 weeks, the doctor explained to Mrs. M. that he might be permanently disabled because of the brain damage caused by the aneurysm. He would have much trouble doing figures, planning, and being aggressive. He would not be able to work at his previous job or probably anywhere else, except in a sheltered workshop. However, the doctor said that Mr. M. could be admitted to a rehabilitation hospital for a retraining program that stood a 50-50 chance of at least partially restoring him. The program would take a number of months, to be followed by a year of training at home. Mrs. M. was shattered.

Mr. M. returned home. The family lived now on disability benefits provided by his insurance. Mr. M. despaired. He spent a good deal of time in bed. He never dressed for the street. He looked at television. He and his wife did not discuss his health, family matters, or plans. She was now on indefinite leave from her job. The children became irritable and disobedient.

After 2 weeks Mrs. M. drove her husband to the clinic where he was to be checked by the doctor. He went into the examining room while she waited outside. After a while the doctor called her in for a brief conversation. He said that Mr. M. had not made up his mind about entering the rehabilitation hospital. She said that it was up to him. She was tight-lipped, not talkative, and seemed tired. The doctor offered her medication for depression, but she said, "Never mind." Later, the doctor asked a mental health worker to call at the M.'s home to help them out in some way.

Explaining roles

After calling for an appointment the mental health worker visited the home. Mrs. M. let her in and then went to the kitchen and stayed there. Mr. M. was interviewed in the bedroom. The practitioner told him that she was visiting him because the doctor thought he was exceptionally depressed.

Explaining problems

Mr. M. was somewhat talkative. In the discussion that followed the practitioner's opening statements, Mr. M. was bitter and hopeless. He could not face going back to the hospital to try to relearn the skills he needed in his work. He asked the fundamental question over and over: "Why me?" Why at the height of success, with a good life, had he been cut down? Because there is no way to explain random acts of fate, there was no answer to Mr. M.'s existential question.

Planning interventions

In response to the practitioner's question, "What are you thinking of doing about the problem?" Mr. M. became angry. He said there was nothing to do; he would be a vegetable.

The practitioner excused herself and went to talk with Mrs. M. in the kitchen. She was preparing food. She was polite but had nothing to say. She refused to go into the bedroom with the practitioner so that all three of them could talk together. The practitioner left.

Explaining problems

Two weeks later Mr. M. was again at the clinic for a checkup. The mental health practitioner approached Mrs. M. in the waiting room. This time the wife agreed reluctantly to go with the practitioner to an office for a talk. Almost at once Mrs. M. said, "Listen, I married a man. He is not the man I married. He is a lump with no future. I can't stand him. I don't want him. I can't figure a way to get out of this." And she wept.

Eliciting information and identifying problems

The practitioner asked Mrs. M. how the marriage had been before Mr. M.'s accident. It became evident that the couple's relationship had been going downhill for some time. The closeness and mutual attraction that had existed in the early years had become a dull routine. But, said Mrs. M., he was "a nice guy," one of the most decent men in their circle of friends. He did well financially. The romance had gone but they had had a stable, secure life—and now this.

Explaining problems

Mrs. M. liked her work at the library. She enjoyed books and discussing ideas with colleagues. Now, however, she was too tired to go back and too worried about the future to be able to think. Besides, there was nothing to think about. Life had ended. She felt responsibility for her children but had stopped being interested in them. Everybody was hanging on her and she was drained. She was angry at the hospital personnel who regarded her as something to be used up for taking care of her husband. Her relatives were OK, but in no way did they understand.

Discussing priorities

The practitioner asked her what kinds of things she would like to do or see happen that would, in her opinion, be most helpful. The answer came immediately: she would like to get rested, to get rid of the awful fatigue, to get away for a while.

Introducing an intervention

The quickly arranged intervention was that Mrs. M. should see a doctor for the fatigue problem. Also, plans were made and executed for her mother to come and stay with her family while Mrs. M. went out of town for ten days to visit her sister in another city.

Discussing additional priorities

Mrs. M. returned from her holiday refreshed and in better spirits. She felt well enough for a joint interview with her husband in which the possibilities and risks of a rehabilitation program were reviewed.

Introducing an intervention

The couple and the practitioner paid a visit to the rehabilitation hospital, looked it over, and talked with the personnel. The practitioner met with the couple and both their children. The children's questions were answered. Everyone began to see the new hospitalization as a good thing. In the end, Mr. M. entered the hospital, and Mrs. M. went back to work.

TECHNIQUES IN FAMILY INTERVIEWING

Family interviewing relies upon the basic techniques already described in Chapters 4 and 5 for the dyadic mode. The family interview is the same kind of discourse as the one-to-one interview. The words, phrases, and sentences used are similar. The practitioner should pay the same attention in family interviewing to such interview attributes as empathy; conventional norms of clear speech; careful listening; and control of body motion, gestures, and facial expressions. However, family interviewing also has some of the attributes of group interviewing. Especially applicable are the group interviewing techniques of scanning, reaching for information and feeling links, and toning down.

The family is preformed; it does not need to be shaped into a group. The formation may need rearranging if family relationships are dysfunctional. The practitioner should pay special attention to the family's patterns of distributing power and sharing intimacy among the members, to love and conflict relationships, and to evidence of scapegoating. It is important for an interviewer to steer clear of taking sides in conflicts or of being drawn into conflicts, to the fullest extent possible.

The form of family interviews is determined by purpose. The kinds of interviews used for service delivery and problem solving emphasize provision of and arrangements for practical services, as in the previous example of the M.'s. Discussion emphasizes clarifying problems, selecting and explaining services, planning and arranging for installing these services, and making decisions about roles to be performed.

Once services are installed, interviews focus on monitoring their effectiveness. If services do not work out, questions should include the following: Was the service actually received? If received, did the client know how to best use the service? Did the service prove to be inappropriate? How the client replies and what information is given uncover the obstacles to problem solving. The next step is to minimize, remove, and avoid obstacles by bettering a poor delivery process, by more and better client instruction on the present service, or by changing the service to a more appropriate one. The example of the M.'s illustrates problem-solving discussions.

FAMILY THERAPY

Service delivery, problem solving, and therapy overlap one another. The differences are ones of purpose and emphasis. Interviewing suggestions in this book emphasize service delivery and problem solving. The chief purpose of family therapy is to alter the client's attitudes and feelings about himself, his relatives, and the interpersonal relations among his family members. Such affective and cognitive changes are considered good in and of themselves and also contribute to desired changes in behavior. Family therapy, like psychotherapy of any variety, is a specialized field that requires practitioners to have particular and detailed training, a long description of which is beyond the scope of this book. Such training is available in many organized courses of study conducted by universities and professional schools and in many workshops and seminars.

A carefully prepared analysis of the different schools of family therapy will be found in a paper by Walsh (1982). Six schools of thought have been identified, each represented by a principal theorist and that theorist's important collaborators. The basic literature is constantly being augmented by practitioners and researchers contributing to several journals. The box below gives an outline of these schools of thought, based on the Walsh analysis, with a bibliography for further study.

MAJOR MODELS OF FAMILY THERAPY*

Model Type and Author(s) (see references for full citations)	Therapy Goals
Structural	
Aponte 1981; Minuchin 1974; Minuchin et al. 1967	To reorganize the family structure
Strategic	
Haley 1976; Selvini Palazzoli et al. 1978; Sluzki and Ransom 1976; Watzlawick, Weakland, and Fisch 1974	To resolve the presenting problem
Behavioral-Social Exchange	
Barton and Alexander 1981; Liberman 1970; Patterson 1975	To improve concrete, observable behavior
Psychodynamic	
Ackerman 1958; Boszormenyi-Nagy 1981; Framo 1970; Lidz 1963; Meissner 1978; Paul 1975; Stierlin 1974	To develop insight into and resolution of family conflict and losses, reconstruct relationships, and stimulate individual and family growth
Family Systems Therapy	
Bowen 1978	To modify relationships in the family system
Experiential	
Satir 1964, 1972; Whitaker 1981	To enhance direct, clear communication and individual and family growth through immediate shared experience

---

*Modified from Walsh 1982, pp. 26-27.

SUMMARY: FAMILY INTERVIEWING

Interviewing family members together is considered to be an effective means for providing services and problem solving. Family interviews are constructed flexibly, taking into consideration the availability of individual family members and their willingness to participate. Practitioner communication is facilitated by speech conventions that are also used in individual and group interviewing. Family interviewing takes advantage of the family social context, which reflects some already formed attitudes, feelings, and interrelationships that may enable interventions to progress. Family therapy uses family interviewing techniques but is usually considered to have goals involving significant change for a wide range of family problems. Much of the family therapy literature is highly informative in formulating interventions that provide services and problem solving.

REFERENCES

Ackerman, N.W. *The Psychodynamics of Family Life*. New York: Basic Books, 1958.

Aponte, H., and Van Deusen, J. "Structural Family Therapy." In *Handbook of Family Therapy,* edited by A. Gurman. New York: Brunner/Mazel, 1981.

Aries, Philippe. "The Family and the City." In *The Family,* edited by Alice S. Rossi, Jerome Kagan, and Tamarak Hareven. New York: W.W. Norton, 1978.

Barton, C., and Alexander, J. "Functional Family Therapy." In *Handbook of Family Therapy,* edited by A. Gurman. New York: Brunner/Mazel, 1981.

Bednar, Richard L., and Kaul, Theodore J. "Experiential Group Research: Current Perspectives." In *Handbook of Psychotherapy and Behavior Change: An Empirical Analysis,* edited by Sol L. Garfield and Allen E. Bergin, pp. 769-817. New York: John Wiley & Sons, 1978.

Boszormenyi-Nagy, I. "Contextual Family Therapy." In *Handbook of Family Therapy,* edited by A. Gurman. New York: Brunner/Mazel, 1981.

Bowen, M. *Family Therapy in Clinical Practice*. New York: Jason Aronson Inc., 1978.

Fanshel, David, and Shinn, Eugene B. *Children in Foster Care: A Longitudinal Investigation*. New York: Columbia University Press, 1978.

Framo, J. "Symptoms from a Family Transactional Viewpoint." In *Family Therapy in Transition,* edited by N. Ackerman. Boston: Little, Brown, & Co., 1970.

Galinsky, Maeda J., and Schopler, Janice H. "Structuring Co-Leadership in Social Work Training." *Social Work with Groups* 3 (Winter 1980):51-64.

Garvin, Charles D. *Contemporary Group Work*. Englewood Cliffs, N.J.: Prentice-Hall, 1981.

Gurman, Alan S., and Kniskern, David P. "Family Therapy Outcome Research: Knowns and Unknowns." In *Handbook of Family Therapy,* edited by Alan S. Gurman and David P. Kniskern, pp. 742-775. New York: Brunner/Mazel, 1981.

Haley, J. *Problem-solving Therapy: New Strategies for Effective Family Therapy*. San Francisco: Jossey-Bass, 1976.

Hartford, Margaret E. *Groups in Social Work*. New York: Columbia University Press, 1972.

Liberman, R. "Behavioral Approaches to Family and Couple Therapy." *American Journal of Orthopsychiatry* 40 (1970):106-118.

Lidz, T. *The Family and Human Adaptation*. New York: International Universities Press, 1963.

Lieberman, Morton A.; Yalom, Irvin D.; and Miles, Mathew B. *Encounter Groups: First Facts*. New York: Basic Books, 1975.

Luft, Joseph. *Group Processes: An Introduction to Group Dynamics*. Palo Alto: Mayfield Publishing Co., 1970.

Magazino, Carmine J. "Services to Children and Families at Risk of Separation." In *Child Welfare: Current Dilemmas — Future Directions,* edited by Brenda Mc-Gowan and William Meezan. Itasca, Ill.: F.E. Peacock Publishers, 1983.

Meissner, W.W. "The Conceptualization of Marital and Family Dynamics from a Psychoanalytic Perspective." In *Marriage and Marital Therapy,* edited by T. Paolino and B. McCrady. New York: Brunner/Mazel, 1978.

Middleman, Ruth R. "Returning Group Process to Group Work." *Social Work with Groups* 1 (Spring 1978):15-26.

Minuchin, S. *Families and Family Therapy*. Cambridge: Harvard University Press, 1974.

Minuchin, S.; Montalvo, B.; Guerney, G.; Rosman, B.; and Schumer, F. *Families of the Slums*. New York: Basic Books, 1967.

Monti, Peter M.; Corriveau, Donald P.; and Curran, James P. "Social Skills Training for Psychiatric Patients: Treatment and Outcome." In *Social Skills Training,* edited by James P. Curran and Peter M. Monti, pp. 185-223. New York: Guilford Press, 1982.

Patterson, G.R.; Reid, J.B.; Jones, R.R.; and Conger, R.E. *A Social Learning Approach to Family Intervention*. Families with Aggressive Children, vol. 1. Eugene, Ore.: Castalia Publishing Co., 1975.

Paul, N.L., and Paul, B.B. *A Marital Puzzle: Transgenerational Analysis in Marriage*. New York: W.W. Norton & Co., Inc., 1975.

Rose, Sheldon D. *Treating Children in Groups*. San Francisco: Jossey-Bass Inc., Publishers, 1972.

Rose, Sheldon D. *Group Therapy: A Behavioral Approach*. Englewood Cliffs, N.J.: Prentice-Hall, 1977.

Rose, Sheldon D. *A Casebook in Group Therapy*. Englewood Cliffs, N.J.: Prentice-Hall, 1980.

Satir, V. *Conjoint Family Therapy*. Palo Alto: Science & Behavior Books, 1964.

Satir, V. *Peoplemaking*. Palo Alto: Science & Behavior Books, 1972.

Selvini Palazzoli, M.; Boscolo, L.; Cecchin, G.; and Prata, G. *Paradox and Counterparadox*. New York: Jason Aronson Inc., 1978.

Sluzki, C.E., and Ransom, D.C., eds. *Double-bind: The Foundation of the Communicational Approach to the Family*. New York: Grune & Stratton, 1976.

Stierlin, H. *Separating Parents and Adolescents*. New York: Jason Aronson Inc., 1974.

Walsh, Froma. "Conceptualizations of Normal Family Functioning." In *Normal Family Processes,* edited by Froma Walsh, pp. 3-44. New York: Guilford Press, 1982.

Watzlawick, P.; Weakland, J.; and Fisch, R. *Change: Principles of Problem Formation and Problem Resolution.* New York: W.W. Norton & Co., Inc., 1974.

Weakland, J.; Fisch, R.; Watzlawick, P.; and Bodin, A. "Brief Therapy: Focused Problem Resolution." *Family Process* 13 (1974):141-168.

Whitaker, C., and Keith, D. "Functional Family Therapy." In *Handbook of Family Therapy,* edited by A. Gurman. New York: Brunner/Mazel, 1981.

Yalom, Irvin D. *The Theory and Practice of Group Psychotherapy.* 2nd ed. New York: Basic Books, 1973.

CHAPTER 7

Specialized settings:
mental health care, hospital and
clinic care, and children's services

Settings as communication networks

A setting is the background or environment of a particular social organization, designed to help implement programs and deliver human services. Settings are classified in various ways, such as by their functions, histories, or auspices. The organizations may be operated by the government, voluntary philanthropy, the private business sector, or nonprofit groups. A setting may be an old organization with long-established and entrenched rules, expectations, and work styles, or it may be a relatively new organization that shows innovation and flexibility.

Social organizations, of which human services organizations are one type, can be viewed from many perspectives such as their politics, their roles in controlling social and physical environments, and their roles in producing a product or service. In this discussion we will look at social organizations as communication networks.

The effect of the organization's communication network is to create a specific culture that heavily influences behavior of people inside the organization. There is also created a wider culture of those who work in different but similar organizations, who become more like one another than they are like those who work in a different field.

This chapter will review some of the distinctive features of selected specialized settings such as mental health facilities, general hospitals and clinics, and facilities with services for children. Features that seem most likely to affect communication between interviewers and clients will be emphasized. Basic interviewing processes are fundamental to all settings. Nevertheless, the way in which clients are viewed, the manner of defining focal problems, organizational structure, and relevant social policies all vary among different organizations and produce unique patterns of discourse.

Interviewing in mental health settings

Communications in mental health settings are distinctive because of the way services are organized, the way mental illness is defined and assessed, and the problems experienced by clients.

ORGANIZATION OF SERVICES

In 1955 public mental hospitals were the main settings for mental illness treatment. In that year they housed 600,000 patients. Within the next 25 years the emphasis shifted from institutional care to community care, or *deinstitutionalization,* as a result of public policy. In 1975 the public mental hospital population had fallen to 200,000 patients, a 65% decline from 1955. Outpatient treatment increased from 27% of patient care episodes to 70%. The total number of patient care episodes increased from 1.7 million to 6.9 million. In 1955 there were 10,000 psychiatrists and a small number of other mental health professionals; in 1980 it is estimated there were 100,000 mental health practitioners, 25,000 of whom were psychiatrists (Klerman 1982). Psychotherapy of all sorts became better defined, more specific, and more accurately evaluated. Presently it is estimated that more than 250 different varieties of psychotherapy are practiced (Parloff 1980).

Antipsychotic, antidepressant, and tranquilizing drugs, administered on an outpatient basis, considerably reduced the amount of institutional treatment of mental illness. Deinstitutionalization was accompanied by the development of community psychiatry and by a governmental policy directed at the prevention of mental illness and expansion of community-based outpatient treatment.

The deinstitutionalization movement was a disappointment in many ways because community services fell short of needs. However, deinstitutionalization expanded and diversified a variety of services. Short-term hospitalization became available in general hospitals. Local clinic facilities expanded throughout many communities. Persons with less acute conditions benefited from the greater availability of help in many localities (Morrissey 1982).

THE MEDICAL MODEL AND MENTAL ILLNESS

Law, custom, and history dictate that the treatment of mental illness is the domain of the medical profession, particularly the specialization of psychiatry. Disease theory is a basic concept in the medical model. The two components of disease theory are (1) the identification of symptoms or syndromes and (2) the discovery, or attempt at discovery, of an underlying biological abnormality. The work of identifying, classifying, revising, and understanding mental disease has been a long historical process and is still going on in a continuous and changing way.

DEFINITION OF MENTAL ILLNESS

To qualify as a mental disease, a condition should have existed over a period of time; that is, the condition should not be a transitory occurrence. The relative stability of a mental disease over time is a necessary part of the diagnosis, according to the American Psychiatric Association's 1980 *Diagnostic and Statistical Manual of Mental Disorders,* or DSM-III. Progress has been made in discovering some relevant biological features of mental disease, but it will probably be a long time before this knowledge is translated into certain and reliable treatment (Snyder 1980).

Whenever mental and behavioral disturbances qualify for diagnosis as a disease, social and physical health factors interact with the disease. The affected person usually becomes impaired, in either an extensive or minor way, in social functioning. People who are handicapped in this way make up a large portion of those who seek help from a mental health service facility.

Klerman (1982) suggests that recipients of mental health services can be classified in three groups: (1) the estimated 30 to 35 million people in the United States with a definable mental illness; (2) the approximately 50 million people per year who have to contend with adverse, disabling life events that do not qualify for a disease label; and (3) a large number of people, difficult to estimate, who have problems in living and desire to increase their well-being.

The modern tendency is to limit the disease label to those who meet the diagnostic criteria found in DSM-III. Persons suffering because of stress in its many varieties are not defined as mentally ill if they do not meet appropriate diagnostic criteria.

Psychological and social treatments are of value to an important number of people coping with stress (Smith, Glass, and Miller 1980). Such people show, for example: depression; anxiety; tension; disturbances in sleep, appetite, activity level, and quality of activity; and sexual dysfunctions. These people may be large users of alcohol, tobacco, stimulants, or sedatives that impair health and social functioning. Psychotherapy and social treatments help them to achieve clarity of perspective, improve their social skills, and expand their interests and horizons. Afflicted people may also obtain help and guidance from services other than mental health programs.

The major concerns of mental health organizations are the mentally ill and those with serious handicaps caused by stress and adverse life circumstances. The most severely ill are in need of sequestering, custody, and care. Drug treatment under medical sanction is important for them, together with receiving training in social skills that enable them to take a reasonable role in the community. Provision of environmental supports is needed to make up for deficiencies in self-management.

People under stress can be offered an array of services to allay conflict, to enhance personal relationships, and to manage overload in such a way as to preserve functioning and move forward to greater productivity and satisfaction.

CLINICAL ASSESSMENT INTERVIEWING (see also Chapter 3)

The assessment interview is the first patient-practitioner encounter in a mental health organization. The dominance of the medical model sets the interviewing tone and determines the speech codes and insider dialect of the staff, the parameters of the assessment content, and the practitioner-client transactions regarding a treatment plan. Assessment interviews shape the interviewee's role as patient, both while she is at the hospital or clinic and after leaving. Memories of and reports about the contact may follow the client into other social living transactions. Although assessments are almost never final and are subject to change over time, the initial assessment is important and has immediate consequences.

Mental health facilities vary concerning which assessment features should receive priority. They vary as to which discipline is used to make the assessment and which system is used for analysis of the assessment. Usually the assessment is a collaborative effort by the staff. An interviewer has to find out the assessment rules for the program that he is part of.

Clinical assessment concepts are currently developed to conform to the new DSM-III, which was published in 1980. However, much of the language and many rules continue to follow an earlier version of the *Diagnostic and Statistical Manual of Mental Disorders,* or DSM-II, which was published in 1968. The current diagnostic classifications are arranged to describe symptoms. These symptoms are clustered into entities called *disorders.* The term "disorder" refers to behavioral, biological, and psychological patterns typically associated with distress and disability. They are classified into descriptive groups. The DSM-III is atheoretical with regard to etiology so that classifications can be used by clinicians of different theoretical persuasions.

The clinical assessment is conducted through interviews and observations with the designated patient and often with family. Information may also be received from social agencies, courts, or other organizations. In some clinics and under some conditions psychological tests are given.

The basic interviewing guidelines described in Chapters 4 and 5 form the essential framework. There are, however, additional features. By voluntarily electing to come to a mental health facility, acceding to pressure from others, or being ordered by a court to come to a mental health facility, the patient has placed himself in a setting where the problem will be seen in terms of mental illness or disorder.

If the patient has come voluntarily, he probably perceives his problem in terms of mental illness or emotional or behavioral disturbance. The patient perceives a need for a psychiatric solution, that is, for psychotherapy. However, some patients are uncertain if the choice is wise, best, or appropriate. A patient may simply want to check his judgment against an expert's. Often, the patient lacks conviction that he has a mental problem that resides somewhere inside himself; he may come to a psychiatric facility under pressure, having been persuaded or coerced by a social authority. Perhaps someone outside the clinic has judged that the patient needs help for a mental problem; this judgment may be correct, or it may be incorrect.

In general, a diagnosis is developed from (1) identification of a particular mental disorder, (2) identification of a particular personality or developmental disorder, and (3) identification of any existing specific physical disorders and conditions. A conclusion is drawn from consideration of these three factors and is aided by (4) consideration of the severity of current psychosocial stressors, and (5) an appraisal of the highest level of adaptive functioning over a few months of the past year.

Mental health clinics are staffed by practitioners from the various professional disciplines to assure that diagnostic judgments are made with technical knowledge and skill. Clinical assessment interviewing can be done by a variety of staff members who obtain information. The actual deciding on the explicit clinical diagnosis usually occurs under the supervision of senior staff. The DSM-III provides authoritative descriptions of the various diagnostic entities. In addition, there are many good psychopathology texts to be consulted for information and study.

The key interviewing question for initiation of the diagnostic process is "What is the matter?" and is addressed to the patient or referral source.

After getting a full idea of the problem as perceived by the patient and, if involved, the relatives and referral source, the interviewer asks how long it has been going on, primarily looking at the past year. Other important questions are, "When did it start?" "What do you think started it?" and "What have the effects of this trouble been on your life, your important personal relationships, your employment, your health, your self-esteem, and your sense of well-being?"

The practitioner should particularly inquire whether the patient has experienced recognized stressors in the past year and how she has reacted to and dealt with them. Attention should be paid to such stressors as difficulties with a spouse, companions, or friends; difficulty in the parental role; difficulties at work or school; moving; arrest, lawsuit, or trial; a developmental crisis; physical illness or injury; a disaster; or serious family distress (DSM-III 1980, p. 28).

In reviewing the patient's experience in the past year the practitioner should ask about social relations, occupational functioning, and use of leisure time (DSM-III 1980, pp. 28-30). A judgment should be based on normal expectable standards and should try to determine whether the person at his best was functioning at a fair level or better, was doing poorly, or was grossly impaired.

The actual diagnostic formulation and treatment plan may or may not be the responsibility of a particular interviewer. How much responsibility the interviewer has depends on her training and position in the organizational hierarchy. Most often such decisions are made by a team. Every clinic and hospital has its own set of rules for dividing up responsibilities; they also have their own rules for deciding what kind of information to acquire from clients. These rules are basic specialized guides for the interviewer.

SPECIAL PATTERNS OF DISCOURSE

Some people who appear in mental hospitals or in outpatient clinics may speak in a florid or unusual manner. Even if their speech shows disturbed ideation, their unusual manner may be limited only to a portion of their communication. The rest of their speech will be standard and intelligible. However, some mentally ill people who are seriously impaired do not speak. Some speak, but unintelligibly. Many patients communicate in normal speech patterns, are wholly intelligible, but are under stress. There are no special rules for clients whose speech patterns are regular and ordinary; the observations about ordinary speech, gestures, body motions, and eye contact described in Chapter 1 apply to them.

In psychiatric settings practitioners will at times observe speech that is different from ordinary speech in both content and manner. This special type of speech is observed in some patients with serious schizophrenic disorders (DSM-III 1980, pp. 181-193). The content of the speech may indicate the presence of markedly illogical beliefs such as *delusions,* that is, false beliefs about being spied on or persecuted. The person's speech may be characterized by "ideas that shift from one subject to another completely unrelated or obliquely related subject, without the speaker showing any awareness that the topics are unconnected" (DSM-III 1980, p. 182). The speech may be incomprehensible because an interviewer cannot follow the loose associations contained in it. Other thought difficulties may be shown in speech that is wordy but conveys little information because it is "overly abstract or overly concrete, repetitive, or stereotyped" (DSM-III 1980, p. 182). The person may invent words or say the same word or phrase over and over again.

A disturbed person may talk about hallucinations, that is, about hearing voices or seeing "visions." It is important to ask hallucinating people what the voices are saying or what their visions look like to try to discern whether the hallucinations are benign or dangerous. Voices that command the ill person to take aggressive action may result in tragic consequences.

Some seriously ill people, especially those classified as suffering from a schizophrenic disorder, will speak in a very monotonous tone of voice. Their facial and bodily gestures will be still. Their speech content, gestures, and body motions will be discordant. Affect may be inappropriate; mentally ill people may smile, giggle, or laugh while talking about sad things.

There are other speech activities of the mentally ill that create interactional problems for the interviewer. There has been some research on interviewing psychotic persons (Shapiro 1979, pp. 155-157). The speech of thought-disordered persons is generally grossly different from ordinary speech. Trying to decipher their speech has been likened to trying to understand difficult, obscurely written poetry. It has been suggested that the interviewer's problem comes from being overloaded with novel talk and not having a blueprint, dictionary, or glossary to make sense of it. The interviewer searches for information about what is being said, but the information is difficult to obtain. The pattern of discourse may sound appropriate, but the interviewer observes that the way the words are put together in sentences does not convey any meaning that ordinary speech norms can interpret. The use of conjunctions is sparse in psychotic talk, making it difficult for the interviewer to grasp supposed connections. For example, disturbed thought may be expressed by stringing everything together with *and,* without appropriately using more explicit connectors such as *but, so,* or *then.* To converse with a person who talks like this, the interviewer must suspend his usual rules of listening to some extent so that the ill person's methods of stringing words together can be deciphered.

One way to handle unintelligibility is to tell the interviewee that you cannot understand. The client can be asked to repeat her words, say them a different way, or at least say them again. Shapiro (p. 157) reports that "some therapists use the technique with psychotics of confronting them with their 'crazy talk,' admonishing them to adopt, if they can, a more standard code."

AN INTERVIEW WITH A MENTALLY ILL MAN

Mr. R. was tall, rangy, and about 40 years old. He walked into the clinic and gave his name to the receptionist. He had to wait 20 minutes before I could see him.

He did not sit down. He paced the waiting room at a fast clip. He stopped to stand in front of other patients and made speeches at them. "You're a junkie," he told one man. The man looked away. He told a woman that he was a mathematician. He asked her to give him a 9-digit number to multiply by any other 9-digit number and said he would give her the correct answer in a flash. The woman got caught up in the game, and Mr. R. started to give her immediate answers to impossible calculations. He circled around the receptionist, telling her what to do. He showed considerable acquaintance with the ways of clinics.

I took him into my office as soon as I could because of the disturbance he was creating. I said to him, "What's on your mind?" He pulled his chair up close, stared, and said, "I just got out of prison. I was in for murder for 15 years." Then he said that he knew many famous murderers, and he started naming them one by one.

I asked him, "What do you want this clinic to do for you?" He said that he had been released from prison a few days before with a small sum of money. Now it was all used up. He had to have some financial help to live on. He said he wanted us to call up his brother in another city to come and get him. His brother, he said, was a well-known, wealthy industrialist. (This last information turned out to be true.)

I said we would need time to decide if we could or should call and that I needed to get some information from him. He said that was all right; he expected it. "Shoot," he said.

I said that this was a clinic for treating people with problems connected to a mental condition of some sort. "Yeah, I know," he said. I said, "Since you see your solution as obtaining financial aid and a phone call to your brother, have you considered going for help to the ex-prisoner's aid organization?" He'd thought of it, he replied, but hadn't contacted the organization because it was just no good. "Well, then," I said, "what good do you think will come of talking to someone in a psychiatric clinic? Do you have a mental or emotional problem?"

"Well, no—but I thought it would be fun," he laughed.

Then the following interchange took place. I began:

"How long were you in prison?"

"Fifteen years," he answered.

"You are out on parole?"

"Yeah."

"Were you taught any job skills in prison?"

"I worked in the kitchen."

"Would you tell me about the offense that got you in prison?"

He stood up, laughed, and took some pencils from my desk and started to juggle them.

"I killed my girl friend," he answered. He went on with a gory tale of a fight and a stabbing.

Pacing the room, juggling the pencils, touching and moving the papers around on my desk, smiling a lot, Mr. R. lectured me on the psychology of murder and talked about the offenses of the famous murderers he had talked to in prison. Although I had no expert knowledge on crimes of violence or prisons, Mr. R.'s story struck me as being fanciful. His narrative sounded more like a soap opera than the reality of prison life as documented in books. Yet I felt alarm about the possibility of having a murderer in my office. I felt I had to be careful in case I was in danger. However, his story was not credible, especially because of his laughter and playing around.

I said to him, "If you have just got out of prison, it would seem that you need to find a job and a place to live." He said: "That's right!"

"This wealthy brother of yours," I said, "would he help you financially until you could get on your feet?" Then I got a long and only partly understandable story about the family business, about how the brother had cheated him and looked down on him. Mr. R. had been given a lowly production job in the factory. He had been drunk a lot. There had been constant fights with his brother. He had constantly changed girl friends. He had never amounted to anything. He had seen a lot of "shrinks," and his brother had paid. He had had several terms in mental hospitals. Nothing had done any good. "Shrinks are dumb," he said.

I tried to see if I could get an agreement with him on focus, and I attempted to get an idea of what he was like. Listening to and observing Mr. R., I considered it possible that he was having a manic episode (DSM-III 1980, pp. 205-224). I asked him, "If I called up your brother and asked him to come and get you, do you think he would come?"

"What do you think!" he said. "Sure he would." He went on to explain that the business was really in his name. He was the oldest. He had the Ph.D. in business. Basically, the brother was his employee. He said, "My brother is a jerk who has arranged with a crooked lawyer to take the business away from me. Look how clever I am with figures. I can run circles around everybody in figuring and running a business." Mr. R. got up. He was scowling. He raced out of the office, circled the waiting room twice, and ran out on the street.

I left my office too and found the psychiatrist on duty, who confirmed my hunch about the diagnosis. When I returned, Mr. R. was in the waiting room. He had acquired an extra-large size box of potato chips and was dribbling potato chips over people in the waiting room, most of whom reacted as if he were a hilarious comic. He followed me into my office as soon as he saw me coming down the hall.

"Listen," I said. "I don't know about this murder offense. What you told me is hard to believe. But for the time being that is not important. What's important is that I think you have a mental illness, and you should be getting treatment for it. Depending on what the doctor thinks, you might need to go into the hospital."

"Christ!" he said. "It's about time you figured that out. Let's go!"

This illustration contains unusual speech accompanied by excessively rapid and irrelevant body motions. The ideas expressed by Mr. R. often lack credibility and substantially diverge from expectable content. The illustration depicts the use of a psychiatric consultant to make a tentative identification of mental illness and a plan for further diagnostic exploration in a hospital.

AN INTERVIEW WITH A MAN UNDER STRESS SUFFERING LOW SELF-ESTEEM

Jim J., 38 years old, came to the clinic complaining of chronic inability to make decisions. A slim, wiry man, he sat hunched over and kept his hat in his hands, turning it over and over as he talked. Sometimes, he rested his hat on his lap and sat rigidly. He was obviously tense, scared, and ill at ease. He came into the room, looked at me glumly, and waited for me to start.

I asked what he thought the clinic might do for him or what he wanted the clinic to do. In a halting manner, stopping frequently and waiting for encouraging gestures and remarks from me, he told me about his problem. He was a construction worker, now out of work because of the economy. When he worked he made good money. Now he was living off unemployment.

Mr. J.'s wife had died 7 years earlier. She had left him with two young children whom he could not take care of. The state had put them in foster care, and now they were after Mr. J. to give up the kids for adoption.

He worried and worried about what to do with these kids of his. He knew he was a complete heel for not being able to take care of them. He owed it to them; what would they think when they grew up?

I asked him if that was what was the matter now; was it about his kids that he wanted help from the clinic? He said, "Not exactly," and then fell silent.

"Well, then," I said, "tell me in your own way what the trouble is." Speaking haltingly and with effort, he said, "I've never done anything right in my life . . . I always do the wrong thing . . . or I don't do anything . . . I can't make up my mind."

"You take a dim view of yourself, then?" I asked.

"It's true, isn't it?"

"In what way?"

"Look—I'm a failure in my job. I've failed as a father. I didn't take care of my wife, and she died. That's enough."

"What would you like to do about those things?"

"Maybe you could find out what's wrong with my mind, why I always fail."

I said, "Is there something going on right now that brings all this up so much?"

It turned out that there was. There was this woman, Ellen. For 5 years, off and on, she and Mr. J. had been dating. He wished he could get married. Once a month the agency let him see his kids; he hardly knew them. He lived in his old father's house. His father took in boarders, all single men. Mr. J. said that from time to time he went job hunting. But it was a dreary business because they all knew him, but there was no work. He looked into getting retrained for something else; he would have to go to school with a bunch of kids and start out with very low pay. He was a top-notch worker, and he could not stand being at the bottom again. So he couldn't decide. If he had a wife, he could have a home again. Maybe *be* somebody. Maybe they would let him have his kids back if he had a home.

"What does Ellen say?" I asked.

He didn't know; he had never asked her. With encouragement Mr. J. told me that Ellen wasn't so great. She was sick and on welfare. She had once been a housekeeper in a hotel. She looked good, kept herself up, and made a nice impression. However, he could not talk to her about marriage because he was nothing. She would certainly turn him down. But he wanted very much to get married—to her. "But it's out of the question—or is it?" Mr. J. asked me. "Would any woman take on a bum like me? Of course not." True, he said with a wan smile, she was no bargain herself, a divorced woman with a lot of sicknesses. Still, he couldn't talk to her about this. What was wrong with him? Why couldn't he be like other men? Could we do something about him?

I said, "Is this what you want to do? Get Ellen to marry you? Is that what's on your mind? Did you come to the clinic to get your mind in order to be able to get married?"

"Yes," he said, "absolutely."

Then he said, "Am I crazy?" I answered right away that he did not sound "crazy" to me. I said that he *did* sound as he were oversensitive to being rejected, easily humiliated, and feeling an awful lot of shame. That did not add up to being crazy, but it did add up to his feeling a lot of pain and not being able to make any desirable changes in his life. He agreed with this. He said he wanted to thank me for not thinking he was mentally ill. I said I thought he could be helped to overcome these feelings enough to make a few necessary decisions and take steps to get out of the dumps he was in. He said that was OK and was assigned to a counselor.

This case illustrates the clear speech and thinking of a man who is under stress but not mentally ill. He knows a good trade but cannot find work in it. In the recent past he has experienced severe pressures because of the death of his wife and the placement of his children.

AN INTERVIEW WITH AN OVERWHELMED WOMAN UNDER STRESS

Mrs. W. came to the clinic because she thought she was losing her mind. A 34-year-old black woman, she was 3 months pregnant and emaciated. Her clothes were shabby and her hair was unkempt. She spoke slowly in such a low tone of voice that she was often inaudible. She seemed exhausted.

As she came into the room, she burst into tears. "I can't stand it," she said. "Can't stand what?" I asked. Weeping, she said, "My life. It's hopeless."

I told her we would try to help. I asked her to please tell me where she lived, whom she lived with, if she had seen a doctor lately, and what had happened recently to make her feel so sad. Speaking very slowly and without embellishment, she told me she was married. A long time ago her life with her husband had been happy, but now he drank too much and didn't do anything in the evening when he came home from work except lay around or go out with his men friends. They had two children already, with a third on the way. Mrs. W. felt that she was a drudge. Lately she could not sleep or eat. Mr. W. reacted to her nervousness with accusations and blamed her for the pregnancy. Yesterday he had thrown a shoe at her head and punched her. He had gone out, letting her lie on the floor unattended, and he had not come home that night. A girl friend had found her, put her to bed, and brought her some soup. The girl friend had taken the kids to her house; they had cried and been upset. In the morning when her girl friend came over, Mrs. W. was lying in bed in a stupor. The friend had driven her to the emergency room, from which she was sent to the psychiatric clinic.

Telling this story totally exhausted Mrs. W. She was now sitting in the chair curled up in a ball. She said, "I can't do anything. It's hopeless."

The psychiatrist admitted Mrs. W. to the inpatient ward. The social worker got on the phone to hunt down Mr. W. and Mrs. W.'s girl friend, who was still taking care of the two children.

This illustration depicts the speech of a person under stress. Mrs. W. has been recently subjected to extreme hardship and is exhausted. Despite her condition she speaks clearly enough to relate an understandable explanation of her problem. The hospitalization will probably reveal whether mental illness is present or not.

INTERVIEWING IN POSSIBLY DANGEROUS SITUATIONS

Mental health practitioners are not often involved with patients who are violent or dangerous. Clinics and hospitals normally employ security personnel in much the same way that any public building does. Only on rare occasions are they needed. Walters (1981, p. 1106), says that:

Violence is an infrequent behavior, even on the part of those considered to be the most violent. They are not violent all the time; in fact, they are not violent most of the time. When a prediction of violence is made, therefore, the 'violent' individuals probably will be deprived of their liberty in the interest of protecting society —when, in the vast majority of instances, these persons will not, in fact, be violent.

Because violent behavior is seldom expressed or encountered, a core issue is how to predict an infrequent event. Since the rules and criteria for doing so are poorly understood, the prediction problem is one of uncertainty. Practitioners are rightfully concerned about protecting themselves and others; however, clients cannot be restrained or deprived of their liberty on vague grounds.

There are provisions that a mental health practitioner can make. The first is to be acquainted with the agency's security services to know whom to contact and where to find people who will help in an emergency. In the rare event that an assault appears imminent, the first rule is to get away and get help. If an interviewee is armed, the interviewer or a security guard should ask him to give up the weapon. Most people will do so. Presumably the person is in the clinic to get help. He is probably frightened and under extreme stress. It is advisable to communicate in a calm manner, with a calm tone and posture, to assure and reassure the person that protection and help will be forthcoming. Repeated statements should communicate to him the idea: "We will take care of you. We will help."

In order to demonstrate that the patient will be cared for and protected, the practitioner should listen attentively to his woe and rage, and to all his fears. Interviewers should be reassuring and respectful and should not argue. It is advisable not to minimize the patient's perceived problem by telling him it's not all that bad or that he is totally mistaken about people he thinks have wronged him. Interviewers should listen to the spontaneous statements the patient makes and be cautious about exploring feelings in detail. The reason is that the patient is probably telling as much as he can bear to. His saying more or trying to look inside himself may increase his stress. People in extreme stress are often absolutely overwhelmed. It is necessary to try to cut down on all stress. The interviewer may give the person food, get him to sleep, sequester him if possible, and take care of him as much as possible. If the interviewer is unable to calm the person in a reasonable amount of time, security services should be asked to help.

Treatment decisions in such cases should always be made by a team involving senior staff members with experience and major responsibility.

If patients are evaluated as dangerous to others, the practitioner and clinic have a responsibility to alert people at risk. There are legal aspects to this responsibility that vary from locality to locality. An interviewer should be informed of proper procedures by the clinic or hospital administration and should conform to the rules meticulously.

In cases of serious suicidal risks a similar responsibility exists to notify relatives or other responsible people. About 2% to 5% of the population attempts suicide; most people are rescued. There does not seem to be any one particular mental disturbance that leads a person to suicide. Some suicidal persons do not appear to be mentally disturbed. Assessing suicidal potential is a complex matter to be undertaken only by experts if possible. However, there is always the possibility that an interviewer may be faced unexpectedly with a suicidal client. If this happens, consultation should be sought. Attention should be paid to people whose depression is prominent, is relatively persistent, or involves recurrent thoughts of death. Suicidal ideation is characterized by rumination about or plans to commit suicide, thoughts of what the world will be like afterward, wishes to be dead, or memories of and wishes to repeat an actual previous suicide attempt. Expressions of suicidal thought or intentions should always be taken seriously.

Assessment information can be obtained from the patient by asking questions and listening to her spontaneous talk. The practitioner does not have to be afraid of "putting the idea (of suicide) in the patient's head." Questions will be interpreted by the patient as evidence that the practitioner is taking her seriously, which is what the patient needs and wants.

The practitioner can simply ask the client if she has thought or is thinking about suicide. Often the person will laugh at the question but take it seriously nevertheless. If the client expresses suicidal thoughts, she should be asked what those thoughts are. The practitioner should also ask what ideas the patient has about means to carry out suicide and whether she has access to them. The interviewer should ask for full details of a previous attempt: when, where, with whom, and what happened. Of those who attempt suicide and fail, 10% succeed later, by accident or design (Snyder 1980, p. 4). The practitioner should try to arrange for family or good friends to see the patient so that she receives messages of concern, interest, and caring. The patient should get confirmation that the practitioner and other important and specific people want her to be alive. In some instances a psychiatrist will admit a suicidal person to the hospital.

INTERVIEWING IN CRISIS INTERVENTION

Theoretically a *crisis* is a state of affairs in which the person is overwhelmed and temporarily experiences confusion, tension, agitation, and perhaps depression. None of his usual problem-solving practices works. The crisis is usually brought on by a sudden event that is perceived as a threat to life goals, a severe loss, or a large and possibly insurmountable challenge. The upset behaviors are not necessarily indicative of pathology or mental disturbance and are viewed as reasonable considering the circumstances. The crisis may trigger the appearance of old problems, which provides a new possibility to resolve them along with the crisis. However, the possibility of some important resolution of an old problem is conjectural, and the empirical evidence to substantiate this idea is nebulous. The important steps in crisis intervention are trying to reach an understanding of the situation ("cognitive restructuring"), proceeding with action to help clients put their lives in order, and proceeding with necessary tasks. Task-centered problem solving is called for (Epstein 1980).

Crisis theory suggests that the crisis state is self-limiting, can be expected to last 1 to 6 weeks, accelerates rapidly, reaches a plateau, and subsides, leaving the person functioning up to par or in adverse circumstances leaving a maladaptive residue. The theory also presupposes that there is a *precipitant* (an event or mental state) that sets off the upset.

Sometimes people in the process of making changes to accompany age-appropriate developmental events, such as retiring, being "empty-nested," getting married, having a baby, entering adolescence, entering school, or graduating, develop a crisis state. Such people are likely to benefit from task-centered problem solving, together with enhanced understanding of their problems and interpersonal relationships and acquisition of new skills.

Crisis counseling is practiced widely. It is found in most outpatient psychiatric clinics, sometimes in specialized units. Crisis counseling is also practiced in many settings other than clinics. The widespread interest in and usefulness of this specialization has merged with the development and acceptance of numerous approaches that concentrate on reducing the impact of present problems in a structured way. These approaches highlight efficiency by intervening quickly and over a short time span to provide practical and useful relief.

Interviewing in a crisis uses the basic techniques outlined in Chapters 4 and 5. However, the following adjustments are indicated:

STARTING UP PHASE

Generally this phase can be abbreviated. Familiarizing can ordinarily be limited to announcing your name and briefly stating your role or position. For example, the practitioner can say, "I am Mr. V., the crisis counselor."

FIRST PHASE

Get to the point right away. Say something to this effect: "I am going to help you get organized." This is possibly the most helpful phrase a person in crisis can hear.

That should be followed with a brief statement summarizing what you already know so that the client will not have to go over it again. For example, the practitioner might say, "I know you were just assaulted on the street and injured," "I know you were just rescued from a fire," *or* "I have been told you were just extricated from a bad accident."

The client should then be asked to tell in her own words what she would like the practitioner to do (and if it is feasible, the practitioner should do it) and exactly what happened to her. In this way the client will spontaneously identify and specify her problems. The practitioner should avoid probing into the client's past history. That can be left for later if it is necessary at all. The practitioner should find out if there are any family or friends who can be contacted right away. The practitioner should also find out if the client has eaten, needs to go to the bathroom, lacks emergency cash, or requires emergency medical care.

Such clients are often agitated and weep. Do not try to shut off tears or the narration of crisis events, even if clients go over them again and again. People have to master traumas; obsessively going over them is one of the tried and true ways to do so.

MIDDLE PHASE

The first phase can dovetail right into the second phase.

The practitioner should find out what the client would like to do and would like to have done. All sensible requests should be acted on if at all possible. Otherwise, the practitioner should immediately make suggestions and recommendations.

The practitioner should give advice, making sure that it is good advice; that is, the advice should conform to the problem and should be feasible with regard to time and available resources. The client should be told how to follow up.

This is all in the interest of getting the client comfortable, cared for, and surrounded with friends and family if possible. For many in acute crisis states, this may be all that is ever done. For other people there will be a few subsequent interviews in which the situation is reevaluated and a more detailed intervention is planned as necessary.

OTHER SPECIAL CONDITIONS

Interviewers in mental health facilities will probably see a range of conditions in addition to those mentioned. The particular requirements for assessment and intervention interviewing can be studied in specialized literature and in coursework. Each clinic and hospital tends to organize its viewpoint and requirements based on organizational function and on the decisions of its leading professionals. To understand procedures it is necessary for the interviewer to become acquainted with the way requirements are established in each organization.

SUMMARY: INTERVIEWING IN MENTAL HEALTH SETTINGS

Interviews in mental health settings take their specialized form because they are conducted from a medical-psychiatric perspective. Interviews deal largely with medically sanctioned problem exploration and assessment of defined mental disorders. Because of the close connection between mental disorders and social problems, interviews deal with patients' social situations in considerable detail.

Clinical assessment requirements are set forth using the particular approaches of various mental health organizations. These requirements are contained in the DSM-III, published by the American Psychiatric Association, and in the individual programs of each hospital and clinic.

Many people who receive services from mental health facilities are not mentally ill but are responding to difficult stress. Interviews need to take account of these stresses, but the communication modes of the intensely stressed are not different from ordinary speech. A proportion of mentally ill persons may not always conform to regular speech conventions, which will pose some difficulties in understanding.

Interviewing in health settings: hospitals and clinics
ORGANIZATION OF SERVICES

The health industry consists of health care workers, public and private hospitals, nursing homes, health insurance companies, medical equipment manufacturers and suppliers, and pharmaceutical companies. The patterns of discourse in health settings are strongly influenced by the practice of medicine. The special interests of health professions, the economics of health costs, the social aims of health care, and the attitudes and aspirations of staff members are also major influences on the patterns of discourse.

The health industry in the United States produces the second largest proportion of the Gross National Product, or GNP, exceeded only by the defense industry (Raffel 1980, p. 341). In 1950 national health expenditures were 4.4% of the GNP. By 1981 they had risen to 9.8% of the GNP. Health care spending more than tripled between 1971 and 1981. Increased health care costs are common in all the industrialized countries.

In the United States the general rate of inflation accounts for more than half the growth in total health care costs. Specific health care system factors that account for increased costs are numerous and complex. The most important of these are (1) demographic changes resulting in increased use of medical care as the population becomes older, (2) the existence of a third-party payment or insurance system with little incentive for cost containment because providers are paid on a fee-for-service and cost-based plan, (3) the development of new and expensive treatment methods and equipment desired by the health professions and the public, and (4) the strong values placed by society on good health and well-being (Freeland and Schendler 1983).

In an attempt to contain health care expenditures, Congress enacted P.L. 98-21 on April 20, 1983. This law provided for a different method of reimbursing hospitals for treatment of Medicare beneficiaries. Hospital charges account for the largest portion of medical care costs. P.L. 98-21 replaced the retrospective method of paying for hospital service on an itemized basis. The new method is "a prospective payment system in which diagnosis related groups (DRGs) are employed by Medicare to determine the amount or rate of hospital funding" (Rosko and Broyles 1984, p. 35). It is intended that this change in payment policy by Medicare will improve efficiency and contain costs in hospitals. Thoughtful people in the health care field note that reorganization of Medicare payments is occurring with a market orientation to producing and dispensing medical service. It is predicted that major changes will develop in the health care field in the near future (Brown 1984, pp. 5-6).

DEFINING PROBLEMS

The power of the medical model defines and sanctions the problem definition and the interview itself. Most patients respect the authority associated with the medical setting and its personnel. In most human services sectors problems in living are dealt with that all people, professional or not, are familiar with. This is not the case in medical settings. When they get sick with anything more than the common cold and need medical service, both sophisticated and unsophisticated people confront an awesome mystery as well as fear of death, maiming, and catastrophic expense.

The accepted criteria for medically defined disease are physicochemical. However, the medical emphasis in hospitals and clinics is modified by social conditions and relations. The consuming activity associated with illness is active struggle to control the environment and life situations. Both the person who is ill and those who care for him are concerned with their own adaptive needs and struggles. "Illness behavior and reactions to the ill are aspects of a coping dialogue in which the various participants are often actively striving to meet their responsibilities, to control their environment, and to make their everyday circumstances more tolerable and predictable" (Mechanic 1968, p. 2).

ADAPTING THE BASIC INTERVIEWING MODEL

STARTING UP

The basic objectives in starting up an interview in the health field are similar to those described in the general guides (Chapters 4 and 5). In a hospital or clinic the patient will be under high stress because of injury, shock, or illness. Sometimes the patient may be so ill or traumatized that putting her at ease is unrealistic. In this case the practitioner needs to minimize the traumatic reaction by adopting, on the one hand, a straightforward and businesslike attitude toward the work to be done and, on the other hand, by reassuring the patient and explaining as much as possible.

Helpful practitioner activities include answering questions, anticipating questions that the patient may be afraid to ask and then answering them, answering very difficult questions with whatever information is available, and conveying feelings of confidence to the extent that the situation permits. For patients who are ambulatory and not extremely sick this part of the process is not much different from conducting the familiarizing process in any other setting. Very sick patients may be frightened or may behave in an objectionable manner because of illness or stress. Patients who are extremely ill should be addressed in an uncomplicated and straightforward manner to avoid putting them under any more stress.

FIRST PHASE INTERVIEWING

The questions about relevant facts that the health interviewer asks are influenced by the particular health care division of labor to which she is assigned. A counselor, expediter, or ombudsman in the emergency room, for example, needs to elicit information about what happened to bring the patient there.

Caretakers who meet the patient on a service or ward want to know about facts and context, patient reactions, and the particular illness and its personal, family, work, and financial consequences. Therefore appropriate questions include the following: How do you feel? What's bothering you most? Have you been visited? Who do you want to see? Are there undone responsibilities that need tending to? Do you have insurance? What does it cover? *and* How do you make your claims? If a patient is too ill to converse, such questions will need to be asked of a relative or custodian. If a patient can tolerate only a limited amount of conversation, questions will need to be parceled out in small amounts over time.

Explaining roles is of the utmost importance. A patient confronted with the busy and confusing bureaucracy of a hospital or clinic needs to know to whom he is talking and why.

MIDDLE PHASE ADAPTATIONS

The major adaptation in medical settings in the middle phase concerns pain, fear, and anxiety. An ill person is mildly to severely uncomfortable and is mildly to severely anxious. Fear and pain accompany illness and arise from genuine and realistic causes. They cannot be made to vanish. However, they ought to be brought under manageable control by means of reality testing and interviewer support. Family and friends ought to be enlisted to offer support whenever possible. Anxiety about being ill and about the machinery of treatment is not pathological; it is normal.

Many people in our society are characteristically anxious. They may develop excessive anxiety in the face of illness and hospital or clinic organization. Anxiety includes fear of the future and dread of the unknown. The repertoire of techniques needs to be adapted specifically to ill people to counteract these fears and dreads to the fullest possible extent. Identification of problems in the first phase needs to be followed scrupulously with discussions of what the patient can do and what will be done to the patient by the medical staff. Understanding should be as complete as possible. Anxiety will be minimized by conveying information and knowledge, facilitating clear decision making, and providing consolation.

A question that seems to trouble many ill persons, particularly those who are severely ill or recently traumatized from such events as a fire or accident, is "Why me?" The fact of the matter is that chance plays the largest part in who gets hurt and who escapes — temporarily.

TERMINATION AND MONITORING

An adaptation in the termination techniques may be called for if the patient is assigned to monitoring status. The interviewer should take pains to tell the patient just what is being watched, why it is being watched, and what the time span involved in monitoring will be.

SOCIAL SUPPORT

Social supports that accompany medical treatment and encourage and reassure the patient often call for involvement from family members, friends, employers, social agencies, and health agencies outside the hospital or clinic. Discussion at termination needs to clarify the roles of participants other than the patient so that support functions can be properly planned and executed (as illustrated in the case of the M.'s in Chapter 6).

EFFECTS OF STAFF SPECIALIZATION

Many hospital and clinic personnel, such as pharmacists, dietitians, and cast-makers, have highly technical duties involving the preparation of essential materials. Others, such as x-ray technicians, conduct tests of many kinds including examinations. Social workers and nurses usually play key roles in preparing patients for discharge, that is, in organizing their exit from the hospital and reentry into normal life. Some discharges mean transfers to other caretaking facilities such as nursing homes and rehabilitation centers. A great deal of organization of family and community resources is involved in discharge processing. The social engineering required to move a patient through discharge is complex.

The many technical functions of different types of workers in a medical setting require specialized knowledge. A common function for many hospital staff members, however, is patient interviewing. Interview content is nearly always organized around a particular technical process that is related to each special job.

SUMMARY: INTERVIEWING IN HEALTH SETTINGS

The substance of interviews in health settings is focused on the patient's illness and medical recommendations for treatment. The focus also includes the person's reactions to treatment and the impact of her illness on such aspects of the social context as her job, her relationships with family members, and her self-esteem.

The basic interview model needs to be adapted to take into account the special features of being ill within the medical clinic and hospital context.

Interviewing in services on behalf of children (see also Chapter 8)
ORGANIZATION OF SERVICES

In a large number of different settings, practitioners deal with case situations involving children in trouble.

There is almost no simple one-to-one communication when children are interviewed. In school settings there are always at least three actors: the child, a parent, and a teacher. The principal, assistant principal, school psychologist, remedial teacher, auxiliary teachers, and other counselors may also be involved. If the child is in a foster home, involved parties include the biological parents, the foster parents, other caretaker staff members, school professionals, and court personnel. In juvenile court cases there are, besides judges and court officials, personnel from psychological and psychiatric services, police officers, and welfare agency representatives. All communication in an interview is influenced by the roles, input, purposes, and reactions of numerous organizations and actors.

PROBLEMS

Interviews in schools, child welfare agencies, and courts occur for one overriding purpose: the attempt to reduce harm to children and enable them to benefit from education, family life, and community life. The Carnegie Council on Children summarizes what harms American children: "Virtually every index of harm to children, from death at birth to poor school performance, is firmly associated with poverty and race" (Keniston 1979, p. ix). Children of affluent families come to harm but not as often as poor children do.

Education, appropriate family life, and the teaching of reasonably good conduct are the aims of children's services systems. These aims are cornerstones for those who strive to provide opportunities for children that will minimize the negative effects of inequality and enable them, when they become adults, to take part in mainstream America in a satisfying and constructive manner.

SCHOOLS

The public school setting for human services work illustrates the complexity of helping children to develop satisfactorily. Public education is a political battleground, and many battles are about funding. The protagonists are those who operate the schools directly; the state and local legislative bodies that allocate funds; the federal agencies that attempt controls, particularly in the area of inequality of opportunity; and taxpayers, particularly those who are parents. In the background but far from insignificant are battles about curriculum, staffing patterns, school security for teachers and students, and educational resources such as textbook type and availability. Major contenders in these battles are teachers and their professional and union organizations (Useem and Useem 1974).

School is the locale for the major portion of a child's day after the age of 6. Children in school are acquiring a theory of social reality. They are developing ideas about what is right and wrong, who gets ahead and who does not, which values make sense, and why they do.

CHILD WELFARE AGENCIES

If a child is removed from his natural home and placed in a foster home, the situation is as complex as a school situation. Placement practices are in the process of being reformed; the federal Adoption Assistance and Child Welfare Act of 1980 (P.L. 96-272) is accelerating the process. The changes are intended to prevent inappropriate placement, to effect greater permanence in placement of children, and to implement new procedures to protect children from harm.

Many questions regarding change in the child welfare system have arisen as child welfare practices change. There is discussion about what changes need to be made in the operating practices to conform to new federal legislation and funding patterns. Questions include: What changes are needed in staffing patterns and staff skills? How long will such a process take? How will families, children, and foster parents react? How will the public and the press react?

The child welfare system is composed of public child welfare agencies in each state and parallel private agencies distributed unevenly throughout the nation. The agencies are tied together by federal government authorities and a standard-setting private agency, the Child Welfare League of America. The system is funded through a combination of state, local, and federal allocations and through funds provided by private philanthropy. The system has been underfunded in the past and in a way that has favored out-of-home placement rather than in-home supports for families and children who had to use child welfare services.

New policies set up in the previously mentioned Adoption Assistance and Child Welfare Act of 1980 are intended to correct six main problems of the system, outlined by Allen and Knitzer (1983):

1. Many children have been placed out of their own homes who probably should not have been.
2. Once placed, children may be in inappropriate settings, such as those that are too restrictive or too far from home.
3. Children are cut off from contact with their natural families.
4. Children "drift" in care because the quality of the care is inadequately monitored, progress is not systematically reviewed, and plans for permanent homes are not made in a timely fashion.
5. Public systems have often been inadequate in their accountability for provided care.
6. The system has not gathered adequate data from which to collect information that could be used to plan and monitor programs.

The following principles guide the reforms now in development (Meezan 1983):

1. There should be early identification of situations that might lead to child placement.
2. Work with parents and children in their own home must be pursued in order to prevent placement.
3. When a child is removed from home, that action must be based on

specific procedural guidelines that make use of all available knowledge and techniques, and there must be clear evidence that the home situation cannot be remedied.

4. The placement should be the "least detrimental alternative available."

5. An intervention plan must be established. The plan's purpose should be to provide a permanent home — either the child's own home, the home of adoptive parents, or the home of long-term foster parents.

6. Proper guidelines must be established for the termination of parental rights if the child cannot be returned to the natural home.

7. Resources must be sufficient to provide for a permanent substitute home if that is necessary.

A new paradigm is emerging in foster home care practice that consists of decision making and case management (Stein 1981; Stein and Rzepnicki 1983). The new pattern conveys the idea that the most important functions are (1) to make critical decisions objectively and (2) to manage services to achieve goals.

JUVENILE COURTS

Juvenile courts rule on questions of child custody when children are removed from their parents and put in foster care, and they also rule on questions of delinquency among youth. Delinquency is an ambiguous concept that is not easily defined (Gold 1977; Rector 1977). The goals of intervention in delinquency problems involve various combinations of punishment, treatment, education, and guidance. One aim is to sequester those who are deemed violent to protect the public, although knowledge about predicting violence is inexact. Another aim is to reform, rehabilitate, or cure those whose offenses are marked by nonconformance. The delinquent population is drawn mostly from those who are affected by inequality in our society; this is also the case with the population served by child welfare agencies and school social services.

Federal departments have attempted to upgrade state standards and have supported considerable research and innovation. Efforts have been centered on the development of major new alternative correctional programs. For the most part these involve attempts to avoid institutionalization of youth while creating a network of rehabilitative services within communities. These programs were begun with federal support in 1967 and have continued up to the present time. It should be noted that the movement to operate alternative programs has occurred not only in the United States but throughout the industrialized countries of the world.

On the whole, these new programs have not met expectations for reducing crime and delinquency. Many who are familiar with the corrections field fear that diversion of delinquents and their families into community services networks creates more involuntary clients who are subject to social control by the state (Hylton 1982; Spergel et al. 1982). There is controversy about the effectiveness of community alternatives to detention; they are less costly than institutionalization but may lack adequate service content.

Most of the human services work done with juveniles at the direct-service level—especially in the alternative programs—has to do with counseling aimed at changing a young person's beliefs, attitudes, self-esteem, interpersonal relationships, physical environment, and attitudes toward schooling. The role of the human services worker is to assist the court by obtaining the necessary background information about the youth to help the judge make a decision. The practitioner may conduct ongoing counseling and secure community resources to aid the young person. More often than not, particularly when the service has adopted a "family focus," the human services worker will also conduct interviews with at least some family members. In current practice the protection of legal procedures is provided in juvenile court. Often a youth and his family will have an attorney to ensure that legal rights are preserved.

ADAPTATIONS OF BASIC TECHNIQUES

The clients most likely to be interviewed by specialized services on behalf of children are the child or young person in question and her family members, particularly her parents. In Chapter 8 there will be a discussion of interviewing considerations related to age, including special conditions that exist when interviewing children and youth. Those considerations will primarily concern the *style* of dialogue. Of concern in this section is *interview content.* The basic techniques outlined in Chapter 5 are also applicable. Adaptations are necessary for the children's service settings just as adaptations are necessary for mental health and medical settings. These adaptations are dictated by the structure of staff-client transactions and by the purposes, aims, requirements, and style of the interview.

MANDATED PROBLEMS (see also Chapter 10)

In all three settings involving children's problems that were just described the problem definitions are often mandated. *Mandated* problems are those that originate with the legal or social authority, whether or not the client is in agreement. The mandate means that the client is obligated to appear for interviews and to attempt to change a situation, sometimes in a manner predetermined by an authority; usually the mandate involves restraining or curbing identified actions and substituting others. There are a small number of voluntary, self-referred clients in the school systems who seek out a practitioner for help. There are a few voluntary clients in the foster care system who initiate service on their own; however, once they are in the system they may lose their independence. There is only a rare and occasional voluntary request in the juvenile justice system, and it almost always comes from a parent, not the child.

Mandated problems arise from sources with varying power. They can be classified by these sources: legislation, police and court orders, professional opinion, and public opinion (Epstein 1980, pp. 184-189).

Legislation

Some legislation requires that agencies and clients act according to the provisions of specific statutes. Problem-solving goals are governed by the restraints and prohibitions set forth in the applicable statutes. For example, assault and theft are legally prohibited. A child who vandalizes a school building and makes off with equipment may be detained by the police and handed over to the juvenile corrections system. When being interviewed this child is the possessor of the problem ascribed to her by legislation, no matter what other problems she might also have. Child abuse reports are another type of situation in which mandated problems arise. No matter what other problems the suspected parent has, the problem defined by authorities is perceived as the most crucial problem.

Police and court orders

A child who is detained by the police or already under a court order will have been advised of the problem as defined by the authorities. The child, his family members, and counselors may disagree on the problem but will all be required to deal with it. A young person may be seen in a police station or an alternative setting, but it is fairly certain that he will be detained and deprived of at least some of his liberty unless he behaves in a specified way.

Professional opinion

Often problems are identified on the basis of professional opinion that a child or adult is afflicted with a mental disturbance. A prediction may be made that if treatment is not obtained, adverse consequences will result. Ordinarily such opinions carry little weight unless they are incorporated into a strong recommendation by a legal or court authority, unless there is a penalty attached, or unless clients choose to accept the opinion. The professional opinion of, for example, a court psychiatrist carries a great deal of weight with other professionals (such as human services practitioners) who may discuss the opinion with the client thoroughly, in order to convince the client of the opinion's value. Many clients respect professional opinion and go to considerable lengths to follow it.

Public opinion

Public opinion is a powerful molder of problem perceptions. Single mothers, for instance, may feel crushed by public perception of their presumed inadequacies. Parents who voluntarily relinquish a child for adoption are often burdened by guilt that is partly caused by their departure from norms of parental behavior.

The best conditions for an interview are under circumstances where there are no mandated problems, where the client can independently decide what she wants to work on, and where the client is free to locate a practitioner with appropriate skills. However, given the actual conditions in those human services that have social control functions, the preferred practice is to discuss the reasons for the mandate with the client and make sure she understands clearly what the undesirable consequences of ignoring the mandate will be. This is possible to accomplish successfully with many clients. The practitioner should then take responsibility for running a two-track problem definition; that is, the client's priority problems, if different from the mandate, should also be placed in a central focus.

INTERVIEWS WITH COLLATERALS

In all three settings where the work is on behalf of children — schools, child welfare agencies, and juvenile courts — there is usually heavy involvement with community resources. Almost no organization has within itself all of the necessary resources, services, and information. Inquiry must be made to locate who has the desired resources, what the requirements are to make the service available, what the conditions are to keep the service going, and how problems that arise in dispensation can be corrected. Thus many collateral interviews take place in these settings.

Collateral interviews are mainly of two varieties: inquiry and negotiation.

Inquiry

An *inquiry* is a telephone call or in-person contact to find out if an organization has a service that can be used by a certain client. Inquiries are straightforward business conversations and are not much different from phone calls to an airline to ask about different types of discount fares. However, an inquiry to an airline involves the possibility of a sale, which the airline wants. In the case of looking for a social resource, the practitioner may be seeking something that is in short supply. The collateral agency may be protective about dispensing its resource. It is advisable, therefore, for the practitioner to be courteous and circumspect, to respect the collateral's caution, and to explain and interpret fully, putting her client and agency in the best light. It is common for some settings to work out referral liaison arrangements with each other. This makes each individual phone call or contact easier. In inquiry communications it is advisable to keep in mind that a "gatekeeper" in another agency is under pressure to conserve resources and may sometimes be critical of those who request his agency's services.

Negotiation

Once past the inquiry stage, the interviews become *negotiations*. The discourse has the purpose of coming to terms with who will give what to whom, and in return for what. If the service is going to be purchased by the inquiring organization, there is little difference in the basic outline between negotiation for use of the service and negotiation to purchase an airline ticket. However, there may be issues raised about function, prestige, esteem, and rank.

NEGOTIATION STRATEGIES. The negotiation strategies described here have been developed by the Negotiation Project, a research endeavor at Harvard University (Fisher and Ury 1981). Practitioners who do a good deal of such work could benefit from studying the full report of the project. In brief, the Harvard project suggestions contain the following:

1. Don't bargain over position. Instead discuss problem-solving alternatives on a principled basis. For example, the *wrong* thing to say is, "I'm calling to get temporary shelter for a couple of weeks." The *right* thing to say is, "I'm calling about a child who needs shelter. I'd like to discuss how your agency might help."

2. Confront the problem, not the person, you are dealing with. For example, a good response to a refusal might be "You are full up? Hm . . . I really think your service would be best for this particular child. I wonder what might be worked out."

Put yourself in the other practitioner's shoes. Don't blame her for your problem. Discuss each other's perceptions. Have the other practitioner participate in the process and help her save face. Allow her to let off steam and don't react to emotional outbursts. Listen actively and acknowledge what is being said. Speak clearly and to the point.

3. Keep the focus on the interests of both agencies and talk about them. Except for personal pleasantries do not stray from the particular purpose of the discussion.

4. Introduce options for mutual gain. Present many tentative ideas; one may catch on.

5. Frame each issue as a joint search for objective criteria. Always

converse from an assumption that the other practitioner is a collaborator of good will, not an adversary.

6. If the other practitioner has more muscle than you do, stand on principle. Bring all your knowledge to bear on the subject. Take your time; use your wits.

7. If the other person turns you down cold, avoid a confrontation and start discussing reconsideration terms.

8. If you feel you have been deceived and pressured, don't be a victim. Be polite but make your principles clear.

This list of negotiating tactics takes time and experience to learn, but the ideas are good. A worked-out example, reconstructed from a real negotiation, follows.

INQUIRY AND NEGOTIATION ABOUT A PLACEMENT RESOURCE

Because a 7-year-old boy was being mistreated in his foster home and was fighting aggressively with the foster mother, the practitioner *(P)* wanted to relocate him. There was a lot of pressure to remove the boy immediately, but it would take time to locate a new placement. What was needed was shelter with people who could handle an upset child who was provocative and aggressive even when not under stress. Thinking over the community resources, *P* decided that Burnside, a moderately large institution, would be best from all angles.

P phoned Burnside's intake worker *(W)*, who was aloof and distant. *P* explained the child's present circumstances and asked if Burnside might take him for an interim period while permanent placement was being worked out.

W asked questions, a good many of which seemed irrelevant. *P* nevertheless answered them. *W* began making numerous comments about actions that might have prevented the present emergency, saying things such as, "It's too bad you didn't know about the foster mother's problems before you put him there."

By this time *P* was getting the impression that *W* was very unsure of himself, was trying to get into a one-up position, and didn't know what kind of a decision to make.

P said that *W* was making some good points and wondered if, under the present circumstances, *W* could help. *W* mentioned a few other agencies that he said would be suitable. *P* now realized that *W* was trying to "pass the buck." Although the reasons were unclear, *P* could tell that *W* was nervous and lacked confidence. *P* then repeated what she knew about the program and staff at Burnside that made her feel it would be good for the child. There was a long silence, after which *W* said that he really didn't think the staff could handle the boy. *P* then asked *W* to discuss the request with his intake supervisor. If any suggestions emerged from that, *P* said, she would be glad to hear them.

Four hours later *W* called back. He was in a very good mood. The intake supervisor had approved temporary place- ment on the grounds that *P*'s agency had done a good job and that the child did need just what Burnside could provide. The intake supervisor thought the child might be hard for the staff but that they would rise to the occasion. *P* and *W* then amicably discussed fee payments. The 4-hour wait had been used by *P* to make another (and highly unsatisfactory) arrangement, which she now reversed. Later *P* learned that *W* was new on the job and very anxious about making any decisions on his own.

ADAPTING THE INTERVIEW TO A SPECIALIZED FOCUS

If the interview is primarily for assessment, the central goal will be to find out what is the matter. If the interview is primarily for taking inter- ventive action, the central points will be to decide what the client wants and can accomplish, what the setting requires and what it will do, what actions should be planned, and how to help the client begin to and con- tinue to take action (see Chapter 3).

In school settings the central focus is on a problem situation that is hampering the pupil in learning. Education is a school's reason for exis- tence; therefore school problems involve obstacles to learning. These obstacles may be, for example, a child's personal deficits, adverse condi- tions in the classroom and school, adverse conditions in the home envi- ronment, poor health, or poor eyesight. The assessment should identify which area is central to precipitating or maintaining the problem. Inter- vention interviews should focus on remedies for the obstacles to learn- ing.

In foster care settings the central focuses for the assessment are (1) deciding on services in the child's own home, a foster home, or an adop- tive home; and (2) organizing the resources needed to effectively carry out the decision.

In delinquency settings the focus is on acquiring information required by courts, which will vary depending on the court's organization and the preferences of particular officials; obtaining assessment information; de- ciding on services; and planning and discussing interventions to remedy problems identified in the assessment.

FAMILY AND GROUP MODES

It is usual and nearly always necessary in settings dealing with children and youth to have family interviews. Because a mandated problem is often present, practitioners have considerable authority in requiring the attendance of parents at an interview. Such interviews are likely to be characterized by fear and resentment from family members because so much is at stake and such frightening consequences may result. (See Chapter 9 for further discussion of involuntary clients.) Family interviews are nearly always useful for assessment. If parents can become involved, they may be helpful for intervention purposes (see Chapter 6). Although the group mode is not often used for assessment in these settings, it is commonly used for intervention. As was illustrated in Chapter 6, many children and young people are quite responsive in group interviews (Garvin 1974; Ladsen and Mitchell 1980; Rooney 1977).

SUMMARY: INTERVIEWING IN SERVICES ON BEHALF OF CHILDREN

Three kinds of human services organizations are responsible for a great deal of the practice conducted to benefit children: (1) schools, (2) child welfare agencies, and (3) juvenile courts and alternative services. The major purpose of these organizations is to reduce harm to children and enable them to benefit from education, family life, and community life. Interviewing in such specialized settings has to take particular conditions into account. There are often mandated problems and interventions that need to be addressed to avoid undesirable consequences. Children's services need to involve many actors, for example, social agencies, parents, educators, and court personnel. Interviews also need to be conducted with other service providers, which necessitates communication that emphasizes processes of inquiry and negotiation.

REFERENCES

Allen, Mary Lee, and Knitzer, Jane. "Child Welfare: Examining the Policy Framework." In *Child Welfare: Current Dilemmas, Future Directions,* edited by Brenda G. McGowan and William Meezan, pp. 93-142. Itasca, Ill.: F.E. Peacock Publishers, 1983.

Brown, Montague. "From the Editor." *Health Care Management Review* 9 (Summer 1984): 5-6.

deLone, Richard H. *Small Futures: Children, Inequality, and the Limits of Liberal Reform.* New York: Harcourt Brace Jovanovich, 1979.

Diagnostic and Statistical Manual of Mental Disorders (DSM-III). 3rd ed. Washington, D.C.: American Psychiatric Association, 1980.

Epstein, Laura. *Helping People: The Task-Centered Approach.* St. Louis: C.V. Mosby Co., 1980.

Fisher, Roger, and Ury, William. *Getting to Yes: Negotiating Agreement Without Giving In.* Boston: Houghton Mifflin Co., 1981.

Freeland, Mark S., and Schendler, Carol Ellen. "National Health Expenditure Growth in the 1980's: An Agency Population, New Technologies, and Increasing Competition." *Health Care Financing Review* 4 (March 1983):1-58.

Garvin, Charles. "Task-Centered Group Work." *Social Service Review* 48 (December 1974):494-507.

Gold, Martin. "Crime and Delinquency: Treatment and Prevention." In *Encyclopedia of Social Work,* pp. 218-238. Washington, D.C.: National Association of Social Workers, 1977.

Hylton, John H. "Rhetoric and Reality: A Critical Appraisal of Community Correctional Programs." *Crime and Delinquency* 28 (July 1982):341-373.

Keniston, Kenneth. Foreword to *Small Futures: Children, Inequality, and the Limits of Liberal Reform,* by Richard H. deLone. New York: Harcourt Brace Jovanovich, 1979.

Klerman, Gerald L. "The Psychiatric Revolution of the Past Twenty-Five Years." In *Deviance and Mental Illness,* edited by Walter Gove, pp. 177-198. Beverly Hills: Sage Publications, 1982.

Ladsen, JoAnn, and Mitchell, Craig. "Task-Centered Strength-Oriented Group Work with Delinquents." *Social Casework* 61 (March 1980):154-163.

Mechanic, David. *Medical Sociology: A Selective View.* New York: The Free Press, 1968.

Meezan, William. "Child Welfare: An Overview of the Issues." In *Child Welfare: Current Dilemmas and Future Directions,* edited by Brenda G. McGowan and William Meezan. Itasca, Ill.: F.E. Peacock, 1983.

Morrissey, Joseph P. "Deinstitutionalizing the Mentally Ill: Process, Outcome, and New Directions." In *Deviance and Mental Illness,* edited by Walter R. Gove, pp. 147-176. Beverly Hills: Sage Publications, 1982.

Parloff, Morris B. "Psychotherapy and Research: An Anaclitic Depression." *Psychiatry* 43 (November 1980):279-293.

Raffel, Marshall W. *The U.S. Health System: Origin and Functions.* New York: John Wiley & Sons, 1980.

Rector, Milton G. "Crime and Delinquency." In *Encyclopedia of Social Work,* pp. 198-208. Washington, D.C.: National Association of Social Workers, 1977.

Rooney, Ronald. "Adolescent Groups in Public Schools." In *Task-Centered Practice,* by William J. Reid and Laura Epstein. New York: Columbia University Press, 1977.

Rosko, Michael D., and Broyles, Robert W. "Unintended Consequences of Prospective Payment: Erosion of Hospital Financial Position and Cost Shifting." *Health Care Management Review* 9 (Summer 1984):35-43.

Shapiro, Theodore. *Clinical Psycholinguistics.* New York: Plenum Press, 1979.

Smith, Mary Lee; Glass, Gene V.; and Miller, Thomas I. *The Benefits of Psychotherapy.* Baltimore: The John Hopkins University Press, 1980.

Snyder, Solomon H. *Biological Aspects of Mental Disorder.* New York: Oxford University Press, 1980.

Spergel, Irving A.; Lynch, James P.; Reamer, Frederic G.; and Korbelik, John. "Response of Organization and Community to a Deinstitutionalization Strategy." *Crime and Delinquency* 28 (July 1982):426-449.

Stein, Theodore J. *Social Work Practice in Child Welfare*. Englewood Cliffs, N.J.: Prentice-Hall, Inc., 1981.

Stein, Theodore J., and Rzepnicki, Tina. *Decision Making at Child Welfare Intake: A Handbook for Practitioners*. New York: Child Welfare League of America, 1983.

Useem, Elizabeth L., and Useem, Michael. *The Education Establishment*. Englewood Cliffs, N.J.: Prentice-Hall, Inc., 1974.

Walters, Herman A. "Dangerousness." In *Encyclopedia of Clinical Assessment*. Vol. 2. San Francisco: Jossey-Bass Publishers, 1981.

Wing, J.K. *Reasoning About Madness*. New York: Oxford University Press, 1978.

CHAPTER 8

Social class, age, and sex

Interviews are affected by client characteristics. Who the practitioner is, how much he knows, and what skills he possesses, as well as the form and structure of the interview and the characteristics of the setting, are all decisive attributes of the interviewing situation (see Chapters 1, 4, 5, 7). However, who the client is and what her attributes are contribute just as much to the interviewing event, its characteristics, and its outcome (see Chapters 9 and 10 for further information).

Some characteristics that influence personal attributes—socioeconomic status or class, age, and sex—will be discussed briefly in this chapter. In Chapter 9 client attributes related to culture and ethnicity will be discussed. Taken together these five factors of contemporary social life are strong determinants of personality, of life-style, and of the type of problems encountered in living. There is an old and currently vigorous debate concerning which of these attributes are related to cause and which are related to effect; there is also debate about what social programs are best for equalizing opportunities (Auletta 1983; Keniston 1977; Thurow 1981). Such questions cannot be explored in detail here; however, a general statement can be made that conditions associated with varying status in society are interrelated and rarely experienced in a vacuum.

Social class and interviewing

Social class, or socioeconomic status, refers to a composite of income level, occupational type and level, educational attainment, and quality of housing and neighborhood. As with most studies of interviewing processes the available research comes from studies of psychotherapy. These studies can be construed as partially applicable to problem-solving processes, although the exact level of applicability is not well conceptualized.

Summarizing psychotherapy research, the authoritative review of Parloff, Waskow, and Wolfe (1978, pp. 258-259) states that:

> *Most studies dealing with the social class of patients have reported that lower-class individuals are less likely than those in the middle or upper classes to be accepted for treatment, are less likely to be assigned to intensive therapy, and are more likely to drop out of therapy early. For those who remain in treatment, however, there does not seem to be much evidence of differences in outcome.*

HYPOTHESES ABOUT INTERVIEWING CLIENTS
OF LOWER SOCIOECONOMIC STATUS

It is widely believed that middle- and upper-class practitioners prefer to interview clients of their own social class. To the extent that this observation is true, interviewers will exhibit a negative bias toward lower-class clients that can be expected to produce a negative reaction. It has been suggested that better outcomes may result for lower-class people if brief treatment methods are used. However, positive results from brief treatment have also been reported for middle-class clients. It is unclear whether the success reported with brief treatment is a function of time or not. Perhaps the most valid comment about these findings is that all clients, regardless of social class, may do better with treatment that is structured rather than passive and discursive (Butcher and Koss 1978; Reid and Shyne 1968).

Numerous findings have suggested that a client's educational level is a factor in achieving good outcomes in psychotherapy, particularly in discursive therapy. It is unwise, however, to draw strong conclusions from these somewhat uncertain research findings, because of the wide individual differences that exist from patient to patient and the large number of variables that might account for different outcomes.

Studies of lower-class patients in psychotherapy often mention that improved chances for good outcomes result from some form of "role induction," which means teaching lower-class patients how therapy is conducted and what to expect from it. Whatever hunches are made about lower-class attitudes and behaviors toward psychotherapy and interviewing, some generally applicable practices can be recommended. Adapting general interviewing guidelines for use with lower-class clients, it appears that effective interviewer behavior will include animated facial expressions and voice tones, a high quantity of verbal output, direct face-to-face contact, friendliness, and spontaneous behavior showing that the interviewer is at ease and self-confident.

Middle-class and upper-class interviewers are often reported to be struck by a certain lack of "psychological mindedness" in lower-class clients (Pope 1979). If this is true, it might be explained by the absence of relevant educational and socialization opportunities. Furthermore, many lower-class people have an occupational status requiring attention to tasks rather than to the fostering of flexibility and autonomy, which are more characteristic of upper-class work experience (Kohn and Schooler 1982). Attention must also be paid to a situational determinant of lower-class life: oppressive and distressful living conditions, the effects of which must be dealt with. The interviewer may be perceived as a representative of a class of people responsible for the inequality and unfairness of the interviewee's circumstances, which might result in client envy and resentment.

Actual circumstances may also be important in explaining lower-class clients' reluctance to engage in the helping process. Clients may need to travel a long distance from home to get to the agency, they may be exhausted after an arduous day's work, or they may need to conduct household and family business in the evening. Many blue and white collar workers are not free to take time off without loss of needed income. These stressful circumstances could well have a negative impact on effective interviewing.

However, other influences may serve to reduce the social distance between interview participants of different classes. Of importance here is the leveling effect of the media, especially television. The media represent human service professionals as benign, interested, and tolerant. Therefore many lower-class clients are prepared by the media, as well as by other socializing experiences, to react positively in helping interviews.

ATTRACTIVENESS

Often interviewers find impoverished people unattractive and have feelings of guilt, pity, and even curiosity about them. Sometimes interviewers may feel an unaccountable anger toward poor people, believing that their poverty is their own fault and that they would not be impoverished if they only "worked harder." Practitioners should be careful about showing such attitudes. The best way to get prejudice of this type under control is to learn more about the structural basis for poverty, which is rarely if ever caused only by personal deficiency.

Nevertheless, no matter how sensitive an interviewer is about social problems, some client characteristics may induce strong dislike. A practitioner does not have to like clients to help them. Practitioners must undertake interventions that are available and that have a good record of effectiveness. It is neither necessary nor advisable to make people over unless they want that. Even if a client is willing to undergo large amounts of change, methods for such achievements do not exist.

GENERAL COMMENT

There is no consensus or firm empirical knowledge to help interviewers construct specific techniques for interviewing people of lower socioeconomic status. There are, however, indications that interviewers may be uncomfortable with types of clients whose experiences and lifestyles are different from their own. Lower-class clients have unique experiences relating to what they do for a living, where and how they live, what they value, and how they feel about those who have more or different advantages. Problems to be addressed in interviews should relate to the adversity a client experiences and how that experience is interpreted. Therefore technique in patterns of discourse is not as important as is sensitivity to problems as perceived by clients.

Age and interviewing
OLDER PEOPLE AND INTERVIEWING
CLIENT CHARACTERISTICS

The client's age shapes the interview, not because of a particular number of years but because of personal attributes and public reaction to older adults. A brief profile of older people reveals that they are a diverse group (Neugarten 1981). The proportion of older people to younger people is rising because of lower birthrates and increased longevity. Improvements in health care and social supports of many kinds have resulted in a population of older people who are well, vigorous, productive, and capable. Because of the new large size of the population, however, the numbers who are ill and disabled have also increased. In fact, the increasing investment in gerontology research suggests that there may not be inevitable decline from an "aging process." Rather, many diseases are treatable now, and their number will increase in the future as more knowledge becomes available (Franklin 1983).

Neugarten (1981), reviewing the economic status of older men, reports that there are as many who have incomes over $20,000 per year as there are those who live below the poverty line. Women live longer than men and are poorer. Very old widowed and never-married women are an extremely disadvantaged group. Older people who have lived under unequal conditions because of minority ethnic status acquire a new set of problems with age.

> *Old age itself does not define a problem group in today's society. Some groups of older people are economically and socially needy; other groups are not. On most socioeconomic measures, it is a minority who are severely disadvantaged. These are, mainly, the very old who, compared to persons born later, have been disadvantaged with regard to education, occupational skills, pension systems, and medical care earlier in their lives* (Neugarten 1981, p. 40).

Not only are older people physically well for the most part, but they are also psychologically well and socially active. Nevertheless, negative stereotypes are strongly entrenched and may interfere with interviewing. If practitioners have these stereotypes, they do not perceive what is actually said or done by older clients but what is imagined. Stereotypes act as "noise" that obliterates perception and meaning. Negative stereotypes may be reinforced by the fact that human services workers are likely to see older clients who are the most needy and who have many troubles. Attributing problems to "old age" is easier than dealing with the real causes: poverty, discrimination, poor education, and illness.

The present interest in and study of social policies affecting older people is the result of the increase in the older population, and will become even more critical as the Baby Boom generation ages. More and more human services interviewers will find themselves interacting with older people as the diverse individuals they are. The most important trap to avoid is classifying clients by chronological age rather than according to social class, education, experience, competence, and individuality.

INTERVIEWING FEATURES

For effectively interviewing older people and putting aside ageist stereotypes, the same practices outlined earlier in Chapters 3 through 7 are applicable. An interviewer should approach an older person in exactly the same way he would approach any other adult. Practitioners take account of illness, disability, educational level, and economic level when interviewing a younger adult, and they should do the same when interviewing an older adult.

However, interviewers need to make adaptations to special circumstances when particular group characteristics are evident. Butler (1975, pp. 405-422) outlines characteristics to be taken into consideration when interviewing older people:

Sense of time

For the elderly the future is shortened. The time for planning and taking action is *now,* the present. An interviewer who is intolerant of the appropriateness and value of a present focus does the older person a disservice.

Sense of the life cycle

Older people are very experienced—they know a lot. They should never be condescended to. They have a temporal perspective that is wider and more complex than that of younger people.

Tendency toward life review

Older people do a good deal of thinking back on their lives in an attempt to get events and processes in explainable order. They vocally "write their memoirs," as it were. This is not a symptom nor is it aimless mind wandering. If anything it is positive—an expression of wisdom.

Reparation and resolution

As Butler puts it (p. 414):

> *Older people are constantly writing and rewriting the scenarios of their lives . . . The old are not served by dismissing the reality of human greed and cruelty in their lives or the variegated fabric of their past. This attitude denigrates their humanness. They often make reparations to resolve their sense*

*of guilt and are more inclined to expiatory behavior than other
age groups.*

Attachment to the familiar

Many older people are attached to familiar objects that symbolize
meaningful people and experiences. Young interviewers may be put off by
this kind of attachment, which they do not share — yet.

Conservatism

The conservatism of old age arises partly from attachment to the familiar and a sense of obligation to pass on that which is deemed worthy. We
live in an age in which tradition is suspect and is sometimes viewed as
reactionary and oppressive. However, maintaining selected traditions can
supply necessary stability in many circumstances.

Desire to leave a legacy

Many older people actively desire to leave something of value behind — objects, traditions, or some marker of their time on earth.

Transmission of power

Deciding when to transfer power to younger people is often a concern
for the older person. A struggle by the younger to take over may also be
involved.

Sense of fulfillment

Sometimes, if not deprived by circumstances, older people acquire a
serenity that comes from satisfaction in life.

Growth

If not deprived by illness, poverty, or the cruelty of others, older
people retain the capacity for continued curiosity, growth, adventure, and
new starts.

Crises

Some crises of old age — threat, loss, and challenge — are similar to
those of any other time. An older adult's emotional reactions, defenses,
and coping behaviors are the same as a younger person's would be.

Identity

Butler, who is perhaps the American guru on this subject, states (1975,
p. 418):

> *The young and middle generations must examine and
> resolve their conflicted feelings toward old age and ultimately
> toward themselves as they grow older. The old must assert them-
> selves in a self-respecting and effective manner. Perhaps even a
> new name is in order. All our terms for old age conjure up
> negative images — some more, some less. Few people are willing
> to be identified as 'aged,' 'aging,' 'elderly,' 'retired,' 'oldtimer,'
> 'gramps,' or even 'old' itself. 'Senior citizen' or 'golden ager' are*

sugary euphemisms. 'Old fogy,' 'old biddy,' 'old gal,' 'crock,' and
'geezer' are putdowns. We can either rehabilitate the least objec-
tionable of these names (perhaps 'elderly' and 'old') to a new
and respected status, or we can come up with a new name
altogether.

TECHNIQUE

There are no special techniques needed for interviewing old people. They have the characteristics that arise from problems with finances, housing, physical health, mental health, work, and family and peer relationships. The focus of interviewing should be on problem-solving processes that relate to their particular problems. The age factor may either minimally or substantially color the way they respond, but their problems will rarely be about "age" alone. They will be about the social or physical conditions that affect them adversely.

CHILDREN AND INTERVIEWING

Most work done by human services professionals with and on behalf of children is not psychotherapy; it is problem-solving work. This means provision of resources and social skills that may sometimes be deficient or imperfect to reduce a problem or enhance the child's opportunities to obtain and use education, form personal relationships, and develop satisfactory attitudes toward self and the world. Usually family members will be the focus of attention in problem-solving efforts, and the involvement of the child will be indirect or auxiliary. Sometimes interviews will give major attention to the child.

Interviewing children, whether as a supplement to interviewing a parent or as a major act of intervention, does not mean that the interviewer has to be a child development expert. The interviewer will benefit from the experience of talking with children and from systematic study of child development as well.

CHILDREN'S LANGUAGE

Although it has not been established with certainty, many linguists and child development scholars believe there are inborn mechanisms that underpin language development. Whether or not this is so, language in children is learned and is the result of experience, teaching, and a wide variety of socialization experiences. Practitioners who interview young children may note that there seems to be a typical and regular development in the way children speak as they mature. Baby talk is "rule-governed" (Aitchison 1978, pp. 160-274). Such children's constructions as "no play that" or "that no mummy" are observed constructions that seem to obey regular speech development. Some mispronunciations, such as "gud" for "duck", occur with regularity. Baby talk or child talk reflects the state of development of the whole speech-making apparatus. Baby talk is not error and should not be thought of as "cute." Most children resent an adult's use of baby talk. The child perceives adult speech constructions accurately even though his speech apparatus cannot reproduce them. From this understanding comes a good rule to follow in interviewing children: Do not talk baby talk and do not mimic the child's inexperienced mode of speech. Speak clearly and in a normal adult style.

Children ordinarily have limited vocabularies and limited experience. Interviewers need to keep their language straightforward and restricted to the child's area of experience. There are no subjects that are off limits unless they are outside the child's experience. It would, for example, ordinarily be silly to discuss the philosophy of science with a child. However, the practitioner can discuss death, sadness, sex, hurt, loss, or fear when they are relevant. If a child has experienced the death of a parent, the facts and feelings can be discussed. The same is true for other painful, frightening, or sad experiences.

However, the adult interviewer has to be prepared to discuss trouble without the circumlocutions that often pervade adult speech. For example:

A 7-year-old client's mother died. The interviewer explained that the mother had been sick for a long time. The child knew that and asked what had happened to his mother after she died. The practitioner said that she was taken away and put in a cemetery. "What happened to her there?" asked the child. The interviewer had learned not to think about such things and found himself without a vocabulary with which to respond. Collecting himself, he said that in the cemetery the mother was in a casket, or large box, and was put in the ground. Next, of course, the child wanted to know if she could breathe. "Well, no, she has stopped breathing," said the interviewer. "Then what happened to her" asked the child. The interviewer responded, "She turned to earth."

"What kind of earth?"

"Dust."

"Dust?? . . . Like the dust under my bed?"

"It's different. Your mother's dust stays in the cemetery."

ADAPTING THE BASIC INTERVIEWING TECHNIQUES (see also Chapter 5)

Starting up

The starting-up and familiarizing phases with children often require substantial time. However, care should be taken to get on with the work as soon as possible. The child knows she is not present just to fool around and that she has been brought or sent for some (possibly unpleasant) purpose. Overextending the familiarizing phase only makes the child anxious rather than putting her at ease.

The kinds of activities that an interviewer can introduce to help the child get started are showing her around the interviewing room or office and explaining where the toilet is. With a child who is overactive or perhaps destructive, it is advisable if possible to have an interviewing room without expensive equipment or gadgets; these distract attention, possibly get broken, and in any case make the interviewer forever watchful.

The interviewer should explain, using appropriate vocabulary, the kind of work that is going to be done. The practitioner should not say, "I am here to help you with anything you are interested in." She should say, "I am here to help you get a passing mark in arithmetic," or "I am going to help you get moved in with a family where you will be taken care of."

The practitioner can play with a child in the familiarizing mode but just to get started. Play therapy ordinarily refers to sets of techniques for psychotherapeutic purposes. Bijou (1976, pp. 26-27) identifies six different theories to explain why children play: instincts, drives, emotional states, mental activity, preparation for the future, and fun. It has been stated that play is whatever children do that is not an essential occupation such as being in school, sleeping, or eating. Whatever play is thought to be, it is a good icebreaker in problem-solving interviews and helps them get started. From play the practitioner often gets interesting and useful insights about what a child thinks. If there is a simple doll family in the room, children often enact little plays about their own families and thereby give a lot of information.

One of the more difficult interviewing interactions with a child is the circumstance where he does not want to be there, does not want to participate, and is suspicious. There is no quick and easy "fix" for this circumstance. The best procedure is to be straight and truthful with the child about why he is there, what the interview is for, and what will be done. Time and experience will subsequently reveal the degree to which the child has become a willing participant.

Introducing and carrying out interventions

The procedures suggested for first-phase interviewing with adults (see Chapter 5) are equally appropriate for children, provided that factors of limited experience and vocabulary are taken into account. However, when it comes to introducing interventions, some children are prototypal involuntary clients. Many children can be influenced and won over to a cooperative enterprise in their own interests, but others remain ambivalent or unwilling. Rarely do children seek professional help on their own; there is almost always a problem that is mandated by others to some degree.

Because of law, custom, and developmental state, children's autonomy is circumscribed. Parents and the state are held responsible for the child's protection, nurture, education, discipline, control, and reform as is deemed necessary (Rosenheim 1964). Features of the relationship between child and state vary depending on historical era and circumstances, but the essential relationship holds. Limits on a child's autonomy are deeply entrenched in social norms and are consequently present in the context of human services interventions. Because an interview is entirely bound by its context, the tendency is to "do to" or "do for" the child in the interview. However, there is credible evidence in research and in practice experience that children are capable of identifying problems, making decisions about activities that they want to undertake, and making choices that are relevant. As with adults, children's cooperation and performance are greatly improved when their choices and self-motivation are respected (Bush 1982; Reid et al. 1980). For these reasons it is advisable when interviewing children to use techniques (see Chapter 5) that emphasize client participation.

However, the status of the child as a minor and the weight of societal requirements necessitate a balance between mandated demands and the choices of the child if these two areas diverge. The preferred avenue is to let the child know what is required, why it is required, and what consequences will probably follow if problems are ignored. The practitioner should also seriously undertake to either merge the child's choice with the mandate or to work with the child in both areas.

All the explorations of a problem and the proposal of interventions can be discussed with children in interviews, taking into account their vocabulary level and experience.

FACILITATING COMMUNICATION WITH CHILDREN

Fear, suspicion, or hostility will make a child "clam up." Interest will help and boredom will hinder communication. The child will want to talk if there is an urgent wish to solve a problem. Embarrassment will make the child avoid discussion. The child must be able to see that the interview is relevant to her problems and that the interviewer can do something about them. The child may weigh the costs of communicating against the costs of keeping quiet. Children are so used to being dominated that many of them expect the worst from adult involvement and learn that silence is golden.

An adult may have learned social skills that allow him to talk without saying anything and still keep the expected interaction going. Many children, however, are not well versed in such dissembling; they simply do not talk at all. It is important to avoid a position of scolding or criticizing the child. Very often this is what he has learned to expect from adults in authority. The child may attempt to turn off the interviewer by pretending, keeping quiet, or suddenly needing to go to the bathroom. The child will probably know that someone has complained about him, so that fact can be put forthrightly on the table. The interviewer should state what he has heard from others about the child but he should state that he also wants to know how the child feels.

Confidentiality

Children sometimes want to extract a promise of confidentiality from an interviewer; that is, they want to know that what goes on will not be told to parents, teachers, police officers, or other authority figures. This promise can almost never be made because it can almost never be kept. Parents can and sometimes will exert pressure to find out information from an interviewer. They may reason that, after all, the child is theirs, and they may be paying the bill or suffering adverse consequences because of the child's behavior. The interviewer may need to use information obtained from a child to discuss problem matters with either parents or authorities.

The difficulty about communicating what one person says to another works both ways. A child may inquire or demand to know what someone else has said, perhaps in confidence. It is important for the interviewer to deal with these situations in a way that inspires confidence and trust. The interviewer should try to be courageous about confronting any conflicts of loyalty that come up. Family interviews or conferences with authorities can minimize trouble. Setting up ground rules about confidentiality—about what may or may not be communicated—will also help, provided that the child and family understand the rules and accept them.

Anger

Adults usually express angry feelings verbally, through facial expressions, or through gestures. However, children will sometimes act on their anger.

Some sensible rules for dealing with an aggressive child in an interview are:

1. Decide ahead of time how much aggressiveness will be allowed— what are the acceptable limits.
2. Tell the child what the rules are.
3. Enforce the rules strictly and fairly. For example, a child may be permitted to throw paint at the walls but not at the interviewer. The

child may kick the wall but not the interviewer. The child may run around and shout in the room but not in the corridor.

4. Enforcement must never involve punishment. Instead the child should, for example, be held on the practitioner's lap and comforted. The correct technique is to resist the behavior but not to overpower the child. The only force that should be permitted is that which originates in personality, command, and firmness of voice. Communication should convey that the practitioner will not let the child hurt herself or any other people. The angry child is a scared child who wants and needs adult protection.

The stubbornly silent child seems to frustrate interviewers unduly. Such a child feels threatened. As mentioned earlier, an adult client in this position often knows how to keep the interviewer at arm's length by irrelevant discussion and may even win favor by talking about the interviewer's interests. The child, unless verbally sophisticated, will just sit there in stony silence. The practitioner needs to be patient and should make sure that the child is clear about the practitioner's intentions, interests, ways of working, and purposes. Interviewers should not be afraid of talking to such a child and should not be insulted if the child keeps quiet. It is all right to take the child on a recreational trip or play a game with him, if he is interested in these activities. However, they may really obscure the issue, which is that the child is afraid.

There is another point to be made about the case of the nonverbal child, which is that some children are just not big talkers. Some children are laconic by nature. If this is true, the interviewer should do most of the talking or find some other way to deal with the problem, such as working with parents, teachers, or child care personnel.

•　•　•

Readers interested in further study may wish to consult Greenspan (1981) and Rich (1968), who deal specifically with the topic of interviewing children.

TEENAGERS AND INTERVIEWING

Young people in our society

> are segregated from adults by the economic and educational institutions created by adults. They are deprived of psychic support from persons of other ages, a psychic support that once came from the family. They are subordinate and powerless in relation to adults, and are outsiders to the dominant social institutions. Yet they have money, they have access to a wide

range of communications media, and control of some, and they are relatively large in number (Coleman 1974, p. 123).

Many interviewers feel uneasy about interviewing adolescents because the rules must be interpreted flexibly. Some adult interviewers have a natural talent for working with teenagers, and some do not. Youthful clients may show many of the same interview behaviors—stubborn silence, fear, and suspicion—as younger children do, and for the same reasons. On the other hand, the adolescent feels pressure to behave independently and may feel awkward and uncertain in fulfilling these expectations.

The adolescent youth differs substantially from the child in an interview because of more extensive experience in interacting with adults. Wanting help from and still depending on adults, young people nevertheless resent authority and are capable of exceedingly acute and hostile interpretations of adult behavior. In interviewing a teenager, the practitioner should try to hold on firmly to her adult role, rights, and responsibilities without assuming a one-up attitude of superiority or righteousness. Full credence has to be given to the teenager's abilities, perceptions, and rights to be different and independent.

Many helping interviews with teens uncover problems resulting from incomplete socialization and failure to conform (see Chapter 5 for illustration). Often such interviews take on an adversarial atmosphere even when both interviewer and client would prefer a cooperative venture. Many young people want adult help but will nevertheless fight tooth and nail if their independence is compromised. One of the keys to productive interviewing with teenagers is getting agreement on focus. Another key is for the interviewer to have a genuine appreciation that the teenager is an able young person. In general the outline of interviewing techniques from Chapter 5 can be used as a framework as long as the special features of youth experience are kept in mind. The actual process of communication with adolescents is not different from the processes normally used in professional interviewing of adults. The content, however, is often of a special nature because the life experience of youth is much different from that of older people.

The adolescent years can be understood as the time of transition from childhood to adulthood. This transition deals with two broad classes of objectives; *self-centered* and *other-centered* objectives. Self-centered objectives include the acquisition of skills necessary for economic independence and occupational opportunities and the development of capabilities for management of one's own affairs. In addition, self-centered objectives include the development of capabilities to effectively use the goods and culture of the society and learning to concentrate intensely on necessary activities. Beyond these self-centered objectives, the transition to adulthood must address other-centered objectives, such as the acquisition of skills in dealing with people who differ from the adolescent in social class, subculture, or age. Other tasks in this category are taking care of others who are dependent and engaging in interdependent activities directed at collective goals (Coleman 1974, pp. 1-7).

Young people come into conflict with the adult world and with adult authorities when they develop difficulties in using the educational and socialization institutions to achieve good performance in these transitional tasks. Consequently delinquency, acting out, violence, and aggression present dilemmas to families, schools, treatment organizations, and the justice system (Feinstein and Giovacchini 1979, p. 421). In the present era of changing perception about women's roles, teen women are appearing with new types of problems, especially those involving stress about life objectives and the handling of sexuality and motherhood (Bassoff and Ortiz 1984). Interviewing of young people is not in itself specialized. What is necessary, however, is knowledge of the experiences that are unique to teenagers and their stage of life in our present society.

Sex: possible effects on interviewing

Ideas about interviewing and research on the subject have largely evolved without attention to sex differences between interviewer and interviewee. There is scant information on differences in patterns of interviewing discourse between men and women and how these patterns might be changed. Although there is little knowledge to differentiate speech and communication characteristics between the sexes, an extensive body of writing has emerged recently about the particular social context and problems of women (Unger and Denmark 1975). This literature and the experience it reflects suggest that many problems are perceived differently by women than by men. Techniques cannot be differentiated at present, but attitudes, priorities, and meanings can be.

Practice theories in the helping professions depend on underlying theories of human behavior in the social environment. In current professional circles human behavior theories are more prevalent than social environment theories. The latter theories are less influential in day-to-day direct services practice and tend to be of interest primarily for policy and program development. The psychological theories that inform direct practice largely ignore differentiations in behavior according to sex distinctions, or else they adopt, often without examination, the sexist evaluations of traditional societies and freudian psychology (Gould 1984). This situation is changing, but it will take time to reexamine the whole body of literature.

Berlin (1976, p. 492) states:

> *Almost every existing sociopolitical establishment — the church, government, health care and educational systems, and the media — has contributed to the systematic undermining of women's capabilities, opportunities, and self-perceptions. The expectations of society have worked on women methodically, influencing them to become dependent, highly emotional, indecisive, and self-effacing. By promoting unhealthy behaviors in them, society limits the roles that women can assume, devalues what they are, and then punishes them if they fail to take charge of their lives and affairs where the circumstances so demand.*

The validity of the preceding quotation is becoming more widely accepted. In recognition of these concerns some general directions, adopted from Berlin, emerge as guidelines in constructing the content of interviews with women:

1. Interviewers can help women clients to specifically identify their strengths, frustrations, needs, and satisfactions. Women need to learn to distinguish between their own authentic perceptions and perceptions that have been imposed on them by husbands, children, parents, and others. For example, when interviewing to explore problems and develop an assesment, the following questions can be asked:

What did you do when your child got sick?

What kind of response did you get from your boss when you made that suggestion?

Why do you think he laughed at you — because you were silly? or because you were right?

Why wouldn't you be disgusted if you have nothing more interesting to do?

Why not go back to school?

2. Interviewers can choose questions that direct women to realize they can achieve influence and personal freedom. For example:

What else could you do?

What made you think (or decide) that?

If you could choose, what would you want?

3. Women can be guided in how to generate alternative problem-solving means. For example, the practitioner might ask:

If you did not feel so limited, what would you like to do, to have, or to be?

If you were not so scared, what would you like?

What would happen if you chose that?

Would it really happen?

What could you do if the worst happened?

What else can you think of to do, even if it seems far out?

4. A woman often needs an interviewer to point out that she can ask for, explain, and if necessary demand what she needs instead of depending on innuendo or deviousness. In other words she can become an advocate for herself.

5. The interviewer can legitimate the work a woman wants to do to solve a problem by accepting the problem as the client perceives it.

Summary

Particular age groups raise issues for consideration in adapting interview techniques. Clients who are old are too often victimized by unjust stereotypes. Interviewing children requires sensitivity to factors such as a child's restricted vocabularies, fear of adult domination, and lack of life experience. Teenagers present problems generated by their developmental need to separate from the society of adults and children, respond to a special adolescent subculture, and learn skills for managing adult responsibilities.

People of low socioeconomic status are sometimes perceived as difficult to interview. However, it could well be that their problems are not sufficiently understood.

Women, as a group, raise special interviewing issues. It seems highly advisable when interviewing women to be especially sensitive in helping them to recognize and legitimate their independent identity and appropriate autonomy.

There are no specialized technologies for interviewing the groups discussed in this chapter. What seems to be needed more than special patterns of discourse is a perspective on people and problems, one which takes into account societal expectations, developmental stages, and explicit attention to problems in terms of the client's own experiences.

REFERENCES

Aitchison, Jean. *Linguistics.* New York: David McKay & Co., 1978.

Auletta, Ken. *The Underclass.* New York: Vintage Books, 1983.

Bassoff, Betty Z., and Ortiz, Elizabeth Thompson. "Teen women: Disparity Between Cognitive Values and Anticipated Life Events." *Child Welfare* 63 (March-April 1984):125-138.

Berlin, Sharon. "Better Work with Women Clients." *Social Work* 21 (November 1976):492-497.

Bijou, Sidney W. *Child Development.* Englewood Cliffs, N.J.: Prentice-Hall, 1976.

Bush, Malcolm, and Gordon, Andrew G. "The Case for Involving Children in Child Welfare Decisions." *Social Work* 27 (July 1982):309-314.

Butcher, James N., and Koss, Mary P. "Research on Brief and Crisis-Oriented Psychotherapies." In *Handbook of Psychotherapy and Behavior Change: An Empirical Analysis,* edited by Sol L. Garfield and Allen E. Bergin, pp. 725-768. New York: John Wiley & Sons, 1978.

Butler, Robert N. *Why Survive? Being Old in America.* New York: Harper & Row, 1975.

Butler, Robert N., and Lewis, Myrna I. *Acting and Mental Health.* St. Louis: The C.V. Mosby Company, 1982.

Coleman, James S. *Youth: Transition to Adulthood. Report of the Panel on Youth of the President's Science Advisory Committee.* Chicago: The University of Chicago Press, 1974.

Feinstein, Sherman C., and Giovacchini, Peter. *Adolescent Psychiatry.* Chicago: University of Chicago Press, 1979.

Franklin, Jon. "Grand Experiment Ends, and Ageless Quest Moves On." Chicago Tribune, June 2, 1983, section 4, p. 1.

Gould, Ketayun H. "Original Work of Freud on Women: Social Work References." *Social Casework* 65 (February 1984):94-101.

Greenspan, Stanley I. *The Clinical Interview of the Child.* New York: McGraw-Hill Book Co., 1981.

Keniston, Kenneth. *All Our Children: The American Family Under Pressure.* New York: Harcourt Brace Jovanovich, 1977.

Kohn, Melvin L., and Schooler, Carmi. "Job Conditions and Personality: A Longitudinal Assessment of Their Reciprocal Effects." *American Journal of Sociology* 87 (May 1982):1257-1286.

Neugarten, Bernice. "Older People: A Profile." In *Age or Need? Public Policies for Older People,* edited by Bernice L. Newgarten. Beverly Hills: Sage Publications, 1981.

Parloff, Morris B.; Waskow, Irene E.; and Wolfe, Barry E. "Research on Therapist Variables in Relation to Process and Outcome." In *Handbook of Psychotherapy and Behavior Change: An Empirical Analysis,* edited by Sol L. Garfield and Allen E. Bergin, pp. 233-282. New York: John Wiley & Sons, 1978.

Pope, Benjamin. *The Mental Health Interview: Research and Application.* New York: Pergamon Press, 1979.

Reid, William J.; Epstein, Laura; Brown, Lester B.; Tolson, Eleanor; and Rooney, Ronald H. "Task-Centered School Social Work." *Social Work in Education* 2 (January 1980):7-24.

Reid, William J., and Shyne, Ann. *Brief and Extended Casework.* New York: Columbia University Press, 1968.

Rich, John. *Interviewing Children and Adolescents.* New York: St. Martin's Press, 1968.

Rosenheim, Margaret K. "The Child and the Law." In *Child Development and Social Policy: Review of Child Development Research,* edited by Bettye M. Caldwell and Henry N. Ricciuti, vol. 1, pp. 509-556. Chicago: University of Chicago Press, 1964.

Thurow, Lester C. *The Zero Sum Society.* New York: Penguin Books, 1981.

Unger, Rhoda K., and Denmark, Florence L., eds. *Woman: Dependent or Independent Variable.* New York: Psychological Dimensions, Inc., 1975.

CHAPTER 9

Culture and ethnicity

The cultural and ethnic backgrounds of clients and practitioners influence how they perceive the interview and what they do.

Definition of culture

Culture was originally an anthropological term, but it has been widely adopted for use in the general vocabulary and in such disciplines as the humanities, biological sciences, and social sciences. Culture consists of the ideas, customs, values, and attitudes shared by a group and transmitted from generation to generation through learning and socialization. Language, other symbolic media, and experience are the chief agents of culture transmission.

Definition of ethnicity

Ethnicity refers to a quality or qualities particular to an ethnic group within a larger society. An *ethnic group* is a minority of people whose culture is different from that of the majority. Members of an ethnic group are bound together by ties of race, nationality, and culture. *Ethnocentrism* is the belief that one's own group has a mode of living, values, and patterns of adaptation that are superior. Ethnocentrism usually contains a generalized contempt for members of other groups and may manifest itself in attitudes of superiority or hostility. Violence, discrimination, proselytizing, and verbal aggression are means by which ethnocentrism may be expressed (*New Columbia Encyclopedia* 1975, p. 898). *Racism* is a term used to identify ethnocentrism that has become embedded in the social and political structure of the community in such a way that victimized groups are forced to endure systematic discrimination and inequality.

Equal opportunity: goal and reality

The United States, like other large nations, is a multicultural society. At different historical periods some sectors of the population, identified by role, culture, and ethnic attributes, have secured a lesser share of success in society. One view—some would say myth—asserts that inequality is a product of deficits in personal effort and ability. Another view ascribes lack of success to inequality of opportunity. Still another view attributes inequality to inherent structural problems of unequal income distribution.

In contemporary America the ethnic, cultural, and racial groups that appear most unequal in social and economic opportunities are most affected by ethnocentrism and racism and by poverty. Large numbers in such groups are locked out of full participation in the economic opportunity structure: blacks, Native American Indians, Hispanics, and Asians. Similar problems are experienced by other groups such as women, homosexuals, and old people.

Hispanics are the fastest-growing ethnic group in this country at present. The mean age of immigrants and black people is decreasing, while the mean age of the white population is increasing. This disparity will affect the way that social resources are distributed in the future. The largest concentrations of ethnic populations are located near their points of entry into the United States: blacks in the South, Puerto Ricans in the urban Northeast, Mexican-Americans in the Southwest, Cubans in Florida, and Asian-Americans on the West Coast (McAdoo 1982). At a time when demand for their services is shrinking, young people are entering the labor market at a rate six times that of the previous generation. Although education is considered to be the basic prerequisite for equal opportunity, the higher education received today by minority youth is mostly concentrated in two-year community colleges. This education does not steer young people into the job markets of the future and tends to prepare them for fields that are already crowded.

The kinds of help that are most needed by minority groups are useful education of high quality, guidance toward areas of employment that are growing, and steering away from employment fields that are stagnant or faltering. Members of minority groups might also benefit from support services designed to mitigate anxieties, depressions, and distress caused by specific traumas that they must deal with. Analysis of services for today's new ethnic populations suggests that priority needs are for employment, housing, translation and language services, self-help minority-run support services, and culturally relevant mental health services.

Various cultures have different ways of perceiving emotional distress and therapy. For instance, Zen Buddhism contains a system of therapeutic thought that is probably more recognizable and helpful to many Asians than therapy based on the American version of freudianism. A group of black psychiatrists take the position that "Freudian theory . . . holds the fallacious assumption that such theory and psychological requisites are relevant to all groups of people, regardless of ethnic or cultural differences" (Chunn, Dunston, and Ross-Sheriff 1983). These psychiatrists doubt the relevance of such approaches to the needs of black patients, noting the tendency to "blame the patient when the freudian treatment approach fails rather than question the validity of the treatment approach, the therapist's competence . . . and acceptance of black patients" (p. xvii).

There is obviously still a great deal to be done in conceptualizing new ways to help ethnic populations deal with the psychic pain and stress inherent in their situation. The available information strongly indicates that major concerns include development of resources and acquisition of skills for managing existing problems.

Interviewing issues

A number of problems exist for a human services professional interviewing a client who belongs to a minority group. One possible problem is a lack of familiarity with general characteristics of the group as a whole. To acquire necessary sociological information takes experience and special study. To assist in this the *Harvard Encyclopedia of American Ethnic Groups* was published in 1980. This 1,076-page volume attempts, with its 106 entries, to summarize ethnic characteristics in terms of 45 factors, examples of which include origin, economic life, and social structure. From a practical standpoint interviewers would be well-advised to consult a reliable expert for interpretive discussion of the features that best explain the culture and life-styles of a particular group. It is also advisable to know about subgroups within an ethnic group to understand group attitudes about age, gender, and internal socioeconomic structures.

Although general characteristics are necessary to know, by themselves they could lead to useless stereotypes. The practitioner needs to keep in mind not only the widely applicable values, attitudes, and characteristics of the group but also the way an individual thinks, feels, behaves, and perceives himself, his own ethnicity, and the wider society. Some personal characteristics of the individual can be expected to match group characteristics, but other characteristics will differ. Furthermore, most clients will also have reactions to becoming acculturated to American ways, which makes the situation more complex.

A number of dimensions in ethnic social and private life may be distinctive. Clients who are part of a minority may react uniquely during an interview to such concerns as illness, helping professionals from the dominant culture, age, gender, cleanliness, housekeeping and home decoration, food, clothing and adornment, extended family connections, child rearing and roles of parents and children, entertainment, philosophies of life and religion, competition, conflict, and intrusion. People from the Far East, Africa, or Pacific Islands will differ substantially from Westerners in the way they view the psychology of the inner person. The freudianization of America and Europe is weak to nonexistent in areas of the world where interpersonal relations are differently conceptualized and lived out. Eastern philosophies have attracted a few Americans and Europeans; at the same time freudianism has attracted elite intellectuals in other countries, but not to the same degree. It must be kept in mind that freudianism is differently conceived, interpreted, and applied in many parts of the world. The interviewer's conceptions about personal relationships and reactions may not be well adapted to the needs of clients from a different culture.

In the United States, where almost everyone is either an immigrant or comes from a family descended from immigrants, ethnic diversity and cultural pluralism are the norm. The length of time since immigration and the degree of separateness that has been experienced greatly affect sensitive client issues. Concern at present is directed not so much toward American people who have long been acculturated but toward recent arrivals whose cultural divergence is a current source of difficulty. An exception to this rule is the case of American Indians, who have always lived in America but whose history as a defeated people has kept alive important issues of rights and status. Another exception is that of American blacks who, despite a long history of living in the United States, have been victims of systematic segregation and are even now undergoing social and political struggles to achieve equality and status.

When interviewing persons from ethnic minority groups, the practitioner must adapt the general interviewing model (see Chapter 5) to take into account the client's relevant ethnic context, background, individual situation, and alternatives. The general interviewing model can be taken as a base. A number of adaptations are suggested below; however, available adaptation strategies are minimal. There is at present no firm research base from which to build a special intervention model or a particularized set of interviewing techniques for ethnic groups. The subject has only recently "come of age" as a field of practice in need of specification, and the problems of arriving at a consensus on what specific definitions should be are monumental (Chunn, Dunston, and Ross-Sheriff 1983). Adaptations should be made based on the client's interpretation of her ethnicity, culture, or race; on how that interpretation relates to the problem of concern; and on the available intervention resources. The specific features of adaptations have to be designed by agencies or settings to accommodate the particular client population because of the important differences among various groups. Expert consultation and familiarization with the literature will help.

SUGGESTIONS FOR ADAPTATIONS

In general, interviewing techniques with ethnic clients are loosely based on the framework that has already been described in Chapters 4 and 5. What should be different and how it should be different have not been addressed from a technical standpoint. There is an assumption adopted in this discussion that practitioners can begin by relying on regular communication processes to carry them through interactions with ethnic clients. Practitioners need to become acquainted with the life conditions of minority populations. The expectation is that increased understanding will give rise to insights and innovations in techniques (Devore and Schlesinger 1981). In the absence of specialized techniques it is necessary for the informed interviewer to make technical adaptations that seem appropriate to the client's ethnic group.

McAdoo (1982, p. 16) identifies five behavioral and situational similarities among those described as "people of color":

1. Close involvement with kin
2. Close relationships with extended family and friends
3. Widespread poverty
4. Conflicts in values with the larger and possibly discriminatory society in which the ethnic people live
5. Awareness of the dominant population's stereotyped perspective and disrespect

Some suggestions for adapting the familiarizing, first, and middle phases of an interview so that they are of more benefit to ethnic clients are discussed in the following section.

FAMILIARIZING

Interviewer statements and observational focus with ethnic clients should reflect the degree of formality and respectful demeanor that is characteristic of their particular culture. Clues to what is characteristic can be obtained from the client's manner of greeting, rate of signaling for turn taking, and manner of changing topics.

FIRST PHASE

With ethnic clients, information may have to be elicited more slowly and indirectly than usual. The degree of difference will depend on particular group characteristics. Roles should be explained as clearly as possible because of the expected gap between the client's expectation of services and the actual capability of the services. The amount of explanation will vary depending on how much information the client and his ethnic group have already. Some minority groups, such as blacks, already have a great deal of information and are not likely to differ from whites in the amount of explanation needed.

Asking for information about problems, personal characteristics, and social context will have to be adjusted to accommodate client attitudes about giving such personal information. Blacks can be expected to have a normative American attitude about these procedures; however, American Indians might consider such inquiries as hostile.

In general it is likely that ethnic clients will appreciate the practicality and concreteness of techniques for identifying and specifying problems. It is possible, however, that the concreteness of planning for priorities, goals, and contracts might counter the philosophy and preference of some groups (Devore and Schlesinger 1981, pp. 118-120).

MIDDLE PHASE: VARIATIONS IN PROBLEM DEFINITION AND
ACCEPTABLE SOLUTIONS

If American interviewers of middle- or upper-class origin confront their ethnic clients by attributing their interpersonal problems to a psychological or pathological cause, they may run into difficulty in the middle phase. American blacks can be expected to react to these discussion areas like other Americans, taking into account each individual's age, sex, and social class. However, foreign people and American Indians may be offended because they operate from a quite different mind-set.

People who do not buy into American value positions about the preponderant influence of mental (cognitive and affective) processes and the assumed value of self-disclosure need to be approached from a different standpoint. Discussion may have to be about other people, what they did or said, what they might be influenced to do differently, and finally what the client may learn to do differently. The usual discussions of client feelings may not be possible. Discussion, of course, can be carried on with clients who understand and value them, but they should not be pushed if the ideas are strange or possibly taboo to them.

An exceptionally fine book by Shirley Jenkins, *The Ethnic Dilemma in Social Services* (1981), reviews the literature about common needs of ethnic clients and reports at length on studies of attitudes, preferences, and expectations of staff and clients in the United States, Great Britain, and Israel. Jenkins calls attention to the significance and variation in family forms, to differing attitudes about parents, and parent-child relationships. She identifies common attitudes among Chinese, Samoans, and American Indians. The thorny question of bilingualism and its effects is examined; whether to maintain communication in two languages or one is a problem of substantial importance and is difficult to solve. The experience of Canada is relevant because the country is divided between anglophones and francophones, which has been accompanied by great social, economic, and political conflicts.

Jenkins provides a thorough and relevant discussion of the problem of stereotypes and prejudgments. There is a not-so-fine line between identifying common group characteristics and freezing these into stereotypes that substantially distort service and cause hardship and misunderstanding between individuals. The problem of stereotyping is linked to difficulty in separating notions of pathology from ethnic clients' versions of an accepted life-style. Stories among clinicians abound in which a client's behavior is mistaken for mental illness when in reality the client is engaging in a religious practice or some other behavior unique to his ethnic culture.

EXAMPLES: PROBLEM DEFINITION

Ho (1982) reports the case of a 65-year-old Hong Kong Chinese widow, Mrs. H., who had recently arrived in the United States to live with her son. The son was married to an American woman of Chinese descent. The older Mrs. H. was referred for help by a physician because of insomnia, weight loss, and depression. She was interviewed by a Chinese practitioner, who showed Mrs. H. the respect and deference due an older person as emphasized in Chinese culture. It turned out that Mrs. H. was suffering from a bad case of culture shock. After being left alone in Hong Kong because of her husband's death, she had submitted to emigration to protect her son's reputation and save face for herself. It appears that the physician's assessment of psychopathology was less important than Mrs. H.'s perturbation about being in a strange country with strange customs.

In another example Ruiz (1982) discusses a Hispanic client who was about to be classified mentally ill because of seizures that, it was discovered, had their basis in his religious practices.

These two examples graphically illustrate the kind of error that could be made by allowing conventional stereotypes of psychopathology to guide assessment interviewing. If the interviewer had emphasized only Mrs. H.'s suspected psychopathology, the interview might have come to a dead end. The conclusion might have been that Mrs. H. was severely disturbed and ought to be institutionalized or simply left to her suffering. She might have had to be taken into her son's home to be cared for by an unwilling daughter-in-law. The quality of her life, as well as her adult children's lives, might have been damaged. However, a practitioner who understood Chinese culture and could communicate with Mrs. H. was able to get appropriate information in answer to the interviewing question, "What do you think is your problem?"

It turned out that, in the Hong Kong community where Mrs. H. lived, it was unthinkable that a respectable son would leave his mother alone when she became a widow. Therefore, to maintain her respectability, Mrs. H. had to emigrate to a strange country to be near her son. She cared more about maintaining her son's respectability in the eyes of her people than she cared for her own comfort and security. Once located in the United States, however, the new experiences were too great for her to accept. On the surface the result looked like "depression." However, Mrs. H.'s sadness was a natural response to being confronted with the totality of the strange physical environment of her new community and with strange family relations with her son and daughter-in-law, both of whom were deeply acculturated to American ways. The interviews had to deal with initiating Mrs. H. into the culture of the Chinese-American community. With her son and his wife, the interviewer discussed ways for Mrs. H. to become involved in their lives without them having to change their own customs too much. By attending to the cultural content of Mrs. H.'s problem, it was not necessary to provide her with psychiatric treatment.

In the example described by Ruiz the interviewer was confronted with a client acting in an extreme manner, moving arms and legs jerkily, falling on the floor with flailing arms and legs, and rolling his eyes as if he were exceedingly distressed or in pain. This behavior could readily be interpreted as a form of seizure that would normally indicate a need for medical and probably psychiatric treatment. Because the practitioner was familiar with the client's ethnic background, the "seizure" was identified as part of a particular type of religious observance.

In both of the preceding examples the client was saved from undergoing the complexities of examination for psychopathology and from running a risk that the cultural factors might never be identified. This is not to say that consideration and evaluation of psychopathology is always ruled out, only that the interviewer should understand that many of the cultural values of the white middle class do not apply to people of different cultural and ethnic backgrounds (Acosta, Yamamoto, and Evans 1982).

MATCHING CLIENT AND INTERVIEWER

For many years there has been exploratory discussion in the literature about benefits or deficits incurred by "mixing and matching" the ethnic characteristics of interviewer and client. In terms of predicting the outcome of psychotherapy, this research is not informative. The methodology of the studies is flawed, and it is not clear whether effect of ethnicity or some other variable is being measured. At any rate, taking the studies at face value, the results are inconclusive (Parloff, Waskow, and Wolfe 1978, pp. 255-258).

However, Jenkins's studies shed light on clients' perceptions if not on outcome effects. Interviews with an extensive sample of parents from 10 child welfare agencies revealed that client preference for a practitioner depended on circumstances; clients did not necessarily always choose a practitioner from their own ethnic group. Interpretation of the information suggests that what the interviewed parents wanted were competent and relevant services offered in an understanding way; any tendency to prefer an interviewer of their own ethnic group was modified by perception of the interviewer's ability. The two examples cited earlier illustrate how complicated such a judgment can become; the ethnic practitioner was superior to the American practitioner in both instances because of knowledge of the culture and ethnic ways. However, there are bound to be instances in which the American practitioner is well schooled in the cultural attributes and quite capable of managing the case. In fact Ruiz, who could speak Spanish and had grown up in a home where he had become acquainted with the religious practices observed in his client, developed an in-service training program to acquaint the staff with this knowledge.

LANGUAGE BARRIERS

There is an immense problem in interviewing when the client and interviewer do not understand and speak the same language. Whenever possible the interviewer should speak the same language as the client. Foreign clients may speak limited English and thus be unable to convey important nuances to an English-speaking interviewer. The practitioner can try to understand basic communication such as client signs and gestures—head nods, shoulder shrugs, arm sweeps, and pantomime. When language is a barrier, interpreters are needed.

Translation of speech is a skilled occupation if performed in a way that accurately conveys the content, tone, and implicit meanings of verbal interchanges in two languages. In human services settings good translator skills are not often available; well-intentioned amateurs are often used. This may lead to problems. For example, the interpreter might listen to a long and emotional speech from a client and translate it for the interviewer in one or two short sentences. The interpreter might leave out the heart of the speech because he does not grasp its importance, feels ashamed to relate what has been said, or disapproves of what has been said. The interpreter and the client may also start a process between them in which the interpreter takes over the helping process from the practitioner without knowing enough to be good at it. The interpreter may disagree with the interviewer and change what is said. It is sometimes better for the practitioner and client to communicate in pantomime or in a verbally limited fashion than to complicate matters with misunderstandings from an amateur interpreter. On the other hand, properly trained interpreters can be of great help.

HENRY

Henry is a 14-year-old Hispanic boy. He came into a neighborhood center by himself and asked to see someone about his weight problem.

Henry and the practitioner conversed in English although Henry was bilingual in Spanish and English. He had arrived in Chicago with his father and brothers only a few days earlier; their home was in southern California. Henry said that he had been walking around the neighborhood, had passed the center, and had decided to inquire if he could get help for his problem, which caused him much embarrassment. Henry seemed shy and reserved. The practitioner asked if it would be all right for her to have a conference with Henry's father about his getting help. Actually, the practitioner suspected that there might also be other problems because the family was newly arrived in the city and living in a neighborhood unlike their familiar rural one in California. Henry was eager to have the interviewer visit his home and talk with his father. A date was arranged, and a Spanish-speaking practitioner was asked to go along.

Close relationships with kin and extended family

The two practitioners visited the family's home, which was located in a poor neighborhood. The family members turned out to be Henry's father, the paternal grandmother, an aunt, two uncles, and two older brothers. One of the uncles appeared to be mentally handicapped. The interview was conducted in Spanish. Coffee was served, and Henry's relatives were very polite and attentive.

The Spanish-speaking practitioner introduced himself and the other practitioner. He translated for the English-speaking practitioner as she explained how this conference was arranged. Henry's father introduced the family and expressed appreciation for the visit. The practitioner explained what Henry had said about his problem and that an appropriate referral could be made for him; however, she said, she had wanted to talk with the father about the situation. After that it seemed that everyone started to talk at once. When the information was sorted out, it emerged that the father, his brother, and his three sons had arrived by truck a few days earlier. They were farm laborers and had been working in Michigan. On the advice of friends they had detoured to Chicago on the way back to California to find out if they could improve their lot by settling there.

Problem of poverty

The apartment at which everyone was staying belonged to one of Henry's uncles, who had been living there with his wife and mother when the other relatives arrived. This uncle was living at present on unemployment benefits. His wife was overwhelmed; she felt that she was suddenly being asked to run a barracks for all these men. She and her mother-in-law had started arguing because of all the tension. Henry's two older brothers had already followed job leads and found maintenance jobs at a nearby factory. They were impressed with what they considered to be high wages, and they were elated about the prospects of things to do and people to meet in Chicago.

Their father, however, was fearful because he had had no luck job hunting. He was a tired and worn-looking man. Another concern was that Henry's mother and two sisters were in California. The father would send for them if he could get established in Chicago. Despite his failure to get a job Henry's father judged their chances for economic well-being to be best in Chicago. An additional concern was Henry's uncle, the one who seemed mentally handicapped. Henry's father asked what might be done for him.

Henry's relatives appeared to be fond of Henry; they were really sorry about his unhappiness. However, they had more important things to look after such as acquiring affordable housing, jobs, good income, and care for the sick uncle. They welcomed this visit by the practitioners because they saw it as a chance to get some advice about problem situations.

Henry was pleased that it was he, by his inquiry, who had caused the visit. He sat with his male relatives, not at all put out with being virtually ignored as the focus changed. When the practitioner mentioned Henry's problem, his father said that Henry was "a sick kid." In California he had been a patient at a children's hospital because of a heart condition, and he had not gone to school because he had always been sick. The father said he hoped that Henry would not turn out to have a mental problem like his uncle. He seemed genuinely puzzled about what to do with Henry; however, he was most preoccupied with the decision that had to be made about whether to stay in Chicago or go back home. Henry's aunt was also concerned about him but too overwhelmed with the present situation to pay any sustained attention.

Value conflicts

Henry's father was worried about his two older sons, the ones who already had found maintenance jobs. They were young, strong, and capable and had been lucky to get work so soon. However, they were already staying out late and coming home singing, laughing, and "full of beer." They were having a good time, and the father was already worried that they would get into trouble; he was thinking they should go back to California. At this the young men laughed at him and said they were staying in Chicago even if he went back. The father looked crushed.

The practitioner started to describe the helping resources that might be available: the employment service for the father, the community psychiatric clinic for the sick uncle, the local Hispanic Society for help with housing and employment, and a pediatric clinic for Henry. At this recital of resources the family's attitude grew cold and disconcerted except for that of Henry's two brothers, who ignored the conversation and looked away. The practitioner asked what was bothering them.

Awareness of stereotyped perspective

The father answered for all. He said he appreciated the suggestions but that they sounded to him like getting caught in a lot of red tape. He had had experiences in California making the rounds of agencies, answering questions, filling out forms, and waiting in lines. He feared that nothing would come of it. Everyone became very sad. They were confronting Chicago, and they feared the coldness, disinterest, and formal provisions of the city. Although the children were all born in the United States, the father was worried that they might be arrested as illegal immigrants. He was now tending to think they should go back home. The practitioner said everybody would have to think more about this, and they could talk again at a later time.

Summary

Interviewing clients who belong to ethnic groups with specific identities and characteristics and who may be part of a minority or group with disadvantaged status calls for sensitivity to many complex issues. Some of these issues have been touched on in this chapter.

When interviewing clients who are members of an ethnic minority, it is advisable to become acquainted with the group's outstanding features and characteristics: origin, economic life, and social structure. This general information has to be interpreted in a way that respects the unique manner in which the individual person thinks, feels, behaves, and perceives himself. In an interviewing situation and in connection with a specific problem, the client's background and status is a source of strength but may also result in strain.

Certain areas have been emphasized to show the kinds of adaptations that modify the general interviewing model. These adaptations, which take into account various types of ethnic realities, are summarized briefly as follows:

1. It is advisable for the interviewer to take into account the normal practices of the client with respect to formality and respectful demeanor.

2. In the first phase, where acquiring information from the client is likely to be strongly emphasized, it is desirable to move at a pace that is familiar to the client and is in keeping with her customary rate of thinking and speaking. It is advisable to focus on present problems and the realistic aspects of those problems and to adopt an attitude that demonstrates willingness to assist with practical problem solving.

3. Minority clients are likely to be closely involved with relatives, extended family, and friends. They are apt to have many problems associated with poverty and inequality, as well as with conflicts of values with the larger society. They may be troubled by awareness of disrespect for them and discrimination against them. The interview content should guide the discussions to deal with areas that are likely to be of considerable concern.

4. There is some reason to believe that ethnic minority clients prefer to deal with a practitioner from their own group, but the greatest likelihood is that competent help from a practitioner is more important to them than ethnic identification. Language is a very important barrier if real communication is thwarted either by the fact that neither party can speak the other's language or by the absence of competent interpreters.

REFERENCES

Acosta, Frank Y.; Yamamoto, Joe; and Evans, Leonard A. *Effective Psychotherapy for Low Income and Minority Patients.* New York: Plenum Press, 1982.

Chunn, Jay C, II; Dunston, Patricia J.; and Ross-Sheriff, Farujal, eds. *Mental Health and People of Color.* Washington, D.C.: Howard University Press, 1983.

Devore, Wynetta, and Schlesinger, Elfriede G. *Ethnic-Sensitive Social Work Practice.* St. Louis: The C.V. Mosby Company, 1981.

Harvard Encyclopedia of American Ethnic Groups. Cambridge: Harvard University Press, 1980.

Ho, Man Keung. "Case Studies." *Practice Digest* 5 (December 1982):4.

Jenkins, Shirley. *The Ethnic Dilemma in Social Services.* New York: The Free Press, 1981.

McAdoo, Harriette P. "Demographic Trends for People of Color." *Social Work* 27 (January 1982):15-23.

New Columbia Encyclopedia. New York: Columbia University Press, 1975.

Parloff, Morris B.; Waskow, Irene E.; and Wolfe, Barry E. "Research on Therapist Variables in Relation to Process and Outcome." In *Handbook of Psychotherapy and Behavior Change: An Empirical Analysis.* 2d ed., edited by Sol L. Garfield and Allen E. Bergin. New York: John Wiley & Sons, 1978.

Ruiz, Roberto. "Case Studies." *Practice Digest* 5 (December 1982):7-8.

Wong, Herbert Z.; Kim, Luke I.C.; Lim, Donald T.; and Morishima, James K. "The Training of Psychologists for Asian and Pacific American Communities." In *Mental Health and People of Color,* edited by Chunn, Dunston, and Ross-Sheriff. Washington, D.C.: Howard University Press, 1983.

CHAPTER 10

Involuntary, unwilling, or hostile clients

The involuntary state: what it means

It is a commonplace observation both in practice and research that the preferred client is the one who comes for help of her own volition and participates readily in discussion, self-disclosure, and action. Not only are such clients preferred but they also will probably obtain more benefit from intervention. However, the truly voluntary client is often not the norm in interviewing. The human services deal with large numbers of people, perhaps a majority, who are labeled "involuntary." It is impossible to know what proportion of clients fall into the "involuntary" category because no figures have been collected on this subject. A 1977 survey estimated that there are approximately 3 million cases in 2375 public agencies serving children and their families (Shyne 1980). Many if not most of these cases are probably involuntary. To this number should be added large numbers of people in correctional settings, mental health settings, and schools. Court-mandated services create a number of involuntary clients. The client population who might be classified as involuntary can only be guessed at.

Human services practice assumes that work with involuntary clients is appropriate. It is public policy to offer help to citizens who are eligible and in need. In North America and Europe during the twentieth century, it has become established social policy that government has a major responsibility for ameliorating conditions that undermine the welfare of individuals and groups who are vulnerable to social problems. Human services are carried out through state programs that are augmented by the private sector. Helping professions provide the personnel to implement these programs.

Since the mid-1960s a critical evaluation of state care has been conducted on the grounds that it is overly intrusive regarding the private affairs of citizens, unfair in its administration, and ineffective in its results. In the 1980s a political tendency to reduce the size of human services establishments emerged. The issues involved in the present movement to reform and limit social programs have stimulated substantial public debate, and they are immensely significant. There is much tension and uncertainty about the amount and type of responsibility that human services have toward clients who are classified as involuntary. This issue has existed for the entire history of human services development, and it will probably continue to exist for a long time.

Interviewing the involuntary client raises some technical questions that are not unlike those regarding ethnic groups in the previous chapter. There is a need to understand the social-psychological context of clients' lives. The words, phrases, and sentences used by clients during interviewing get their meaning from client living conditions, perspectives, and aspirations; clients are also affected by the purposes, intentions, and behaviors of interview settings and the personal attributes of practitioners.

Clients who are called "involuntary" are not a part of a rigid, undifferentiated collection of people. They vary on a continuum from being somewhat voluntary to very involuntary. They will involve themselves in services to varying degrees, especially those services that offer counseling.

VOLUNTARY CLIENTS

Clients who are voluntary have acquired a belief in the value and effectiveness of counseling. They have probably acquired knowledge about and belief in psychotherapy from their parents, peers, teachers, books, magazines, television, or newspapers. They have sought psychotherapy from a private practitioner or a fee-charging agency or clinic and have a modest desire to be better off afterward. The most voluntary clients rarely have illusions of extraordinary benefits to be obtained. They usually fear personal disclosures but are hopeful. This hope is probably warranted; only a few will reap remarkable benefits, and a few will not be helped at all, but most will indeed get better.

Some voluntary clients will not come entirely under their own steam. They may be strongly persuaded by parents, friends, spouses, or employers. They are still considered voluntary; however, a degree, perhaps a strong degree, of coercion has been used to persuade them to seek counseling. They may be worried that they will lose their spouses or jobs if they do not shape up. They may worry that they are jeopardizing their futures by staying away from counseling although commitment to it is weak.

Barriers hamper the whole helping process and interviewing itself for a large segment of voluntary clients. Analyzing voluntary clients leads to a possible conclusion that issues faced with voluntary clients are not necessarily all that different from issues faced with involuntary clients. Barriers to getting the work done are ubiquitous. The helping professions are preoccupied today with study, research, and development of approaches and techniques to improve the effectiveness of services. The immediate effort to provide available and relevant services is of paramount importance. Running a close second in importance, however, is the need for innovation and revision of services to improve effectiveness and minimize barriers for clients.

Some people who come to human services agencies voluntarily are simply seeking information. They are interested in collecting facts about available resources, rules for obtaining them, and choices that can be made regarding them.

An example of this type of voluntary client is a man whose wife is facing a long hospitalization. He wants to know how to find reliable and affordable child care. He chooses to come to a reputable private child welfare service. He assumes that experienced professionals will be able to present him with safe and reliable child care options from which he can select one that is suitable for his children, income, and life-style. He is willing to listen to the opinion and advice of an expert. However, he is totally unwilling to permit exploration into his feelings about his wife and her illness, the details of his financial predicament, the availability of relatives to cooperate in child care, the personalities and problems of his children, or almost anything else. He is a well-educated man who is successful in his occupation, concerned about his wife and children, and able to function competently as a person. He wants information and no intrusion into his personal affairs. When he learns that the agency's services will include mandatory supervision of the placement of his children by the staff, he discontinues contact with the agency. He locates a child care service by consulting his friends. He ultimately chooses the home where he places his children, pays for it directly, and supervises his children in his own way.

Other voluntary clients want straightforward advice about problem-solving methods for reducing a problem. For example, a divorced father wants to know the range of possible things that can be done to keep his child from dropping out of school. Another example is a woman who wants to find out where she can obtain an easy job while recovering from surgery. Another example is a couple married 20 years who want information about hiring a reasonably priced and competent divorce lawyer. Another example is a married couple besieged with debts who want information about how they can pay them.

These people are voluntary clients because they are, of their own will, looking for problem-solving methods (in combination with problem-solving resources) to achieve a goal they have established. This does not necessarily mean that they are determined to obtain the goal if it should prove unfeasible. It also does not necessarily mean that they will refuse to consider an alternative goal if available problem-solving methods are uncertain or if needed resources are unavailable. What this kind of client problem definition does, however, is pose the distinct possibility that the client will not easily be persuaded to review and discuss the situation. He may well turn away from extensive exploration of alternatives and follow his own ideas about acceptable methods and resources for solving the problem.

INVOLUNTARY CLIENTS

Involuntary clients tend to be individuals or families who have come to public attention because they are part of a social problem that is currently of official public concern. They are likely to be poor and to have problems that are associated with poverty, such as those common to one-parent families, elderly people, and people from minority or ethnic backgrounds. These problems include poor child-rearing practices, violent behavior among family members, public misbehavior resulting from mental illness and chemical substance abuse, and other similar forms of social deviance.

Examples of involuntary clients include parents who willfully neglect or physically abuse their children, husbands who assault their wives, and young people with severe conduct disorders involving assault, theft, or drug abuse. Another type of involuntary client might be the mentally disturbed person who needs to be committed to a mental hospital.

SOCIAL DEVIANCE

Two conditions that often accompany involuntarism in a client are the client's exhibition of public behaviors that are strongly disapproved of, or *deviance,* and the client's need of resources that are publicly funded. Involuntary clients are treated as a result of the social role that human services organizations are expected to play; this role has both a social control function and a problem-solving or therapeutic function. These two functions are traditional in human services. The goals associated with them may sometimes clash; however, the degree of dissonance experienced by many practitioners who provide services to involuntary clients is more extreme than it needs to be. Agencies are vested with authority derived from law, public policy, and custom, and staff members have authority delegated to them by their agencies.

The various models of counseling provide a means for dispensing direct service. Because voluntary participation is most conducive to the success of professional help, interviewers attempt to persuade an involuntary client to change her mind and to assume as many of the attributes of voluntarism as possible. A change from involuntarism to voluntarism is possible to varying degrees.

People who do not freely choose to go to a helping organization may become attached to one, nevertheless, through a complaint or referral. A complaint may come from another professional person, from another setting, or from a private citizen on a "hot line" (as is the case when complaints are made about suspected child abuse). A referral may come from a health, correctional, or educational organization and may have strong authority backing it; this is the case when a court orders a person to submit to psychotherapy, hospitalization, or child placement.

Social deviance "is the departure of human beings from rules" that establish the norms of roles and statuses (Shoham 1976, pp. 4-5). The deviant is viewed as a heretic, someone who is

> . . . *different in a way that infringes on the group's normative system . . . . The social and economic consequences of this stigma depend on the severity of the infringement of the norm, and are determined by the inner strength of the norm, as measured by the public's indignation when this norm is infringed . . . . [The] more severe the stigma, the stronger the social norm* (Shoham, p. 13).

The Judeo-Christian concept of "free will" leads the dominant society to view the deviant's offense "as a malicious act, perpetrated out of a free choice to do bad" (p. 13). In recent times the view of the offender as "bad" has been transformed into the view of the offender as mentally disturbed or needing therapy. However, the characterization of mental disturbance as the cause of deviance is currently under a cloud of doubt. The "rehabilitative ideal" as the major means to ameliorate deviance has lost some of its appeal. A more sophisticated viewpoint has emerged that attributes deviance to many complex determinants.

From a practical standpoint this present viewpoint suggests an approach that encourages maximum client voluntarism; the practitioner can concentrate on problem solving as it is perceived by the client while adhering closely to mandated requirements. With this viewpoint it is entirely possible to arrive at a mutually agreed-on problem definition to which both practitioner and client can subscribe. When this is done the client's voluntarism is maximized.

There is credible research evidence to support the idea that congruence between practitioner and client on the problem focus (or target problem) establishes the best condition for achieving a good outcome (Blizinsky and Reid 1980). However, this should not be interpreted as a guarantee for all cases. In particular cases other variables may turn out to be stronger than congruence. For example, too much pressure may be used to force agreement. Clients may have unstated reservations that were not sufficiently perceived by the practitioner in early sessions. The intervention experience itself may uncover information or teach lessons that result in the client's change of opinion.

The following excerpts are from the seventeenth and eighteenth interviews between the practitioner and Mrs. Dora N. (Rooney 1983). These interviews take place at Mrs. N.'s home during the middle phase, deep into problem solving (see Chapter 4, Figure 5).

Mrs. N., a black woman of 40, is the single head of a household. She has been receiving public aid for 15 years. She has 10 children. Two years ago Mrs. N. was advised to have surgery for a benign tumor. She agreed to have the operation and arranged to have her children placed in foster care while she was incapacitated; then she changed her mind.

Nevertheless, the public aid agency went into court and obtained temporary custody of nine of her children, ages 2 to 15, to protect them from unsuitable and neglectful conditions. Mrs. N. had been reported several times by neighbors because of alleged frequent intoxication and absence from home. The children were reported to be dirty, unfed, and roaming the streets. Public aid staff members visited the home on a few occasions and found the neighbors' reports to be true. The public school reported that the children's school attendance was poor. It was felt that Mrs. N.'s preschool children were endangered by her unexplained absences. Mrs. N.'s eldest daughter, Wilona, a 15-year-old, had disappeared from home.

Mrs. N.'s version of the events surrounding the children's placement was that she had had no knowledge of the plan until police cars arrived and took away the children. The public aid staff stated that Mrs. N. had been missing for several days prior to the children's removal. An emergency court order had been obtained, granting authority to remove the children for their own protection.

Wilona reappeared, stayed in foster care one night, and then ran away and went back home. A second daughter, Aileen, was released from foster care after 3 months' stay; she also returned to live with her mother. The other children remained in care where they have been for a year at the time of the present interviews. Mrs. N. has repeatedly asked for visits with the children, who are dispersed to several different foster homes in the suburbs. Mrs. N. has been able to see her 3-year-old and 5-year-old children only once; she has seen the others a few times.

Mrs. N. had lived for many years in a public housing high-rise apartment. After Wilona had returned home, the girl was raped in the building's vestibule. Mrs. N. became determined to get out of a building that was so dangerous, and she moved a few weeks later. All she could get for the money she had was an extremely deteriorated apartment with no phone, no heat, and a landlord who sometimes turned off the gas.

This was the state of affairs when the public aid service purchased care from the private sector to determine what might be done to rehabilitate the family and return all the children to Mrs. N.

Because Mrs. N. had no phone, the new practitioner wrote to her, giving the date and time when he proposed to visit her. She never got the letter, mail delivery being an uncertain thing in housing like hers. When the practitioner came, Mrs. N. was drunk and incoherent. It was a hot day and the apartment smelled. Piles of clothes lay around on the floor. There was almost no furniture. The door was broken and hung on its hinges; window shades were tattered. The roar of the express-way was loud through the open windows. It was a very depress-ing scene.

Narrating this case, the interviewer says: "I asked Mrs. N. as a beginning task to attempt to be sober for the next session. I also asked her to clean her house since we knew that the condi-tion of the home was seen by the court as an obstacle to her children coming home. I wrote down clearly for her the day and time I would be returning. She said over and over how much she wanted her children home. When I returned a week later, Mrs. N. was sober and clean and the house was remark-ably tidy. Since that time Mrs. N. and I have met 16 times. Over 80 tasks have been developed between us; 47 of them have been carried out by Mrs. N. and 28 of them by myself. That's about 60% worth of client tasks."

The following interchanges are taken from Interview 17. There has already been much discussion about the hopeless inadequacy of Mrs. N.'s present housing. The interviewer has told her that it is almost impossible to expect the court to discharge the children to her if she is still living in her present deplorable apartment. She has looked at other places; either she cannot afford them, or the landlords refuse to rent to her because she has so many children. She has insisted firmly that she will not move back into public housing. However, she now has had to confront the fact that she seems to have no alternative but public housing. She is still totally unwilling to apply.

The practitioner and Mrs. N. first make some introductory remarks:

Interviewer (I): What do you think will happen if you apply at public housing? *(analyzing obstacles)*

Mrs. N.: That they're not going to accept us because when I moved out of there I owed them $260. Because they kicked me out of the apartment I was in. So I moved out, but they also took me to court.

1. **I:** They did! *(empathic sounds)*
2. **Mrs. N** *(Adjacency pair responses proceed from Interchanges 2 through 14).* They did. *(obtaining needed information; identifying, specifying, and explaining the problem)*
3. **I:** Since you moved out?
4. **Mrs. N:** Before I moved out.
5. **I:** What for?
6. **Mrs. N:** For not paying rent. *(Her voice drops; she looks down at her hands, which are clenching and unclenching.)* I was all tore up. I didn't have no stove where I could cook. So . . . there was a stove there but all I could use was one burner. The other one didn't work and the oven would never come on. *(explaining problem)*
7. **I:** Uh huh.
8. **Mrs. N:** The refrigerator was broken. I couldn't store any food. I kept telling them to do something but they wouldn't. So I decided I would hold the rent and see if they would give me a refrigerator. So then when they sent me to court and the judge asked me why I didn't pay the rent, I told him. Then he asked the investigator why they hadn't given me a stove and refrigerator that worked. *(explaining problem)*
9. **I:** So public housing wouldn't do anything for you until you paid your back rent?
10. **Mrs. N.:** Yeah. But I never could get them to fix anything when I did pay.
11. **I:** So when you moved out—did they still try to get the rent from you that you owed?
12. **Mrs. N:** Uh huh. I went down and talked to them and I asked them could I pay so much every month and, you know, he said no. I had to pay all of it at once, so I didn't pay.
13. **I:** They haven't gotten in touch with you again?
14. **Mrs. N:** About the money? No.
15. **I:** Well, it sounds like you are right. All that trouble is going to make it tough for you to get accepted again in public housing. I talked to the official at public housing. He just kept saying you were uncooperative. I stuck with it and kept

on explaining your condition to him, how you might not be able to get your kids without decent housing. He softened up and said I should put the whole thing in writing. I wrote a letter on your behalf to public housing. Here, I brought you a copy so you would know what I said about you. *(introducing and pinning down the interventions)*

16. **Mrs. N:** *(She looks over the letter; then she speaks very softly.)* I had a lot of trouble when I was living in the project. My daughter Wilona, the oldest one, she ran away after she got shot in the project. She got raped there. I just don't want to be there. . . . I had a gun put to my head there. *(telling new information; explaining problem more thoroughly)*

17. **I:** You're talking about any of the high rises? *(keeping focus on target problem, which is the need for new housing)*

18. **Mrs. N:** I think all of them are about the same. If I could get back, I would like to have a walk-up.

19. **I:** You mean one of the low rises? *(pinning down information)*

20. **Mrs. N:** Uh huh. My kids could get outside. I wouldn't let my kids out in the high rise because I was afraid.

21. **I:** Well, you're caught now in a circle. We still have a long way to go to change the public housing authority's attitude toward you, to get them to allow you to move back, to negotiate some kind of a deal about the money you owe them. But then you are afraid to move back, and we don't know if they will get you space in a low rise. It's almost impossible to get you a big enough place outside of public housing that you could afford. What do you think we should do? *(analyzing obstacles, discussing what client wants to do)*

22. **Mrs. N:** I don't know.

23. **I:** Listen. Will you do this? You keep making the rounds of the buildings and real estate offices. Maybe you'll get lucky and find an OK apartment. That's what you prefer. Meanwhile I'll negotiate for you with the housing authority to see if I can get some kind of agreement that they will take you back, especially in a low rise. I'll see if I can get them to let you pay back your debt to them in small installments. What's standing in the way with them is that they think you are unstable and uncooperative. In the end you are going to have to show up and talk to them in person after I pave the way for you. They are going to have to satisfy themselves from seeing that you are going to cooperate. *(reviewing, advising, informing, instructing, encouraging, guiding)*

The following interchanges are taken from Interview 18.

24. **Mrs. N:** I went to the doctor after you left last week. *(Adjacency pair responses proceed from Interchanges 24 through 35.)*

25. **I:** You did? I didn't know you were sick.

26. **Mrs. N:** I didn't know I was sick either. I got high blood pressure.

27. **I:** You have? Did they give you anything for it?

28. **Mrs. N:** Uh huh.

29. **I:** What were you feeling like that caused you to go? *(identifying problem)*

30. **Mrs. N:** Well, I went for my side. See, I've been having trouble with my left side for a long time, so I went to the doctor to see what he could tell me about it. Instead of him telling me about my side, he told me about my blood pressure.

31. **I:** Uh huh. Is he going to tell you what to eat?

32. **Mrs. N:** I have to go back to him in 2 weeks.

33. **I:** Well, you definitely have to watch your health. You've been trying to do too much. But you can't do it without your health. *(identifying problem, responding empathically)*

34. **Mrs. N:** I know. The doctor told me last year I had to stop drinking. And I never did really pay attention, you know. *(In the 17 previous interviews Mrs. N. has never been drunk; this is the first time the subject has been raised.)*

35. **I:** That contributes to all your problems, doesn't it? *(formulating meaning)*

36. **Mrs. N:** Yeah. All that whiskey and wine and stuff. It runs your blood pressure up. See, I always did have trouble with my blood pressure. And then when I started getting drunk and falling out, and, you know, on the street and things, wind up in the hospital—you didn't know that, did you. *(sardonic laugh)* Yeah, I did that a couple of times last year. Got drunk and fell out on the sidewalk and wind up in the hospital. *(After 17 interviews and the sustained action of the practitioner to stay with her, be on her side, and offer practical help and advice, Mrs. N. has enough confidence in him to talk about a serious drinking problem that has contributed to criticism about her child care and her loss of her children.)*

37. **I:** You were in bad shape the first time I visited you.

38. **Mrs. N:** *(Sardonic laugh)* Yeah. If I didn't stop it, I would wind up with cirrhosis of the liver.

39. **I:** Probably right.

40. **Mrs. N:** When I start it, I stop eating. I don't have an appetite to eat; I just have an appetite to stay drunk.

41. **I:** What about now?

42. **Mrs. N:** I don't want to drink cause I might not survive the next time I fall out, and I want to get my kids back so I put myself to a test.

43. **I:** Good Lord! All these weeks we have been struggling with these terrible problems, and you have been all by yourself testing your strength to stay off drink! *(highly empathic; formulating meaning)*

44. **Mrs. N:** I don't think it's always going to be easy. Two of my friends just left outa here before you came; they are stoned alcoholics. They just don't know it. Some of my friends have been drinking all this week. I haven't taken any of it because I don't drink and take medicine. That's one thing I don't do. *(explaining problem)*

45. **I:** How can you see them, stay with them, and keep from drinking?

46. **Mrs. N:** *(very softly)* The guy I got a crush on, he drinks too. But it don't bother me. It's a strange thing — it don't bother me. It used to — would make me want some, but now I just don't have any interest. I guess I'm going through a phase. *(She has developed an extraordinary amount of confidence in the interviewer if she can tell him not only that she used to have a drinking problem but also that she now has a boyfriend. Both things could elicit disapproval. Also, she might be trying to see if the practitioner will still stand by her when he knows all about her.)*

47. **I:** A good phase. *(He is impressed and reveals his true feelings.)*

48. **Mrs. N:** Yup. I don't want no more. I don't want to drink no more, period. Alcohol has caused me everything bad that has happened to me in my life. Caused me to be drunk, get my TV stolen out of here, my radio.

49. **I:** People took advantage of you? *(formulating meaning)*

50. **Mrs. N:** Of course.

51. **I:** You see, that's the thing that public aid doesn't know about. They have been here only once in 5 months. They don't know that you haven't been acting like the person that they thought you were before. *(informing, instructing, formulating meaning, providing incentives and a rationale)*

52. **Mrs. N:** I know that.

53. **I:** What they've been saying to me and to you is: "Why should we make any special efforts for somebody who is

not going to hold up, pull their own weight, fly right?" *(informing, instructing, formulating meaning)*

54. **Mrs. N:** They say once you do something you always have to do it, but that's wrong. A person can change. *(confirming incentives and providing a rationale)*

55. **I:** They asked you to go to Alcoholics Anonymous a while back.

56. **Mrs. N:** I think I'll go this Saturday. Because when I went before, I will be honest with you, you know I always like to tell you the truth.

57. **I:** I know you do *(empathic response)*.

58. **Mrs. N:** When I went there I was so drunk—I didn't even know what I was doing there. So I'm going back. This time maybe I can understand what they're talking about. I know one thing. There are lots of people going there, so there must be something to it. The doctor told me, "Don't fool yourself. Once you're an alcoholic, you're always an alcoholic." But being alcoholic is a sickness, and that's the problem, see. I've been so weak all my life, till I just can't stand to hurt anybody. *(whispering)* I would let them hurt me and then go and get drunk, and forget about it—but you don't forget about it. You forget about it while you're drunk because you're out.

59. **I:** And then?

60. **Mrs. N:** When you get sober, it's the same thing.

61. **I:** The same all over again. *(empathic)*

62. **Mrs. N:** Right! So it doesn't make sense to get drunk. Just stand up and speak up for your rights. That's all I say. But see, I never did that because—I left my husband years ago, I mean before he died. *(She is whispering.)*

63. **I:** Do you mean it took you years before you stood up to your husband—and left him? *(formulating meaning)*

64. **Mrs. N:** Yup. My life and my kids' life could have been different if I hadn't hung on so long to him.

65. **I:** Well, that's a hard decision to make, though, to leave like that. I don't think you should fault yourself too much. You knew if you did that you were going to carry a lot of responsibility alone. *(empathic; formulating meaning)*

66. **Mrs. N:** No, it was my fault for staying with him. He didn't work. When anybody worked it was me. *(She is formulating what the relationship meant to her.)*

67. **I:** Well, the fact is that now—maybe it was true in the past. Maybe it is still true about you now sometimes that you don't stand up for yourself. But I haven't seen it. When you

needed to stand up for yourself since I have known you —
well, you have done it. *(informing, instructing, formulating
meaning, encouraging)*

68. **Mrs. N:** Well, I'm trying to gain . . . stand up for myself and
stand up for my kids, and stand up *to* my kids when I know
they are wrong.

69. **I:** That's another problem. That's something we're going to
have to deal with when your kids come back home.

Mrs. N. has not been required by a court order to work on her problems with the agency, but the view of the court is known. She cannot
expect to have her children returned home unless her deviant mothering
behaviors are changed. Wanting her children is strong motivation to work.
Furthermore, Mrs. N. is an intelligent woman who has shown that she is
capable of raising children under adverse conditions, of leaving a husband
who had hurt her, and of moving. She has some severe weaknesses and
she is pulling herself together at present. She is perceptive, and she trusts
the interviewer. The interviewer respects her, does not judge her, and is
compassionate.

This example illustrates that the interviewing process with an involuntary client proceeds according to regular basic procedures. The interviewer emphasized several interactive qualities: (1) respect and compas-
sion for Mrs. N., (2) affirmation of her problems as she understood them,
and (3) either providing advice and explanations to confirm what she
already understood or providing information she lacked to avoid misperceptions.

The multiproblem family

Dora N. is an example of a type of client defined as *multiproblem.*
Multiproblem people are said to make up large numbers of the involuntary client group. (Mrs. N. could be termed involuntary because the decision to rehabilitate her was not her own but that of an official agency.) The
multiproblem label is pejorative and contains no assessment information;
it simply states that a family has many problems, which is something that
could be said about nearly any family. The peculiarity and drawbacks of
this much-used term have not gone unnoticed in human services. Although the term is little used today in written literature, it is prevalent in
spoken communication.

It seems advisable to examine briefly what kind of family is generally meant when the term "multiproblem" *is* used. Discussions of
resistance and of *authority,* which are terms related to the term "multiproblem," will appear later in this chapter. The characteristics of in-

voluntary clients are often not well understood, so a brief description may prove useful.

The term "multiproblem" came into use in the human services around 1947. At the close of World War II the Pacifist Service Units in England identified and wrote about the first multiproblem families in Liverpool. In the United States projects such as the Family Centered Project of St. Paul, Minnesota were set up; attempts were made to deal with "families with serious problems in more than one of the following areas: social adjustment, health, economic behavior, and recreational needs" (Geismar and La Sorte 1964, pp. 19-20).

The main characteristics of families likely to be designated as "multiproblem" included:

lack of cleanliness
mental and physical illness
poverty and dependence on public aid
delinquency and crime
alcoholism and drug abuse
having numerous sexual partners
child neglect or abuse
school truancy
mental retardation
husband-wife conflict
parent-child conflict
presence of only one parent in the home
failure to respond to help or treatment

By 1970 the concept of the "multiproblem" family had been all but exhausted. Numerous projects had been established to provide specially designed services for multiproblem situations, but the results did not live up to expectations. In fact most of the projects failed (Mullen and Dumpson 1972). The literature accumulated and many practitioners participated in projects, both formal ones and more informal spin-offs. Between 1946 and 1965, 322 books and journal articles on the subject appeared, mostly in the United States. However, by 1970 specific literature on the subject almost came to a halt.

What emerged from this twenty-year engagement with the multiproblem family idea was the realization that multiproblem families were not identifiable by one specific pathology common to all of them. Rather, multiproblem families were made up of people of many different types under great environmental stress. It was found that people needed and often could accept and use specific interventions. Preferred interventions were concrete, specific, and congruent with problems as perceived by the clients. These clients often took advantage of learning better ways to view themselves and their world while improving their social skills in dealing with a variety of interpersonal problems (Epstein 1977).

Today there is a more sophisticated way of thinking about families who used to be referred to as "multiproblem." This new viewpoint sees families as being handicapped by a large load of environmental stress, discrimination, and inequality. Family members may lack some or many of the skills needed to negotiate their lives successfully in this very complex society. They may have the cards stacked against them (see examples in Chapters 8 and 9). They sometimes do lack cleanliness and are accused of having other flaws that would stigmatize them if old multiproblem definitions were adhered to. (It is interesting to note that many people are, for example, not very clean and yet are not stigmatized.)

Failure to respond to treatment does not justify a pejorative label for the client. It simply indicates that the field of practice does not yet know how to understand the client's problems and design corrective programs. The problem may not be conceptualized properly even though the best information available is used. Detailed and tedious attention to specific problem solving is clearly useful, as it was in the case of Dora N. It is appropriate to try to help these clients to attain feasible goals so that they obtain real benefit. Practitioners have to be humble about trying to make massive life-style changes quickly—or at all—with the techniques that are available. The limited capability of individualized direct service to perform miracles is well known. Services can and ought to be improved. Clients should not be blamed or given pejorative labels if the treatment to which they are not responding is inappropriate for their condition.

In summary, the notions about multiproblem families that were formulated in the fifties are naive from today's perspective. Problems are now better understood as extremely entangled products of social structure, socialization, and personality. Some clients respond to helping services and some do not. There are no simple, quick, or inexpensive solutions (Auletta 1982).

Unwillingness and resistance

In the literature on involuntary clients and the related "multiproblem" phenomenon, an outstanding feature is unwillingness or resistance in clients. Resistance is thought by some to account for involuntary clients' unreadiness to cooperate; to actively commit themselves to plans, actions, and self-disclosure; and to think about and emotionally experience problems in the interviewer's presence. It is commonly thought that if clients could engage themselves in these ways, they would benefit.

Concepts such as resistance and ambivalence have been developed in an attempt to explain the minimal or shifting commitments of some clients. It is very common in case discussions to identify a client's unwillingness as *resistance* and a client's uncertainty as *ambivalence*. The concept of ambivalence will be further discussed in the section following this one.

The idea of "resistance" was borrowed from psychoanalysis and then broadened. In psychoanalysis resistance is defined as an unconscious process that opposes ameliorative change. The idea of resistance gained wide popularity in the human services, but its meaning departed from the original. The psychoanalytic theory of resistance as an unconscious process has been explored theoretically and in detail; the broadened meanings, however, have not been well developed. At best the term is heuristic; it alerts the practitioner to something perceived abstractly but lacks particular meaning in a specific instance.

Tension is produced when the client becomes unwilling — reluctant, hesitant, evasive, withdrawn, hostile, sarcastic, or overly submissive. These reactions may all be identified as "resistance." Commonly an interviewer perceives resistance when a more accurate judgment is that there is an impasse, deadlock, or barrier to proceeding in a certain way. The plans that a practitioner maps out as appropriate, desirable, or advisable are influenced by his own views of what should be happening. These personal views are mixed in varying proportions with the practitioner's ideological persuasions and preferred practice theories and with the aims, intentions, preferences, and obligations of the service organization. An assumption is often made that professional status immediately confers adequate knowledge to decide the best way for the client to proceed. This may sometimes be true. The assumption, however, ignores the tentativeness and uncertainty of intervention practice knowledge.

The client's attitudes may reflect his fear, justifiably or not. The client may feel insulted or put down, again justifiably or not. The client may have an essentially different view of how matters should proceed and may, if allowed, make a good case for his position. If the client is mandated or obliged to take the service or if grave consequences will ensue from his lack of cooperation, he may pretend or may become "persuaded" — pragmatically — to agree with the practitioner; his resistance may appear to melt.

It has been suggested that tension about how to proceed with interviews grows out of the efforts of both practitioner and client to control what is going on and what is planned in helping processes (Gitterman 1983). Clients may try to control the interview process through such behavior as dropping out; submitting, or yielding to authority without conviction; not talking; feigning instant improvement; changing the subject; with-holding information; forgetting; or minimizing concerns. Under these con-ditions, interviewers may try to control by reassuring the client before knowing that it is justified; interpreting the meaning of client actions before having enough information or before the client can tolerate an interpreta-tion; imposing values and solutions on the client; being impatient; avoiding an area of proper concern; exploring problem areas inadequately and jumping to conclusions; and going too fast when checking for client con-gruence, agreement, and interest.

Clients are sometimes subjected to long waiting lists, long waiting room delays, rudeness and insensitivity in admissions procedures, harass-ment, overcrowding, and discrimination. They might very well feel hassled and might throw up roadblocks to the interview. Furthermore, if the client is not there of her own volition, the tensions are going to be even greater. It is therefore important not to write off unwilling clients as "resistant," which suggests pathology, when they might have very valid reasons for their behavior. There should instead be scrutiny of possible occurrences, both attitudinal and physical, that might arouse embarrassment, humili-ation, shame, fear, resentment, or anger in the client. A wise interviewer will talk to the client about tensions so that they can be explained by the interviewer and understood by the client. If in the past practitioners have conducted themselves in an abrasive way with the client, the present practitioner must encourage the client to discuss hurts or unpleasantness that might have been experienced. Low-status and involuntary clients are often unable to express their anger, resentment, or fears; they are too strongly socialized to view such behavior as negative and "dangerous." Even though discussions may not seem to be particularly successful, an attempt must be made to enhance the interview with as much courtesy and sensitivity as possible.

For problem-solving interviews in the human services it is advisable to identify why the client exhibits unwillingness to participate, to respect and legitimate the client's viewpoint, to openly discuss practitioner and agency actions that are seen as hurtful, and to avoid solidifying a negative attitude about the client by using the term "resistant" in a pejorative sense.

Ambivalence

Also borrowed from psychiatry, the term *ambivalence* refers to the coexistence of antithetic emotions, attitudes, ideas, or wishes toward a given object or situation. Extreme degrees of ambivalence are sometimes observed in psychotic patients, but the presence of ambivalence does not signify pathology. Ambivalence is a usual and ordinary state of mind for everyone at one time or another. It is a confusing condition only if it is perceived as abnormal—which it is not. It is true that some poorly adjusted people do not manage to acquire any useful ways to consider the pros and cons of situations and are therefore perpetually troubled by ambivalence. Most people, however, learn to specify a problem, figure out alternatives, and decide on a solution (after agonizing about it). Even after a decision is made, reservations may remain. This also is normal; individuals do not have crystal balls that assure them that their choices are the only right ones. Like resistance, ambivalence—evidenced by a client who is unsure of which way to go, is being swung first this way and then that, or has second thoughts and often changes his mind—should not be interpreted as pathology. In those instances where ambivalence *is* part of a pathology, other symptoms that are more concrete should be used to make the final diagnosis.

With the exception of interviewing a mentally ill person with a thought disorder (see the example of Mr. R. in Chapter 7), ambivalence in clients can often be observed. Ambivalence is present when a client is unclear on what she wishes to do. Clients often say, "I do not know." This may mean several things. The client may be fearful of saying what she thinks; these fears need to be explored and tested to see if they are justified or not. Or the client may be depressed, with slowed-down thought processes; when the depression lifts, the client will probably think more clearly. Or the client may be confused by many contradictory ideas that need to be discussed to organize thoughts more clearly. Or the client may be engaging in the normal problem-solving process of generating alternatives. Ambivalence can be revealed when a client changes her mind easily. When confronting problems, everyone does this. It may take time to sort out alternatives and try them out to actually decide which is best.

Authority and the involuntary client

The role of human services providers is vested with authority, although that attribute is sometimes ignored or regarded as undesirable. In fact, authority is a feature of the interviewing process that is sometimes considered to be detrimental to a proper helping posture. In some instances, as in child abuse investigation, the practitioner has certain authority conferred by law. In other instances authority is delegated by officials who are sanctioned by law to do so. Public sanction and custom also confer authority on various service organizations and their staff members. Even when practitioners act as if they do not have authority, their clients and the public are aware that they do.

The authority of practitioners rests in their power to give and withhold resources and counseling and in their ability to influence clients to change. Although social science experts do not agree on an exact definition of authority or on theories about its development and effects, the concept is generally recognized as necessary to help explain social processes. Most scholars agree that authority is a component in all helping relationships and results in the practitioner's ability to influence the client and the situation.

An influential analysis of the bases of social power was done by French and Raven (1968). They identify five types of power that underlie authority: reward, coercive, legitimate, referent, and expert.

REWARD POWER

Reward power is the power that the practitioner has to reward the client with services and with elements of interpersonal relationships. This power increases the potential of the practitioner to influence the client.

COERCIVE POWER

Coercive power comes into play if the client senses that he will be adversely affected by failure to conform to expectations. Independence may tend to be undermined, and negative attitudes may come to the surface. Although coercion may achieve desired conforming behaviors, it is the type of power that is most alien to and disliked by practitioners in the human services. Nevertheless, it is a fact that in drastic situations, such as the protection of children, the use of coercive power may become necessary if all else has failed or if there is no time to develop other avenues of influence. The least possible amount of coercion should be used to put a stop to behaviors, slow them down, or eliminate them.

LEGITIMATE POWER

Legitimate power can be built on the client's own values, which often lead her to the conclusion that the practitioner does in fact have the right to influence her and that she, the client, has an obligation to accept this influence. It is theorized that the bases for legitimate power are derived from cultural values (for example, the value that therapists know best, are experienced and intelligent, "look the part," and have credentials); from acceptance of the social structure of the organization (that is, the clinic is seen as the right place to go for getting rid of depression); or from designation by a legitimating agent (for example, the government has set up this clinic for this purpose). To the extent that she contests the legitimacy of an interviewer's authority, the client will be disaffected and unwilling to accept influence.

REFERENT POWER

Referent power is based on the interviewer's prestige and attractiveness to the client. An interviewer's authority is increased if the client has a high opinion of her because of these two factors. (For example, a client might say, "I have a good counselor; she is the chief of the service agency, and she is thoughtful and kind.")

EXPERT POWER

Expert power is evident if the client has confidence in the knowledge and perception of the interviewer. (For example, a client might say, "My counselor really knows his stuff.")

Practitioner authority in an interview is conveyed through multichannel communications and revealed through a collection of facial expressions, body postures, and tones of voice. The foundation for expert power is the personal recognition on the part of the interviewer that he possesses necessary qualities for interviewing and will be able to communicate them as needed.

Power and authority are closely related. Power has been defined as the capacity to control the behavior of others, either directly by decree or indirectly by manipulative means. However, authority—the established right to make decisions on pertinent issues—is a transactional concept and includes the committed consent of another person who is responsive to the authority (Palmer 1983).

In interviewing clients who are involuntary, it is necessary for the practitioner to know exactly how much authority she has and how much power she is vested with to exercise control of the client. The degree of respect, belief in expertise, and legitimation that the client gives the interviewer are in the realm of affect, values, and perceptions; therefore they affect practitioner authority more indirectly. The ability of the practitioner to give and withhold resources and to coerce the client against her will is more direct.

It is important for the interviewer to communicate the real limits and derivation of her power to the client. This is necessary to provide the client with a realistic measure of the practitioner's power and to cut down on false ideas about imaginary powers.

For example, a practitioner might say, "Under the terms of the Child Welfare Act I have the right to see the condition of your child"; *or* "I cannot force you to take this medication but I can warn you of adverse effects if you don't. This treatment is well documented by the medical profession to relieve your symptoms to a reasonable degree." Another example can be found in the interview with Mrs. N., in which the interviewer tells her that a clean house will be in her favor when she appears in court to try to get her children back.

Client rights

The reliance on authority, especially with clients who are involuntary and unwilling, needs to be balanced against an emerging body of law and opinion concerning clients' rights. There is an influential body of opinion in the child welfare services field that supports the concept of least intrusion; that is, using interventions in private family matters should utilize means that intrude least on the privacy and autonomy of the family. Many believe that clients should be in a position to make an informed choice about procedures, goals, and possible side effects of psychotherapy, about the credentials of a therapist, and about other sources of help (Thomas 1983, p. 619). In recent years the judicial system has involved itself in attempts to develop procedures to protect clients from unwarranted, unfair, or unequal decisions made in human services systems about the nature of, quantity of, and reason for services (Gaskins 1981). Implementing informed consent precipitates problems about values and procedures and creates conflicts between competing directives; significant decision-making problems are created (Parry 1981; Raider 1982).

These various issues fortify interviewers in being clear about explaining the limits and extent of organizational authority to clients. This should include explaining the content of proposed interventions, reasons for them, and probable risks and benefits. Taking the time to check repeatedly with the client about other choices he might want to formulate, how well he understands, how much commitment there is to a plan, and what his reservations are — these efforts are important. An interviewer should find out the administrative policies and rules of his organization, the organization's attitude toward the extent of and limitations to client rights, and what practitioner positions will and will not be backed up.

Hostile client reactions

Hostile client reactions are most likely to occur with involuntary or unwilling clients and pathologically suspicious people. It has been suggested that interviewers "need to handle anger as an electrician handles current, respecting its force and potential for danger but not being fearful because they have knowledge and experience" (Palmer 1983, p. 124).

The term "aggressive acts" usually calls up images of bodily assault and property destruction. However, these are not the kinds of behaviors that ordinarily concern interviewers; verbal complaints and angry facial and body motions are the worrisome events that more often cause the interviewer to feel humiliated and rebuffed. Trying to understand why some clients are hostile, the practitioner might come up with what seems to be an obvious explanation: they are participating unwillingly. However, many or most involuntary clients are not aggressive in interviews.

There are groups of theories that offer explanations of aggression (Bandura 1973). Instinctual theories posit the existence of an innate striving for destruction. Drive theories suggest that aggression is produced by frustration. This theory has achieved widespread public popularity but has not withstood the test of scientific study. Frustration is a complex idea with many different attributes but it does not always predict aggression. Both the drive theory and the instinctual theory suggest that aggressive behavior may be regulated by ventilation of built-up pressure. Ventilation is a logical regulatory device if the aggressive tendency is considered to be a bottled-up force of energy that comes from an innate instinct or drive. However, the value of catharsis is not supported by research; catharsis may even maintain the aggressive behavior or increase the likelihood of its expression.

Social learning explanations suggest that aggression is aroused by an unpleasant, thwarting, offensive, or painful experience. Most people under aversive conditions, however, intensify activities to overcome these conditions in one way or another. Whether or not a person will react aggressively depends on learned patterns of coping and the particular details of the instigating experience. The social learning explanation of hostile behavior in an interview is the most useful; it suggests that if aggressive reactions occur, the interviewer should discuss ways to deal with the unpleasant, thwarting, offensive, or painful experiences that the client has had.

Comments of the following type may be useful:

"What are you bothered about?"

"What happened to hurt your feelings?"

"Was it something I said? What?"

"I know you will have to wait and that is going to cause trouble for you. What kinds of trouble are you expecting?"

"I saw the security man yelling at you. What did you make of that?"

On rare occasions an interviewer may confront assaultive behavior (see Chapter 7). Should that happen a number of actions are called for. Try to calm the client by a diversion. Stop the action, if you can. Do not make interpretive remarks that could be understood as criticism. Stand up and move close to the door or leave the room. Get another staff person to participate. If you cannot calm the client, activate as quickly as possible the security system that the setting employs. Do not rush matters; these incidents take a lot of time. Do not argue with the client. If he is armed, get the police. Keep onlookers away; the fewer people present the less likely somebody will inadvertently escalate the situation or get hurt.

A few additional suggestions can be made. Don't make home visits alone in neighborhoods that are known to be dangerous or at hours that are dangerous; the police can provide information about this. Do not be afraid of your intuition. If you start to fantasy getting assaulted, if your breath almost stops, or if your mind goes blank with fear — don't ignore it. You are getting a message and you should obey it. You may on occasion make a fool of yourself by being scared of nothing. It doesn't matter; better to be embarrassed than in the hospital.

If a setting has a history of violent or aggressive incidents, there should be an administrative plan. Great pains should be taken to eliminate office conditions — such as long waits in crowded rooms, close or uncomfortable quarters, and discourteous staff members — that are likely to produce such incidents.

Summary

Many clients do not come voluntarily to a human services setting. They are reluctantly persuaded to come and are only tentatively committed. Some are influenced by authoritative recommendations, and some are required to participate by courts or other social authorities. Clients who are involuntary to a high degree are not only difficult to engage in the helping process but may also be actively unwilling and occasionally hostile. Dealing with involuntary clients poses a dilemma: on the one hand, an interviewer's professional posture involves helping; on the other hand, it is expected that the practitioner will overcome the client's perceived deviance. When conducting interviews with involuntary clients, the practitioner must realistically appraise her power and authority. Furthermore, the interviewer should not only be nonjudgmental but should also discuss mandates clearly and accurately.

REFERENCES

Auletta, Ken. *The Underclass.* New York: Random House, 1982.

Bandura, Albert. *Aggression: A Social Learning Analysis.* Englewood Cliffs, N.J.: Prentice-Hall Inc., 1973.

Blizinsky, Marlin, and Reid, William J. "Problem Focus and Change in a Brief Treatment Model." *Social Work* 25 (March 1980):89-93.

Epstein, Laura. *How to Provide Social Services with Task-Centered Methods: Report of the Task-Centered Service Project,* vol. I. Chicago: School of Social Service Administration, University of Chicago, 1977.

French, John R.P., Jr., and Raven, Bertram. "The Bases of Social Power." In *Group*

Dynamics: Research and Theory, by Dorwin Cartwright and Alvin Zander, pp. 259-269. New York: Harper & Row, 1968.

Gaskins, Richard. "The Role of Discretion in the Legal and Social Service Systems." *Social Casework* 62 (September 1981):387-397.

Geismar, Ludwig, and La Sorte, Michael A. *Understanding the Multi-problem Family.* New York: Association Press, 1964.

Gitterman, Alex. "Uses of Resistance: A Transactional View." Social Work 28 (April 1983):127-131.

Mullen, Edward J., and Dumpson, James R. *Evaluation of Social Intervention.* San Francisco: Jossey-Bass, Inc., 1972.

Palmer, Sally E. "Authority: An essential Part of Practice." *Social Work* 28 (March-April 1983):120-126.

Parry, Joan K. "Informed Consent: For Whose Benefit?" *Social Casework* 62 (November 1981):537-542.

Raider, Melvyn C. "Protecting the Rights of Clients: Michigan Sets a Model for Other States." *Social Work* 27 (March 1982):160-164.

Rooney, Ronald. Private communication, 1983.

Shoham, S. Gora. *Social Deviance.* New York: John Wiley & Sons, 1976.

Shyne, Ann W. "Who Are the Childlren? A National Overview of Services." *Social Work Research and Abstracts* 16 (Spring 1980):26-33.

Thomas, Edwin J. "Problems and Issues in Single-Case Experiments." In *Handbook of Clinical Social Work,* edited by Aaron Rosenblatt and Diana Waldfogel, pp. 603-622. San Francisco: Jossey-Bass Publishers, 1983.

CHAPTER 11

Planning, organizing, and recording

An interview is not a solitary or unique event. It is one component of service delivery, which is the process through which a human service is transferred to a client. This transfer can take place in many ways: by mail, by phone, or in person. All these transfer mechanisms involve reflection and communication. The interview is the communication structure that effects the transfer of the service.

Interviews are components of a case strategy, which is a plan to achieve a goal. The plan is a method devised to implement activities that are expected and intended to facilitate reaching the goal. Intervention tactics—specific, particular, and detailed actions and attitudes—are the means to carry out the strategy. Interviews use multifaceted tactics to carry out or implement plans. Interviews are aimless and meandering without plans.

Planning processes

A case plan is derived from a collection of information from various sources: a practice theory recommended by the service setting or professional discipline; an assessment of the problem, the people involved, and available resources; and information about the content and effectiveness of intervention designs that might ameliorate the problem, change the people involved, or shed light on the social context of the problem.

The elements of an intervention plan are:
1. *Defining a change target:* identification of what is to be changed.
2. *Identifying goals:* identification of the end result or intended goal to be achieved.
3. *Choosing intervention activities:* identification of what is to be done.
4. *Formulating a sequence:* identification of the duration of the intervention and the order of activities.

THE CHANGE TARGET

The change target can be a person, a problem, or a condition. These three general categories are completely interrelated because one does not exist without the other. However, priority should be given to one over the others to organize the work efficiently.

Changing people directly is theoretically possible but often practically difficult. It requires a client who has given informed consent, knows what the procedures are, and is able to undertake them. Changing people is a developmental undertaking. This undertaking may involve reviving old experiences and reinterpreting them or providing a strongly felt, intimate relationship within which the client may experience necessary support to alter the way she feels and perceives herself and the world. Theoretically people may also change through experiencing novel encounters with caring friends, through a decrease in stress, or through stimulating occurrences. They may also change because of increased knowledge of themselves and a better understanding of their world. These various approaches to changing people are usually designated as *psychotherapies*. These therapies require rigorous specialized training.

In most human services work the change target is a problem or several related problems. Adequate problem solving or problem reduction requires a clear definition of the problem, that is, naming the problem; describing it; specifying its components; and identifying when the problem occurs, with whom it occurs, where it occurs, what happened before it started, and what its consequences are. The various problems of concern need to be listed and put in order of priority. Then they can be taken up in this order, limiting them to approximately three for practical purposes.

Problem conditions are composed of interrelated problems with an emphasis on the stresses and deprivations specific to each problem. The change target may be any aspect of the problem or condition that is judged to be amenable to change and is likely to reduce the condition if changed to some degree. Change targets may be feelings, emotions, attitudes, interpersonal relations, physical environments, social environments, or some combination of any of these.

Whatever change target is chosen, it is important that the client be as free as possible to select that target or to agree to a target selected by others. This can be accomplished primarily by focusing the discussion on the problem as perceived by the client. The practitioner may modify the client's perception by her professional expertise and authority, but only with the demonstrated understanding and agreement of the client.

GOALS

The goals of an intervention strategy should be specific. They should state what the end result is intended to be, taking into account selected aspects of the person, problem, or condition. The goals must address the targeted problem. Goals should be formulated as a result of an individual client's problem and not to fit in with a predetermined, generalized idea of service provision.

INTERVENTION ACTIVITIES

Intervention activities are the general categories of actions expected to ameliorate a problem. As much as possible they should be selected from among intervention activities that have been tested in research or in codified practice and have achieved good records of success. Experimental and innovative practice should also be encouraged, but with the informed consent of clients. Processes and effects should be studied systematically. Types of intervention activities are practical help; provision of resources, advice, information, and direction; clarification; referral and linkage; emotional support; negotiating, bargaining, and advocacy; task formulation and guided performance; overcoming obstacles; teaching and enhancing social skills; reinforcement-based procedures; and modeling, rehearsal, and feedback (Epstein 1980; Loewenberg 1977; Pinkston et al. 1982).

The parts of an intervention plan should be summed up verbally or in writing. This summation constitutes a contract. The plan should identify which interventions will be attempted, their approximate order of priority, and the people who will be included.

SEQUENCE

The sequence — that is, the order of activities — as well as the length of time that an intervention plan takes has to be individually decided on. Administrative regulations limit the length of contact in many settings. The particular circumstances in the case also often limit the available time. Brief durations are usually as effective as lengthy encounters, although there are exceptions. A reasonable rule of thumb for planning the duration of an ongoing case is eight interviews over 2 or 3 months. (This of course does not refer to a one- or two-interview sequence for immediate information-giving.) Open-ended duration is favored in some practice models. The nature of some problems and the social responsibilities of some organizations necessitate long or ongoing durations.

Organizing processes

Every interview has a slot in the practitioner's total workload and is affected by how much time the interviewer can allow and how heavy his schedule is. How the caseload of an individual interviewer is organized is at bottom the result of administrative practice. Within that practice, however, practitioners have leeway and autonomy. The crucial element seems to be how priorities are set; there is always more work to do than there is time. To cover a caseload entails making decisions, following up on them, and revising priorities.

The difficulty experienced in trying to efficiently organize a caseload lies in the extremely large number of variables involved in processing cases and in the "state of the art" of technical processes and program requirements. What an individual practitioner must do is select priorities from among a complex group of many contending activities and allocate time so as to emphasize the highest priorities. Because of the impossibility of making firm predictions about the outcome of complex decisions involving human affairs, assigning priorities involves a calculated risk that nevertheless must be taken.

Three basic processes come into play when deciding on priorities. First a predictive judgment is made to answer the question: If this is done first, what is likely to happen and what will the benefits be? Second, a choice is made among competing values in answering the question: If this is done first (or left until later), what good (or harm) can be expected to result? Third, criteria are used to assign priority value when answering the question: What rules should be applied for organizing the activities?

The last question about criteria can help to put the other two questions in perspective. The various criteria that can be used for organizing caseload priorities are:

1. Actions of most immediate and clear benefit to the client
2. Actions of possible benefit to the client in the long run
3. Actions of the most immediate and clear benefit to the service organization as a whole
4. Actions of immediate and clear benefit to important leaders in the service organization
5. Actions most compatible with professional statements of values
6. Actions most compatible with professional practice standards
7. Actions preferred by the practitioner as the most satisfying and personally rewarding
8. Actions most congruent with the client's interest and choices

These decision criteria are bound to result in conflicts that have to be worked out by making a series of trade-offs. But decisions must be made. If no decisions are made or if the decisions are flimsy and infirm, Criterion 7 will prevail by default. Indiscriminate reliance on practitioner preference as the main criterion can be expected to create as many problems as it solves.

Any set of priorities for managing a caseload needs to be flexible. Priorities may have to be put aside in deference to unforeseeable future events. However, putting aside priorities should be temporary; the practitioner should have the intention of either returning to the decision when the emergency ends or making a different decision. Practitioners who work under conditions of continual emergency must manage by making emergency intervention their major priority; they have no other choice.

At present there are three general systems for organizing a caseload: (1) individual supervision, (2) team supervision, and (3) case management. All the systems "bleed" into one another; following one does not exclude the use of another. There are differing emphases among the systems, but the amount of overlap is often so great that two or more of the systems are sometimes in operation at the same time.

INDIVIDUAL SUPERVISION AS A MODE OF OPERATION

In individual supervision the practitioner has considerable leeway for decisions on priorities. The practitioner's autonomy is constrained by agency directives and regulations, by the supervisor's interpretation of those directives and regulations, and by the practitioner's interpretation. Allowing for the constraints of the agency's reward system, the practitioner has a good deal of freedom to make priority judgments. At her own discretion the practitioner may be subject to influence from professional peers, for example, in meetings where consensual rules are stated.

TEAM SUPERVISION AS A MODE OF OPERATION

In team supervision the individual practitioner's judgment is usually either somewhat or greatly circumscribed because the team meeting will probably reach a consensus on priorities that will bind the practitioner through the cohesive effect of group processes. Team decisions can arouse a good deal of resentment in individual participants; however, they are safer than individual decisions because responsibility is shared. Team decisions are preferred when situations are grave ones on which highly significant or public matters depend.

CASE MANAGEMENT AS A MODE OF OPERATION

The theory on which case management rests is that client benefit is the central criterion for assessing priorities. Case management supervision, only recently developed, is concerned with assessment, planning, purchase or referral, and monitoring a set of activities (Johnson and Rubin 1983; Spitalnik 1981). Taken at face value, this system is meritorious because of the obvious value of its prioritizing scheme. Whether it will achieve its goals or not remains to be seen; the system is too new to make firm judgments about it.

It is theoretically possible to develop models for achieving successful caseload coverage. Such models would have to be clear about a setting's exact requirements, preferences, and major priorities. The ability of such models to capture all the important variables is an important consideration. Certainly in the foreseeable future priorities will continue to be defined as judgments that a practitioner makes in cooperation with his own conscience, colleague opinions and instructions, and choice of professional viewpoint. It is clear that the individual interview is a central function in deciding on coverage of any caseload by any method. Caseload coverage decisions focus on such things as the following: In which cases should interviews be scheduled first? How many interviews should be scheduled in a given month? How much interview time should be allotted per case? Where should the interviews be held? What should the interview's major focus be?

Recording

Planning and organizing lead to case action and recording. The need to account for case action is what makes recording an essential function.

A record should contain factual data that identify those problems that the service is set up for and sanctioned to work on. The record should provide succinct and coherent formulations, definitions, and assessments of these problems in acceptable professional form and language and should be based on credible facts, relevant theory, and professional judgment. The record should contain the treatment plan and goals, actions to implement them, information about client progress, and in conclusion a statement of the client's condition at the time of closing. Rumors, chat, loose speculation, and unwarranted inference should not be recorded. The record is a business document; it is not an artful literary device. In many ways it is a public or potentially public document.

The record of an interview rarely stands by itself. In virtually all recording systems the individual interview substance is merged with a comprehensive record that provides usable data about what the client's problem was, what was done about it, who did it, how the client responded, what further service is needed, and how that service will be provided (Ryback, Longabaugh, and Fowler 1981).

Keeping records in human services settings is expensive. The largest costs are in salaries that pay the staff members for time and effort used in recording and processing. Keeping records is time consuming; there are numerous complaints about "too much paperwork." Time spent in recording takes staff members away from direct client contact, which practitioners and administrators regard as the most important activity of the work. This discussion will show that it is not the least bit simple to design, test, and revise recording systems that are efficient. Many demands are put on these systems, which have to capture an enormous amount of detail some of which can be easily misunderstood — in an understandable fashion.

PURPOSES OF RECORDING

The primary purposes of recording are case continuity, documentation of services, and interprofessional communication (Kagle 1983). There are also auxiliary purposes for recording: supervision, intervention process decision making, and research.

CONTINUITY

Continuity refers to recording entries that collect the actions and events of the interview as they occur chronologically. These entries are needed to inform staff, supervisors, and administrators of the status of cases if some action needs to be taken. The primary practitioner may be absent or busy, or the case may be transferred. Consultants or specialists may be called in. An understandable set of reports should always be available so that someone with a need to know the answers to questions — such as who the client is, what is being done, or where the process stands at the moment — can be fully informed. The primary practitioner also needs a ready reference for the times when she has to review the situation to answer questions, prepare for an interview, or make further plans.

DOCUMENTATION

The need for documentation in modern human services bureaucracies is simply enormous. This need arises because funds such as government grants, fees, third-party payments, contributions, and philanthropic grants must be accounted for. Documentation must also be provided to verify compliance with legal and statutory requirements and regulatory agencies that oversee the maintenance of standards.

Documentation in records serves both managerial and professional purposes. The information in these records "must be easy to retrieve, compile, and interpret" (Kagle 1983, p. 151). It is for this reason that documentation is made on "forms," which are formally constructed instruments that encourage specificity and cut down on vagueness and ambiguity. The practitioner "fills in short, explicit answers or, better, checks off responses from a list of mutually exclusive and exhaustive alternatives" (p. 151). These forms become the data base for monitoring key events and transactions of not only an individual case but also a whole caseload. Hence the data can be used to monitor and improve service delivery in an organization. If they are integrated into an organization's management information system, these data are best handled by computer processing.

INTERPROFESSIONAL COMMUNICATION

A record can also be used for interprofessional communication, that is, the sharing of information with other professionals. This is done especially between interdisciplinary colleagues in settings such as hospitals and clinics, where numerous practitioners might collaborate on work. The Problem Oriented Record (POR) has been in development for a number of years to improve interprofessional communication by making the information more easily read and understood, thereby facilitating service to clients.

SUPERVISION

A recent survey of a random sample of social agencies and social work departments in the United States found that supervisors use records kept by new practitioners to assess if client needs are linked to goals and plans and to document the progress of service (Kagle 1983). Although the record may play some role in the development of the worker's interviewing skills and analytic thinking, it acts principally as a monitoring device, providing feedback to the worker and supervisor so the service plan can be modified as the transaction develops. With experienced workers the record was found to be used primarily in the supervision of problem cases.

INTERVENTION PROCESS DECISION MAKING

The purpose of reviewing the intervention process in the course of a single case is to check on the effectiveness of interventions, to attempt to identify barriers to progress, and to make corrections and changes in a timely fashion to improve the effectiveness of the interventions.

RESEARCH

Unfortunately it has not proved feasible to use the record (as produced in the work process) for research purposes. There is too much data recorded from different viewpoints and times; a record nearly always lacks information that the researcher needs but the practitioner does not. It is essential that instruments be designed for the delimited focus of research purposes (Seaberg 1970). It is possible that new designs in computerized recording systems will make it easier to extract viable research data from regular recording at a reasonable cost.

TYPES OF RECORDING

At present numerous recording systems exist. Most systems combine two or more of the possibilities to make up a suitable recording package. For purposes of this discussion, the world of recording is divided into five main types: minimum basic, logs, narratives, structured recording, and process recording.

MINIMUM BASIC RECORDING

Minimum basic recording is a simple, economical mode of recording that is suitable for a single practitioner. The record contains minimum identifying information: the client's name, address, and phone number; if necessary, a few other bits of information such as the name, address, and phone number of one or two close relatives; and the fee, if any. Depending on need the card or sheet can add information about work, income, or other topics.

This record accumulates information on dates of interviews and other interventions, where they are held if not in the office, major client problems, major goals, the planned schedule of contact, running notations on major subjects of the interviews, major interventions, client responses, areas for exploration needed, resources needed, important actions taken on behalf of the client, collaterals, and status at termination.

This kind of minimum basic record is suitable in notebook form for a practitioner's own use. It can also be used for an extremely small organization with minimal accountability needs. Notebook data can be recorded in the course of conducting the interview, or just after the interview is completed, or some combination of both.

LOG RECORDING

A log is a device for keeping track of case activities that occur each day or during another time period. Logs are usually on sheets of 8-1/2 by 11 ruled paper with a few or many columns. If logs have few columns, the practitioner can write out notes. If logs have many columns, notes are made in code. An example of an ordinary case log is shown on p. 281.

Logs should be handwritten legibly. They can be typed, but that might be unnecessary because in due time log information has to be reduced to a summary. As information accumulates, its bulk makes it inaccessible. Logs should be kept so that practitioners have access to details that might be needed later. A brief summary should cover the essentials in typed form.

NARRATIVE RECORDING

Narrative recordings are of two types: *chronological and summary*. A chronological narrative is similar to a log but less usable. The probability is that a log can be kept up-to-date. It is therefore thoroughly useful as a reminder, for service continuity, and for interprofessional communication. If there is no log, the narrative, which is written some time after the events,

CASE: THE P. FAMILY

Date	Type of contact	Practi-tioner	Recording
11/4	HV*	EN†	Visited, request of school (James Elem.). Saw Mrs. P. No money for rent. Husband unemployed. Mrs. P. cannot work because no child care. One school-age child and an infant. No relatives in Chicago. Parents both have health problems, diag. uncertain. School says Sally, their school-age daughter, has academic and conduct problems. Mrs. P. strongly interested in plans to avoid such crisis in future. *Plan:* Mr. and Mrs. P. to come to office 11/5 to apply for public assistance. Longer range planning soon.
11/4	O‡	EN	Alerted RG, PA (fellow practitioners).
11/5	O	EN	Couple in. Set up emerg. food. Planned for them to find out if they can remain in apt. See LLD (their landlord) or start apt. hunt. Explained rules for rent assistance. Contract pending.

*HV, Home visit.   ‡O, Office visit.
†The practitioner's initials.

will have to be reconstructed from informal jottings or from memory. Such recording is immensely unreliable. The log is a contemporary document and is much more accurate and credible than a narrative reconstructed a long time after the events.

Summary recording is a form of narrative made at stated intervals and is constructed from logs and notes. Ordinarily settings that use summary recordings make rules to govern when they are made. There are many variations. A summary may be made only once, when the case is closed. Continuity is a big problem in such an instance unless there is also a log. However, if the case is active for over a month, the log is likely to be so bulky that information will be hard to retrieve if it is needed in a hurry; in this instance summary recording is helpful.

If time allows, it is preferable (and safer for accountability and continuity) to make a summary by phases. The first summary should be at the time the problem focus is decided on, the goals are set, and the plan is made. One or several summaries of the intervention process should follow. A closing summary completes the process; it states the status at termination, makes plans for any follow-up or monitoring, and makes an evaluation.

Summaries should state all the dates of contact and show where and with whom the contacts took place. Summaries should also state the date of the recording and should be signed or initialed.

An example of an outline for a summary covering an entire sequence of intervention is shown on pp. 283-284. That outline can be subdivided into smaller summaries at shorter intervals. The example outline was constructed to illustrate brief service with contacts over a period of 2 or 3 months, involving approximately eight client interviews and a number of additional collateral contacts.

STRUCTURED RECORDING

Structured recording uses preset instruments, which eliminates logs or narratives or retains them as supplementary. There is no single set of "forms" in use today for structured recording. There are numerous systems, each one having its own advantages and drawbacks. Structured recording is intended to increase the relevance and accessibility of information and to comply with essential accountability needs. The conditions of each organization (and sometimes each department) are so variable that it is necessary to adapt recording structures to fit each one.

Three general types of structured recording will be described: the structured narrative record, the Problem-Oriented Record (POR), and the Goal-Oriented Record (GOR).

The structured narrative record

The structured narrative record is an outline that covers the content considered most essential to account for service, documents facts and events, and guides the recorder for future action.

The example shown on pp. 285-287 is taken from one type of structured narrative used in the Task Centered Project at the University of Chicago. Numerous versions of structured narrative recording instruments were designed at various times during the course of that project. This instrument was designed to record either the first contact, the first two contacts, or the initial start-up phase of a case. There are other instruments to cover such things as identifying information, middle phase and termination phase narrations, assessment of progress in problem reduction, and research information for a special project. If required, financial and man-

CASE RECORDING GUIDE FOR INDIVIDUALS
AND FAMILIES: SUMMARY

A. Contacts (dates, who, where)
B. Problem exploration
   1. Problem(s) initially stated
      a. By client(s)
      b. By collateral(s), including referral sources and mandates
      c. Practitioner's judgment
   2. Assessment information
      a. Social context
      b. Health and psychiatric conditions
      c. Personal traits
      d. Problem circumstances
      e. Assessment summary
C. Target problem specification, contract, interventions, and reviews
   1. Introduction to intervention
      a. What client(s) was (were) told
      b. Client reactions
      c. Practitioner's judgment of client commitment
   2. Supplementary and revised assessment information: social context, health and psychiatric, personality, circumstances, other
   3. Intervention strategy: summarized
   4. Contract conditions
      a. Client target problem priorities
      b. Mandated problems
      c. How priorities established
   5. Contract
      a. Target problem(s)
      b. Date contract established
      c. Dates/times/place of sessions (schedule)
      d. Parties
      e. Duration
      f. Goals (general tasks: client and practitioner)
      g. Intervention plan

Continued.

CASE RECORDING GUIDE FOR INDIVIDUALS
AND FAMILIES: SUMMARY – cont'd

D. Intervention
   1. Client performance
      a. Tasks stated
      b. Degree of achievement
      c. Obstacles
      d. Reduction of obstacles: interventions planned and taken; results
      e. New or revised tasks: how developed
   2. Target problem status
      a. Changes from the original
      b. State and explain status of target problem(s)
      c. Status of problem situation as a whole
   3. Practitioner performance review
      a. Tasks stated
      b. Degree of achievement
      c. Obstacles
      d. Reduction of obstacles: interventions planned and taken; results
      e. New or revised tasks: how developed
      f. Other
   4. Interventions report
      a. Social network actions
      b. With client(s) directly: resource provisions; social skills development; counseling
      c. Agency system constraints and opportunities; actions indicated, taken
E. Termination
   1. Problem status (practitioner's, client's, and others' assessment)
   2. Planning for remaining problems and circumstances
   3. Extension and monitoring plan, if any
F. Other pertinent information

agement information can be recorded on forms designed for those specific areas.

STRUCTURED NARRATIVE

Client(s) Name: _____Sally P._____ Case no. ___65___

Session no.'s in which data collected: ___1___ thru ___2___

Dates of data collection: ___11-4___ thru ___11-6___

Approximate no. of minutes spent in interviews no. 1 — 1 hr., 40 min.; no. 2 — 45 min.

1. *Problems initially stated:*
    a. *by client(s)*
    Seven-year-old Sally's mother, Mrs. P., does not have enough money to pay the rent. Lack of money for rent is chronic so that the family finds it necessary to move often. This has had bad effects on Sally, who is having problems in school. Mrs. P. was offered a job recently but had to turn it down because there was no one to care for her 2-month-old baby.
    b. *by collateral(s)*
    Sally's teacher feels that she should be sent back to first grade because she does nothing in class. Teacher is not sure that Sally understands English very well because until last year she was raised by her grandmother, who does not speak English.
    c. *practitioner's judgment of problems*
    Problems are related to the family's frequent moves. Instability has adversely affected the children's school work. I think that the main reason that it has been necessary to move is Mr. P.'s lack of concern about paying the rent and also possibly other family matters.
    d. *main problem:* (check) first brought up by client ___X___
    by practitioner _____ other _____ (explain)
    Most immediate problem is with the apartment. The manager said they will have to move; they have to find a new apartment. There will be a problem about how long they can stay in a new apartment. They often have trouble paying rent.
    　　　Client would like to get a job but she can think of no way to handle baby-sitting.
2. *Initial assessment of target problems*
    Problem 1:
    Client needs to find adequate housing. Expecting eviction in next few weeks.
    Problem 2:
    Mrs. P.'s unemployment. She recently turned down a job because she did not have a baby-sitter. Baby-sitter needs to be found.
3. *Context of problem(s): brief summary*
    a. *duration and history of problems*
    The P.'s have moved several times in the last couple of years because Mr. P. does not pay the rent regularly. He uses the money to buy alcohol for himself and his friends, according to his wife. Mrs. P. worked as an assembler up to

the time she had a baby 2 months ago. Since then she has not worked because she can't get a baby-sitter.

b. *client social situation*

Mr. and Mrs. P. seem to be well informed about resources, that is, they have a "milk subsidy card" and are familiar with neighborhood health care facilities. Mr. P. has visited legal aid with regard to their current eviction threat. They seem to be getting quite a bit of help from Mr. P.'s sister, who lives in the neighborhood and gives them both money and counsel. Currently the apartment where they live costs $272/month, but it only has one bedroom and is small. It was in good order. One problem is a big dog that they keep for protection; he is not housebroken. Mr. P. works at a good restaurant as a cook, but this job is not regular. His hours are from 3 to 11 PM.

c. *client health, medical and psychiatric problems, and care*

Mrs. P. is in touch with the Neighborhood Health Center and is receiving care for the baby and Sally. Mr. P. may have an operation (at City Hospital). Mrs. P. said he is going to have a boil removed, but it sounded as if he would have to be in the hospital for awhile (I will check further on this). Sally had an operation on her hand during the summer, and there is a bill for $650 that is unpaid.

d. *client's dominant personality characteristics*

Mrs. P. seems very open and easy to talk to. She has a great deal of interest in and concern for her children. Seems to be willing and capable of taking action on her problems — if given assistance on what to do. Have not met Mr. P. yet. Can't get a picture of him from her.

4. *Concrete resource assessment and provision*

a. *needed?*   Housing

b. *what and how provided? If not, why not?*

I gave Mrs. P. several numbers to call regarding housing. Also gave her a map of the school district so that they can keep Sally in the same school if they move. I also found out from the principal that Sally could continue to attend the same school even if the family were to move out of the district (depending on his discretion).

5. *Preliminary assessment of problem*

I first asked about Sally. As Mrs. P. talked, it seemed to me that I should make her (that is, Mrs. P.) the client. When I suggested this she seemed very receptive. Seems to see my position as assisting her to think about her problems. She and her husband also seem to be taking their own measures to deal with their problems. I am supporting this strongly.

The major problem I faced was a large number of problems that all seem to be interconnected. My difficulty is to assist Mrs. P. to focus on the most important problems. At times she begins to think about (or at least, talk about) several of her problems, and at this point it is necessary to return to the point.

Previously Mrs. P. apparently took care of the baby-sitting problem by sending Sally out of state to stay with relatives. Prior to living in their present apartment the family lived with Mr. P.'s sister-in-law and her family. Mrs. P. is receiving some advice from Mr. P.'s sister-in-law and her daughter, who has a college degree. I am supporting the continued use of this resource.

Client would like a bigger apartment and would like to be able to be more stable. For this she feels it is necessary to work.

I think that if client can arrange for a baby-sitter (possibly by getting her husband to take some responsibility here) and if she can get a job, the money problem will be less critical. Hopefully, this will allow the family to be more stable, which will go far toward helping Sally. In any case, the point now is for Mrs. P. to get a job and to stabilize the housing situation.

6. *Intervention contract*
   a. *target problems*
      (1) Unsuitable, unstable housing
      (2) Unemployment (Mrs. P.)
   b. *goals*
      (1) Apartment will be found and rent will be paid on time so that it won't be necessary to move again soon.
      (2) Client will attempt to find a job that ends early so that she can take care of the baby after her husband goes to work.
   c. *duration of service and schedule*
      Ten weeks, one time a week

7. *Next steps*
   Client will attempt to straighten out the situation with regard to housing, either by (1) arranging with landlord for her family to stay where it currently is or (2) finding a new apartment.

   Mrs. P. will attempt to arrange baby-sitting (will explore this with husband) so that she can take a job.

   Conference with Mr. P. and wife to explore his rent nonpayments and devise plan to correct this.

8. *Others*

Similar instruments could be designed to fit various styles of practice. The major benefits of structured recording are that it succinctly records the information deemed most relevant and useful, it eliminates information selected idiosyncratically, it minimizes redundance, and it keeps the focus clear. Space is allotted for the practitioner to record important information not covered by the headings. Recording is done on the instrument. The spacing ordains the amount of writing and restrains verbosity. The demand that this instrument makes for discipline and focus was almost universally experienced by practitioners as unpleasant and too constraining. The information obtained, however, was generally considered satisfactory by staff members who administered the project. The original version was developed from a research instrument (Westbury, Simon, and Korbelik 1973). There was almost constant revision. In part the revisions were made to accommodate the practitioners who wanted more space and less structuring; later versions tended to become less focused. Revisions were also made because of the insatiable demands of administrators, who never stopped thinking up additions that they wished to have. The "Structured Narrative" on pp. 285-287 shows a version from the middle years of the project and is a compromise between the "tightest" and "loosest" versions of the instrument.

Two more examples will be given of this same type of structured recording to indicate how to construct it. The example beginning on this page is a recording of the fifth session, that is, of a single interview. This kind of single-interview recording is suitable for training staff members. It is unnecessarily detailed for an experienced practitioner with a large caseload. Single-interview recording of this type is really a structured log. Too much paper is generated to do such recording regularly; the record would be too bulky for easy comprehension. Normally many interviews would be combined for such an instrument. For illustration, however, having only one interview to deal with helps to visualize how this recording system works.

MIDDLE PHASE

Name of Client(s) and Date Seen: _____Mr. & Mrs. P., 12/11_____ Case no. ___65___
Session no.: ___5___   Recording Date: ___1-19___
Length of Session (in minutes): ___60___

1. *Problem specification and review*
   Mr. P. did not see getting Mrs. P. a job as a major problem. Instead he had a couple of other ideas: (1) budgeting, which would help alleviate the need for Mrs. P. to work; and (2) getting himself a better job (or possibly an additional job). With regard to the apartment: this is still a problem because they have a court date on 1/23 regarding eviction.
2. *Task review*
   Mrs. P. had gone to get the food stamps and they had bought some food. Also the budgeting idea had been tried (however, not thoroughly because of the short time span involved). They had also been careful to have someone at the apartment all the time to wait for the verification worker from the welfare dept. Mrs. P. had gotten the previous job verification that the dept. needed.
3. *Treatment contract:* No Change _____
   If changed, describe:
   The contract was changed to include Mr. P. but we retained the earlier agreed-on number of appointments (i.e., 5 more after this one).
4. *Task planning*
   The first task this week was for Mr. P., who has had his operation, to take sitz baths as often as possible as recommended by his doctor, to stay inside and off his feet to help heal the operation, and to return to work as soon as possible. Second task was for Mrs. P. to go out and look for an apartment.

Third task was to stick to the food stamp budget that they had set up.

Fourth task was to go to court (they had another court date that was preliminary to the January 23 date mentioned above).

The reasons for these tasks were all fairly clear to the P.'s and they proposed them after I prompted them with, "What else do you need to do this week?"

5. *Establishing incentives and a rationale*

The P.'s saw these tasks as being crucial to their situation. Mr. P. had to get well to return to work. The food stamps had to be budgeted to assure food for the next month. Finding a new apartment and going to court were both necessary to maintain some kind of adequate housing for the family.

6. *Obstacles*

The main obstacle was still Mrs. P.'s timidity. However, she seemed up to the apartment hunting task. This removed a possible obstacle to Mr. P.'s health improvement; if she can hunt for an apartment, he can stay at home and recover.

7. *Reaction to interview and intervention*

Mr. P. doesn't want his wife to work; he would rather have her go to school, as he would also like to do. Mrs. P. accomplished the task of getting the job verification. This is good; she is getting involved in doing more things. I'm still not sure whether she can apartment hunt or not; I am simply encouraging it at this point, and I am not going further into task planning because I want to see if she can look for apartments by herself.

8. *Changes in assessment of target problem(s) (if any)*

Clients still need to find housing, but it may be that the budgeting is really more important than Mrs. P.'s finding a job.

The following is also a single interview—the final one at case closing.

FINAL SESSION

Case no.: ___65___   Session no.: ___16___
Name of Client(s) Seen: _____ Mr. and Mrs. P. _____ Date: ___3/9___

1. *Description of situation at closing*

Clients are now in a new apartment. Sally, the P.'s older child, now has her own room, which she keeps very clean. Sally caused the first referral because she was so far behind in school. She has, according to her teacher, caught up in class (this is in a new school) and has begun to bring home "good" papers. Sally and Mrs. P. are getting Sally's glasses today. Mrs. P. is now attending adult school. The P.'s have continued budgeting. The P.'s contract was extended to six additional interviews that are needed to get the work done.

2. *Review of client's accomplishments in the interview*

a. New, nice apartment in good neighborhood

b. Budgeting

   (1) Mr. P. has joined credit union

   (2) Family is now covered by group health insurance

c. Mrs. P. is going to school

d. Betty (the baby) and Sally have eye problems that are being taken care of

    e. Mr. P. and family have gotten through the ordeal of his operation and all that involved — getting on welfare, getting food stamps, and Mr. P.'s recuperation

    f. Mr. and Mrs. P. are now getting along with their children well and feel much better about how to deal with them.

3. *Planning clients' and collaterals' work in remaining areas of difficulty (strategies, tasks, etc.)*

We discussed that there might be future problems with budgeting and problems getting Sally to wear her new glasses and agreed that the P.'s should continue to be systematic about setting goals and monitoring.

4. *Plans for additional or future help, if any*

We discussed availability of school counselors, welfare staff, our agency, and other sources of help.

The problem-oriented record

POR, which stands for the Problem-Oriented Record or Problem-Oriented Recording, is a considerably more advanced and sophisticated means of structuring recording than the system that was just discussed. The POR involves more than record keeping; it also reflects, mirrors, and shapes the problem-solving approach to practice. The POR originated as a way of standardizing medical records in hospitals and clinics and monitoring compliance with standards. Basic standards in hospitals are set by the Joint Commission on the Accreditation of Hospitals (JCAH) and the United States Department of Health and Human Services (HHS).

POR was introduced in hospitals and clinics in the 1960s; it was introduced into psychiatry and mental health care a decade later. Because of interdisciplinary practice in medical and mental health hospitals and clinics, POR has been or is being adapted for use by all the disciplines found in these settings. Many POR ideas have spread at least in part to other sections of the human services.

POR is still in the process of development. It is not a complete or unchanging set of procedures. It has been a powerful shaper of practice because it emphasizes the following areas: "(1) collection of a data base in order to identify problem areas; (2) formulation and definition of the patient's problems; (3) planning treatment for these problems; and (4) monitoring treatment interventions until problems are resolved or constrained" (Ryback, Longabaugh, and Fowler 1981, p. 1).

POR systems have different degrees of structure. One way to create a POR system is by writing a narrative that follows an outline; this closely resembles the example shown on pp. 283-284. The outline varies with requirements of individual settings. Another way to create a POR system is in a semistructured manner; this resembles the structured narrative shown on pp. 285-287, adapted to meet the requirements of a specific setting. An extreme POR system is the fully structured record that contains forms composed of a series of checklists and rating scales and is set up for the purposes of data collection, formulation, planning, and monitoring. One of the strong points of POR in an interdisciplinary setting is that the entries (checks and notes) are made according to topic; it is not necessary to keep separate records for different disciplines.

Essentially POR is recording through some combination of instruments and notes. A POR is organized to reflect the problem-solving process, showing the condition at the start-up phase in a clear and definite manner. The record then proceeds to state plans for the case, to describe what is done and how the client responds, and finally to depict the condition of the client at the end of the process. In multidisciplinary settings all the disciplines' recordings are interwoven to show how the interventions are articulated. This kind of recording maximizes focus, enhances relevancy and efficiency, and shapes intervention practices that follow the problem-solving process.

Monitoring or follow-through recording is made in progress notes. Quantitative information is recorded in flow sheets made up of checklists, tables, and graphs and is augmented by notes that make the instrument intelligible.

The virtues and drawbacks of POR have recently been summarized by Ryback, Longabaugh, and Fowler (1981, pp. 6-9). The fact is that hospitals and clinics are heavily monitored by standard-setting bodies. The data to comply with these standards and also with insurance payment requirements must be generated in one way or another. If these data are not recorded through the regular procedures of the system, they have to be provided by special data-gathering means. The child welfare system is becoming more closely monitored by statute and court reviews. Here also, the information is either going to be generated on a write-as-you-go basis or else it will need to be secured by special efforts. It *must* be gathered unless the organization wants to jeopardize its reputation and funding.

Structured recording of all types, and especially POR, is meant to obtain and preserve client data in such a fashion that they can be efficiently utilized to provide good service and to minimize idiosyncratic or biased information, conclusions, and planning. To what extent this objective has been achieved is not well understood at this point.

POR and other types of structured recording were intended to make recording efficient, to cut down on the time used to record, and to make information retrieval easier. When a new recording system is introduced, most staff members react as if it will be more time consuming than what they have been used to; however, their perceptions also depend on what they have been used to. For some POR will save time; for others it will not. POR is exceptionally time consuming if the prior system is retained and POR is added to it.

Some users complain that structured recording is too mechanical. This complaint is a reflection of a value system held stongly by some practitioners who wish to relate to a total person in a total situation. They see structured recording as a dehumanizing endeavor that reduces the client to bits and pieces of artificially analyzed problems. Supporters of structured reporting claim that these negative aspects need not exist if the practitioner who writes the record has a clear conception of the client's wholeness and an investment in problem solving.

Although the POR is intended to cut down on redundancy, some users perceive that the forms require them to be repetitive by continuously commenting on or checking the same things. This objection is hard to combat.

Introducing structured recording into a system that is accustomed to individualistic unstructured logs and narratives is difficult. Structure is resisted by practitioners who are used to what they perceive to be less restrictive recording. It is probably best to phase in such a new system in installments and to accompany it with considerable in-service training.

POR forms vary a great deal because they are created by individual organizations and are tailored to particular needs. Manual POR records may be voluminous; consequently it is impractical to give examples of POR in this book. Fortunately computer assistance is coming into use. Two excellent references can be examined for details and examples of POR (Ryback, Longabaugh, and Fowler 1981; Wilson 1980).

The goal-oriented record

The concepts of goal-oriented intervention and the Goal-Oriented Record or Goal-Oriented Recording (GOR) emerged during the 1970s. Unlike POR, which originated in the field of medicine, GOR evolved from parallel innovations in the U.S. Department of Health, Education, and Welfare, or HEW (now referred to as Health and Human Services, or HHS); from the task-centered model of practice developed at the University of Chicago (Epstein 1980; Reid 1978; Reid and Epstein 1972; Reid and Epstein 1977); and from Goal Attainment Scaling, a device for evaluating outcomes of psychotherapy (Kiresuk and Sherman 1968). Although goal orientation to practice has firmly established itself as a result of widespread dissemination during the 1970s, its recording system has not become as complex as the POR system, in which the infinite detail of medical settings must be captured. The particular feature of goal-oriented recording is the specification of goals. The activities (practitioner tasks) that are expected to assist the client in achieving these goals are also featured. The task-centered practice model and its structured type of narrative recording seek to combine both the problem-oriented and goal-oriented approaches to recording. There is a dual emphasis: being specific about problems to be reduced and being specific about goals to reduce those problems. Both client and practitioner tasks to achieve goals are monitored. Similar combinations to those just described are advocated in community mental health (Ryback, Longabaugh, and Fowler 1981, pp. 119-126).

PROCESS RECORDING

There are two types of process recording: electronic and written. They are both used for training. They are too cumbersome, expensive, and time consuming for use in busy organizations that deliver services. Process recordings of either kind allow for detailed teaching and learning of interviewing and other intervention skills.

It is generally assumed in human services training that study of as much detail as possible is a valuable learning experience because it calls in-depth attention to all the client-practitioner transactions. However, besides being expensive and time consuming, process recording may also encourage learners to ignore the social and organizational context of a case or interview, thus distorting an accurate perception of the situation. There is no research on the merit or lack of merit in process recording as an educational device; however, it is almost always used at some time in a training process, which suggests that many perceive its value.

Electronic recording uses either audiotaping or videotaping equipment. A whole interview can be recorded. It is standard practice to obtain written consent from the client for taping and to assure as much confidentiality as possible. The benefit of a tape is that the practitioner can view the whole interview and analyze its features thoroughly. Trainers can provide detailed and accurate feedback about information. The major drawback to taping is that trainers never seem to have enough time to view and comment on whole tapes in any numbers. It has therefore become common practice for trainers to view short segments of tapes, for example, 5-minute sample segments from the start, middle, and end of an interview. Students can identify on the tape counter any segments that they are particularly interested in examining with the trainer. Because the thinking and planning that underpin an interview are so important, some teachers follow the practice of having the student write a planning outline and a brief summary — one paragraph — stating the major interview content. The instructor may comment in writing or may view or listen to the tape along with the student, thus allowing for lively discussion and a fresh response to what is shown on the tape.

Written process recording is a retrospective attempt to make a type-script of the interview, that is, to "type up" as accurately as possible a verbal record of the interview. This is an exceedingly time-consuming process and seems unwarranted if electronic devices are available. Audio-taping equipment is inexpensive today, and most people have it. Retro-spective recording is not always an accurate transcript of what actually occurred. However, written process recording is indicative of mental se-lection and organization, shows the writer's interpretation of what hap-pened, or shows what the writer would like the trainer to believe hap-pened. Written process recording also encourages the learner to identify his own thoughts and feelings. However, thought processes can be written down in a memorandum that accompanies the tape or can be recorded on tape.

Whereas clients must give their consent to taping, no similar require-ment exists when interviewers write down in retrospect what their clients have said (see following section on confidentiality). Written process re-cording was common before tapes came into use and before sensitivity to a client's informed consent became as great as it is today. Some inter-viewers are concerned about client reactions to taping. It is extremely rare for a client to refuse permission if he is given the reason for taping. Clients often play back the tape and learn about interesting and possibly useful aspects of themselves. Practitioners who are not used to taping may get stage fright, but it is usually short-lived. Playback, however, can be a shock-ing experience because the tape is so accurate and does not hide things the practitioner might be uncomfortable about. However, in a short time the practitioner will begin to be accustomed to the whole thing. People today have been reared on taping, and they usually pay little attention to these discomforts.

Confidentiality

Human services professions all recognize that communication occur-ring in interviews between a practitioner and client is confidential — not to be disclosed. The reasons for this ethical position are obvious. Practition-ers must be discreet to encourage trust from clients as an essential basis for securing necessary information and making the helping relationship secure. It is accepted practice that a practitioner share client information with any supervisors, consultants, trainers, or colleagues who are col-laborators in the whole effort to reduce the client's problem, secure resources, and conduct other activities in the client's interest. Signed consent of the client is commonly obtained to share information—even with colleagues, if they are in other organizations. It is also generally understood that disclosures of information without consent can be made in cases of emergency such as homicide, suicide, or other extremely threatening situations.

This kind of confidentiality seems straightforward, reasonable, and thoroughly in keeping with accepted standards of proper professional conduct that clients have a right to expect. However, there are two broad types of complications: unauthorized access problems and unsettled and developing legal issues.

In large bureaucracies client information, both verbal and recorded, is unfortunately sometimes accessible to unauthorized people on the premises—for example, support staff, visitors, occasional people who are passing through, and delivery personnel. Curiosity seekers should not have access to client files and should not be able to overhear professional conversations. People with wrongful intentions might gain access to and use client information for harmful purposes. Records contain information that can be used (and abused) to subject a client to ridicule, slander, stigma, and accusation.

An inquiry from an insurance company is a special case. Insurance companies must have certain kinds of verifiable data to process payments. Almost always a diagnosis has to be given. Often a diagnosis can be inferred from a straightforward statement about treatments that are reimbursable. However, there is never any need to reveal more to an insurance company than the information it specifically wants and needs.

The legal aspects of confidentiality are problematic. Only attorneys and ministers have complete immunity from disclosing client information. All other helping professionals are subject to requirements to disclose client information in some circumstances, which are established by statutes, judicial decisions, and public health service needs. Physicians' rights to confidentiality are in much the same jeopardy as other professionals' rights, even though it is commonly believed that they are not.

One of the circumstances that may require a breach of confidentiality is a court-issued subpoena. These can be issued to demand the appearance of the professional and the client's record at a court hearing. Subpoenas might be issued in cases where there is a contest about child custody or in any other type of litigation in which client case information is deemed useful. The quandary is that under certain circumstances disclosure might be in the client's interest, but under other circumstances the client might be harmed.

If a practitioner is served with a subpoena, the administration of the organization must be informed, and legal counsel must be obtained. Counsel is needed especially if the practitioner and agency do not wish to comply. A lawyer can advise on the numerous options available, which depend on particular state laws, any federal laws pertinent to the case, and relevant judicial decisions. The extent to which a professional is entitled to privileged communication is set by state laws; these vary considerably from state to state. No human services professional should ever assume expert knowledge in this area and should proceed only on the advice of counsel.

The Federal Privacy Act of 1974 established principles to safeguard client rights, as well as the rights of all citizens. This statute governs federally funded and administered programs. Agencies are required to have regularized procedures for the handling of records and the safeguarding of confidentiality. Client information should be restricted only to that which is relevant and necessary. A client has access to her records and has the right to bring a person of her own choosing when examining the record. A client can correct or amend a record to make it complete and accurate. The act requires a client's written consent for release of record information except when this information is exchanged between employees of the agency, conveyed to researchers in disguised form, given to another governmental agency for law enforcement, released in an emergency to protect the health and safety of the client, or ordered by a court. Programs that are governed by this law will have established regulations to assure compliance and will have the necessary counsel to make decisions about happenings that come up under the terms of the law. Some states have also passed freedom-of-information statutes and statutes that protect client rights. Even where such laws are on the books, however, all matters pertaining to confidentiality are not settled. There are usually provisions in other laws that conflict with these statutes or complicate the matter (Levick 1981; Raider 1981). Again, in case of contest or litigation legal counsel should be obtained.

Client access to records is seldom used, although in time it may occur more frequently. Client access statutes were a novelty when first passed. They changed the former position, which held that the record was the private property of the organization and was therefore off limits to clients. The openness of records to clients and their chosen representatives is in keeping with the modern attempt to protect everyone from the potential misuse of vast files of private information, both written and electronic, that exist today. One important rule for human services record keeping is that records should be free of vague, ambiguous, biased, slanderous, or erroneous data, speculation, and accusation. They should be factual and objective. Records are not a proper place for the free play of imagination.

CONFIDENTIALITY AND THE TARASOFF DECISION

A 1976 decision of the California Supreme Court has had repercussions throughout the mental health field. The decision held that when a psychotherapist appropriately determines that a "patient presents a serious danger of violence to another, he incurs an obligation to use reasonable care to protect the intended victim against such danger . . . to warn the intended victim or others likely to apprise the victim of the danger, to notify the police, or to take whatever steps are reasonably necessary under the circumstances" (Weil and Sanchez 1983, p. 114).

This decision raises numerous issues for practitioners. One of the most obvious is the possibility of a clear breach of confidentiality (by warning a potential victim of a threat revealed by the client in confidence to the helping professional). The Tarasoff decision is controversial. Practitioners confronted with such a problem need to know the position that their employers will back and should consider legal advice. Many practitioners apparently have no difficulty with this decision, but a breach of confidentiality is worrisome. A study of social work practitioners' attitudes in California indicates that less than 6% of the practitioners surveyed made it a point to discuss confidentiality with their clients (Weil and Sanchez 1983). It may be that the dilemma experienced in such instances would be eased if practitioners were candid with clients about the ethical position supporting confidentiality and also about the conflicts of interest that might under specific circumstances limit the right to confidentiality.

TEACHING AND RESEARCH

Research into questions concerning human services is obviously necessary and must be pursued. Monitoring bodies exercise scrutiny to assure that client information is never divulged in research in a harmful way. It is not difficult to protect clients when information about their cases is used in teaching; this is done by never using real names and by presenting cases with appropriate disguises.

Summary

Interviews are events within an intervention process. Planning is necessary to identify change targets, goals, intervention activities, and sequence. Organizing is needed to be efficient and enhance effectiveness. Recording fulfills needs for continuity, documentation, and interprofessional communication.

There are a number of different systems for recording. What system is used depends on administrative factors. Confidentiality of records must be guarded; this complex subject has many legal and practical ramifications.

REFERENCES

Epstein, Laura. *Helping People: The Task-Centered Approach.* St. Louis: The C.V. Mosby Company, 1980.

Johnson, Peter J., and Rubin, Allen. "Case Management in Mental Health: A Social Work Domain?" *Social Work* 28 (Jan.-Feb. 1983):49-56.

Kagle, Jill Doner. "The Contemporary Social Work Record." *Social Work* 28 (March-April 1983):149-153.

Kiresuk, T.J., and Sherman, R.E. "Goal Attainment Scaling: A General Method for Evaluating Comprehensive Community Mental Health Programs." *Community Mental Health Journal* 4 (1968):443-453.

Levick, Keith. Privileged Communication: Does It Really Exist?" *Social Casework* 62 (April 1981):235-239.

Loewenberg, F.M. *Fundamentals of Social Intervention.* New York: Columbia University Press, 1977.

Pinkston, Elsie; Levitt, John L.; Green, Glenn R.; Linsk, Nick L.; and Rzepnicki, Tina. *Effective Social Work Practice.* San Francisco: Jossey-Bass, 1982.

Raider, Melvyn C. "Protecting the Rights of Clients: Michigan Sets a Model for Other States." *Social Work* 27 (March 1981):160-164.

Reid, William. *The Task-Centered System.* New York: Columbia University Press, 1978.

Reid, William J., and Epstein, Laura. *Task-Centered Casework.* New York: Columbia University Press, 1972.

Reid, William J., and Epstein, Laura, eds. *Task-Centered Practice.* New York: Columbia University Press, 1977.

Ryback, Ralph S.; Longabaugh, Richard; and Fowler, D. Robert. *The Problem Oriented Record in Psychiatry and Mental Health Care.* New York: Greene & Stratton, Inc., 1981.

Seaberg, James R. "Systematized Recording: A Follow-up." *Social Work* 15 (October 1970):32-41.

Spitalnik, Deborah M. "The Case Manager Role and the Naming of Case Managers." In *Case Management: State of the Art.* Proceedings of the National Case Management Conference, National Conference on Social Welfare, Indianapolis, Indiana, 1980 (Washington, D.C.: Administration on Developmental Disabilities, 1981).

Weil, Marie, and Sanchez, Ernest. "The Impact of the Tarasoff Decision on Clinical Social Work Practice." *Social Service Review* 57 (March 1983):112-124.

Westbury, Ian; Simon, Bernece K.; and Korbelik, John, eds. *The Generalist Program: Description and Evaluation.* Chicago: The School of Social Service Administration, the University of Chicago, 1973.

Wilson, Suanna J. *Recording.* New York: Free Press, 1980.

INDEX